REASONING
AND
ARGUMENT
IN
PSYCHOLOGY

REASONING AND ARGUMENT IN PSYCHOLOGY

PHILIP BRIAN BELL

**Lecturer School of English and Linguistics
Macquarie University**

PHILLIP JAMES STAINES

Lecturer Department of General Studies
University of New South Wales

Routledge & Kegan Paul

London, Boston and Henley

First published in Great Britain and the USA in 1981
by Routledge & Kegan Paul Ltd
39 Store Street, London WC1E 7DD,
9 Park Street, Boston, Mass. 02108, USA, and
Broadway House, Newtown Road,
Henley-on-Thames, Oxon RG9 1EN

Printed in Great Britain by
Billing and Sons Limited,
Guildford, London, Oxford and Worcester

British Library Cataloguing in Publication Data

Bell, Philip Brian
Reasoning and argument in psychology.
1. Reasoning (Psychology)
I. Title   II. Staines, Phillip James
150'.1   BF441   80-41280

ISBN 0 7100 0712 4

To Janet and Penny

CONTENTS

PREFACE

THIS BOOK is a response to what the authors consider is the most common problem confronting students of introductory psychology. Although common, it is largely ignored by those involved in teaching undergraduate psychology courses. Generally, the difficulty concerns the nature of psychological argument – its conventions and idiosyncrasies. More than any other single aspect of psychology it is this that students fail to understand. Perhaps the best way to emphasise the dimensions of the problem is to look at it from the student's point of view.

One of the obvious initial difficulties which strike the student of psychology is that he[1] cannot classify the subject in a precise way. It cannot be placed neatly into the usual educational pigeon-holes which have served so well in his earlier education. Psychology, he may feel, is not quite a 'science' (meaning that it appears somewhat different from physics), although it is not like the study of literature or art. And yet at times the subject matter is like that of *both* the sciences and the more conventional 'humanities'. It includes fields as diverse as existentialist theories of man's place in his social world, philosophical speculation about the 'mind-body problem', as well as methodologically rigorous experimental studies of behaviour and physiology. A second aspect of the student's initial difficulty is the fact that most undergraduate courses in psychology are not explicitly vocational. There is no single 'practical' or 'relevant' body of facts or techniques to be mastered. It is hardly surprising then that many students appear confused as to the most fruitful approach to the course of study they have undertaken.

Failing to find any clearly defined guidelines in these areas of confusion, the student may adopt the only approach with which he is familiar. He then regards psychology as similar to, say, high-school physics or biology, assuming that the safest solution consists of accumulating a large body of 'facts', techniques, and precisely stated generalisations which can be reproduced on demand (i.e. in essays and examinations). He may soon realise that matters are not as simple as this, and become perplexed, hostile or cynical about the lack of 'correct' answers to complex questions which psychology raises. The student may fail to see the situation as a challenge typical of those which tertiary education ideally should provide, and react against the subject by becoming only superficially involved in it.

1.   Throughout this book we have referred to the hypothetical psychology student as 'he'. In following this (perhaps sexist) convention we do not wish to imply that we are unaware that (at least) half of the undergraduates who study psychology are, of course, female.

Such indifference may partly account for the low standard of work which students frequently submit in essays, reports and examinations. When this work is assessed, and critical comments made, the student may become aware that his general approach to psychology is inadequate or misguided. But in most instances there is no provision made for properly rectifying such inadequacies or redirecting the student's effort.

In the large, rather impersonal institutions in which psychology is quite often taught, contact between student and assessor is usually only superficial and may be entirely lacking. Even if an assessor goes to the trouble of writing copious notes on an essay or report, the advice is frequently directed only at the most obvious shortcomings and is expressed in quite vague terms. Comments such as 'poorly organised', 'badly argued' or 'you have not supported your case', etc., do little more than suggest general areas in which some (quite unspecified) improvement is needed. They certainly do not demonstrate specific ways of improving the student's ability to present extended psychological arguments. In short, comments pointing out what is wrong with an essay do not show how to construct a well-argued case.

Perhaps more importantly, other fundamental problems may be overlooked in such comments. Much of the student's difficulty may be that he simply cannot comprehend or critically evaluate the literature relating to the topic, or else he lacks the ability to organise what he has read according to a coherent plan. There is little an assessor can do to alter this.

We believe, therefore, that one of the major aspects of studying psychology which students fail to appreciate is the need to present, analyse and evaluate sophisticated scientific argument. This is so at all levels of psychological study, but is particularly obvious in the introductory years.

We do not wish to suggest that all the blame for this state of affairs should be laid at the door of the psychology student. On the contrary. Only a small minority of these students receive any formal training in the basic concepts and techniques of argument relevant to their course of study. If a student does not happen to study logic or general philosophy as part of his degree course, he will probably fail to acquire any real sophistication in this basic area, at least until late in his course. Moreover many students appear not to recognise the need for such skills, while those who do frequently come to the realisation only when it is too late for any real improvement to be possible. Then, during the later stages of their degree, they find theoretical questions intruding into their complacent acceptance of what they have previously been taught. Yet such theoretical questions are not integrated into the student's general understanding of psychology; theoretical controversy is compartmentalised as something additional to, or separate from, the ordinary concerns of psychology. It might be added that psychology departments frequently confirm and extend this compartmentalisation by teaching distinct subcourses called 'Theory', 'History and Philosophy of Psychology', or

'General Issues in Psychology', as though such issues did not naturally develop within particular areas of study. Other departments do not make even this concession to theoretical discussion, ignoring such questions altogether.

The motivation for this book, therefore, arises from our belief that most undergraduates studying psychology are merely *assumed* to know, rather than explicitly taught, how to construct, analyse or evaluate the kind of argument which is characteristic of psychological discussion. We feel that it is unrealistic to expect students merely to 'pick up' such an ability by some apparently magical process. Rather, the ability requires explicit instruction and practice — that is, familiarity with a variety of arguments, concepts and the techniques of analysing these.

Therefore, this book presents basic concepts and techniques involved in advanced argument in an informal, practical manner to enable students consciously to develop the ability to construct worthwhile written and oral presentations in the field of psychology. What follows is entirely informal, requiring no knowledge of logic or allied disciplines. Without assuming that there is a unique, simple approach to constructing and expressing arguments, we have tried to present both general principles and specific techniques, illustrating these by numerous examples and exercises.

The first part of the book deals with the nature and uses of argument in psychology, with problems in the definition of terms, and with the evaluation of evidence and some theoretical issues of fundamental importance to psychology. The second covers the research, preparation and presentation of essays and empirical reports. Although the latter is the more 'practical' of the two sections, it presupposes an understanding of much of the preceding material. Of course the chapters need not be studied in their given order if particular information or assistance is sought.

ACKNOWLEDGEMENTS

For help typing the manuscript, our thanks go
to Maureen Kelleher, Fay Colman, Leanne Reid
and Alice Yau. For reading part of the manuscript we thank Peter Boyle and Jim Mackenzie.

PART I – THEORY

PART II – PRACTICE

PART I THEORY

1

UNDERSTANDING AND EVALUATING STATEMENTS

'don't criticize what you can't understand'.

Bob Dylan

1.1 INTRODUCTION

TWO MAIN skills are required of the psychology student: (1) comprehension and (2) evaluation of verbal material. In most courses on psychology students attend lectures, participate in seminars and tutorials, read texts and references, write theses, essays and reports, and conduct or observe experiments. In each of these areas almost all the psychological ideas to be considered will be provoked by the written or oral offerings of psychologists. For attending lectures and reading the literature this is transparently the case, but it is also true when one is conducting experiments. Even if the ideas formulated on the basis of the results of experiments do not derive directly from what someone else said or wrote, the ideas or theories which prompted the experiments and which give these results significance almost certainly will.

Two major features of this situation put a premium on understanding or comprehending verbal statements. Firstly, most of the material considered is presented linguistically, being written or spoken; second, most of the ideas come from other people (which is not to deny that students are required to think in an original manner!). For both these reasons quite sophisticated skills are required at the receptive end of linguistic communication. One is required to *understand* — literally, to make sense of — psychological theories and facts received in the form of (often complex) verbal statements. This can be particularly difficult as these theories and facts are sometimes presented in idiosyncratic language, using unfamiliar terms or, if not, employing familiar terms in unfamiliar ways. *Evaluation,* the second skill, presupposes the first: one cannot properly evaluate what one has not properly understood. Evaluation is particularly important in the social and behavioural sciences, including psychology, where alternative theories compete for acceptance. Faced with this situation, the student is forced not merely to understand but to evaluate theories — to consider reasons for and against accepting them, to judge them true or false, well supported or unsupported, etc.

Accordingly, in this chapter we undertake the deceptively simple task of introducing certain fundamental distinctions between the types of statements which are the elements of all argument. We emphasise the need to understand thoroughly and evaluate carefully these statements if one is to appreciate the complex and subtle verbal detail of psychological literature.

1.2 UNDERSTANDING STATEMENTS

Understanding what someone has said or written is the everyday ability of coming to know what he means. It is an ability we all share as users of the same language. Someone who can understand English is someone who, in general, can understand what people are proposing or 'getting at' when they use English. Why then should we devote a section of this book to discussing something that everybody who is able to read it can do already?

The answer is: First, even though we all understand English, we do so with differing degrees of competence, at different 'levels', and second, that more than the routine ability to understand informal or colloquial English is required of someone tackling abstract material presented in technical language. A number of quite special demands are made of someone who is trying to understand the technical discipline of psychology.

We will distinguish two levels of understanding. The first, which we call the *linguistic level,* concerns the comprehension of statements to the extent of being able to paraphrase them – to 'translate' them into one's own words. This level is concerned with identifying what is being communicated. The second, deeper or *conceptual level,* involves seeing the significance and implications of what has been communicated. This second level presupposes the first.

What, then, are 'statements'? Clearly, they are to be contrasted with questions, requests or orders. Put very simply, statements say or assert something to be the case (i.e. true), while questions ask whether something is the case, and requests ask that it be made the case. Since ideas, or theories and facts, are presented in the form of statements, our concern is with understanding these, not with questions or requests. (However, as we shall emphasise later in this chapter, understanding questions also plays an important part in studying a discipline like psychology.) Thus we might contrast the statement 'More boys than girls were tested' with the question 'Were more boys than girls tested?' and both with the order 'See to it that more boys than girls are tested'. A statement is typically made by producing a simple declarative sentence, although a single word uttered in reply to a question may also constitute a statement (e.g. 'Yes', in reply to 'Were more boys than girls tested?', asserts the corresponding statement above). Similarly, two different sentences can make the same statement. The sentence 'Less girls than boys were tested' can be used to make the previously mentioned statement also. Sometimes such sentences are said to have been used to assert the same *proposition,* but we shall adopt the more familiar 'statement' and speak of different sentences being used to make or express the same statement.

The statement expressed, because it depends on the meaning of the sentence, is a difficult notion to make precise and is best referred to via the sentence that expresses it. In the course of this book we will follow the convention of placing sentences in quotation marks to refer to the statements they would, in their context, be used to make. As we have pointed out above, it is the statements, *not* the sentences expressing them, which are taken to be true or false, plausible or implausible. Hence if the meaning of a sentence is understood, then what was meant can usually be reformulated in other words: being able to put what someone has said or written into one's own words is central to the task of understanding what he said (that is, what he meant).

For the purposes of illuminating some of the difficulties involved in understanding verbal material, let us briefly outline a simple account of what is involved in communication. The assumptions underlying this theory have been strongly criticised by a number of recent thinkers — most notably Ludwig Wittgenstein and Willard Van Ormond Quine — but as a theory it will serve our purpose. We will exemplify it by discussing the communication between a psychologist and someone studying what he has written.

The psychological author has an idea in mind which he wishes to share. He formulates or 'codes' it into words forming sentences which he then writes. His reader 'decodes' the words, and if he does so properly 'gets the idea' — or understands what the psychologist means. The sentence he wrote is said to express the idea, 'proposition' or 'statement' he had in mind. He could have used another sentence, but only if it had the same meaning as the original. On this account, successful communication occurs when the reader understands what statement or proposition the writer is expressing.

1.2.1 'Technical' Language

Since the words used in sentences are the common coin of communication, we need to distinguish what the author means by them from what they are conventionally taken to mean and from what the reader takes them to mean. This is particularly important where the author and reader do not share the same theoretical predilections although they may use similar words which also have a conventional, 'non-technical' use (e.g. a behaviourist and a psychoanalyst discussing 'anxiety'). For communication to proceed smoothly, the writer's intended statement and the statement the reader takes him to have made must coincide. Unfortunately, in technical disciplines it is often difficult to tell if this has happened. Although the psychologist may assume that his words are conventionally understood and not idiosyncratic, they may mean something radically different to the student just beginning to learn the 'language of psychology'. We have mentioned the word 'anxiety', but any number of other examples might be cited: 'intelligence' has a (vague) conventional meaning as well as a number of technical ones, as do terms such as 'instinct', 'drive', 'introversion', 'identification' and 'neurotic'.

The differing interpretations of the words used by author and reader mean that the former's words may need to be, quite literally, *translated* from his English to that of the reader. This is not to say that the grammar or form of technical language is necessarily obscure — it is the vocabulary which causes the problems. This may include everyday words used in a precise, technical sense or coined words or phases (like 'cognitive dissonance', 'eidetic imagery', or 'negative reinforcement').

Since word or phrase meaning is the major source of trouble in this special form of communication, we shall now consider it in more detail. Perhaps the best way to begin is to ask what motivates psychologists to use a technical vocabulary. Oddly enough, for something which causes trouble in communication one of the main reasons for using technical terms is that they facilitate communication. They, at least, serve as abbreviations for longer phrases. Thus if a learning theorist uses the term 'operant extinction' for 'the process during which a response becomes less and less frequent when reinforcement is no longer contingent upon that particular response', he saves a great many words.

More troublesome, perhaps, than cases like the above in which no non-technical meaning is apparent, are those words or phrases taken from day-to-day discourse which are adopted by theoreticians for a more restricted use. The word 'authoritarian' is a good example. In everyday language this means, roughly, 'inclined to be dogmatic, aggressive and assertive of one's authority'. However the technical meaning proposed by Adorno *et al* (1950) in their book *The Authoritarian Personality* is much more complex and, in some respects, quite paradoxical. For instance, being submissive to authority is a characteristic of being generally authoritarian. This is certainly not part of the word's more common meaning.

Given that the special vocabulary of psychology can lead to serious mis-understanding, how can one detect if one's interpretation of an author's words is inconsistent with his intended meaning? Unfortunately, sometimes one cannot tell. Although at other times it is possible to know that you have misunderstood, the clues usually lie outside the sentence or passage that is misinterpreted. For example, if a Freudian author states that 'the young boy, during his Oedipus complex stage, wishes to possess his mother sexually, and is jealous of the father', then the reader might regard this as absurd, depending on what he understands by the phrase 'possess his mother sexually'. If he interprets this to mean that the child consciously desires sexual intercourse with his mother, then this is to misunderstand the statement. However he can only realise that this is so if he compares the statement with the whole paper or theory of which it is part. The reader, having associated one interpretation with the sentence, will need to be alerted to his error by clues he can gain about both the author and his ideas independently of the disputed statement. In our Oedipus complex example, he may learn that the child's desire is hypo-thetically unconscious and relates to sexual (or 'sensual') possession of the mother in a way that need not include any idea of copulation. Hence the original unreasonable interpretation of the statement was really a misunder-standing.

The problems involved in communicating technical ideas require that special care is taken to make meanings explicit. This is why considerable space is often devoted to defining, analysing and clarifying the meaning of words in psychological literature. Indeed this topic is so important that we devote an entire chapter to it later. Here we concentrate only on those aspects which are of general importance for understanding statements.

1.2.2 True 'by Definition': true 'in Fact'

One important way of misinterpreting an author is mistakenly to take some statement which he proposes as *trivially true* to be a significant factual claim, or, conversely, to confuse a factual statement with one that he takes to be true by definition. In other words, even though each word of the sentence may be understood, the reader may not be clear as to the status or significance of the statement it expresses: even if one understands each word of the sentence, and can satisfactorily paraphrase it, one will still not fully understand the intended statement until one is clear which of two alternative purposes the sentence was intended to serve. The sentence may either specify how the author wishes to use words (i.e. it is essentially definitional), or be intended to make some claim about the world, not merely about the use of language. For example, a behaviourist might state that 'a reinforcer is any event which increases the probability of a response after which it occurs'. This statement is readily understood at the linguistic level. However it is also important to understand what *type* of statement this is. Is it intended to be true merely as a result of the way the proponent chooses to employ words, or does it express some fact about the nature of learning? Is the statement true by definition or true in fact? This is a critical distinction if one is to understand the statement in relation to others that the author makes.

Despite its importance, this distinction is not difficult to understand in principle, as the following pairs of statements indicate. Read each pair carefully and attempt to define the way in which the members of each pair differ from each other.

(a) (i) A bachelor is an unmarried male adult.

    (ii) Bachelors are happier than non-bachelors.

(b) (i) The shortest distance between two points is a straight line.

    (ii) The distance between Sydney and Melbourne is 600 miles.

(c) (i) No surface can be both wholly red and wholly green simultaneously.

    (ii) Green apples are less sweet than red apples.

As the heading of this section suggests, the first of each pair of statements is true regardless of 'what the world is like'. One cannot conceive of a world in which they are false. By contrast the second statements are not true in the same way. (We will assume for argument's sake that each is true.) Their truth depends upon, or is *contingent* upon, the state of the world. Let us try to clarify this distinction. The former statements could not be denied unless one contradicted one's self or unless one misunderstood the conventional meanings of the component words. In that sense they are *tautologies*, or are true *by virtue of their verbal formulation alone.* If someone denies that a bachelor is an unmarried male adult, there is nothing that can be done to correct his error except to reiterate that, in English, the words of his statement are conventionally used to make a statement that is unquestionably true. No evidence (e.g. examples) is relevant. On the other hand, the sentence 'Bachelors are happier than non-bachelors' would be conventionally used to assert a contingent statement: it may be denied or affirmed according to evidence. Unlike the tautology, denial of this contingent statement does not involve self-contradiction. It is an empirical question whether bachelors are happier (although a very difficult one about which to gain reliable evidence).

Although this distinction is a matter of some philosophical controversy, and there are some cases where classification is controversial (even for those who accept it) it is generally accepted that the distinction between tautologies and empirical statements is fundamentally important to understanding the functions of language. Members of the former class are more accurately referred to as *analytic* truths, and of the latter class as *synthetic* statements. The truth or falsity of synthetic statements is an empirical matter, and hence these are the main subjects of scientific debate. Analytic statements are also important, although mainly as part of theoretical analysis or definition. Let us consider these in more detail.

Since the main function of definitions is to help in the understanding of other sentences, it is important to be able to distinguish which statements are definitions and which are not. It is usually clear when someone is defining a word or phrase. He will write sentences like 'We will use the word . . . to mean . . .', or 'Let us define . . . to be . . .', etc. Sometimes, however, it is not clear whether an author intends a sentence merely to indicate the way he is using words, or not. This is because the same linguistic form can be used to provide definitions, as well as to make significant empirical statements. Thus instead of saying 'I will define X as Y', an author may write 'All X are Y'. Here it is not clear whether he is telling us that X's (as we would use the term) are the same things as those we call Y's, or whether he is implicitly telling us that he intends to use the word 'X' to mean 'Y' – i.e. to make it trivially true that 'All X are Y'. If the former is his intention, we can meaningfully ask if the claim that all X's are Y's is true or false. But this is not so in the second case. Here one can only use the statement as an indication of what the author means by 'X', to help understand other sentences in which he has used the word.

There are two main classes of definition: *descriptive* and *stipulative*. These correspond to what might be called 'conventional meaning' and 'writer meaning' respectively. When proposing a descriptive definition, a writer attempts to spell out the usual meaning of a term he is using (e.g. after referring to a psychological or conventional dictionary), whereas in a stipulative definition he specifies the meaning he intends for the word or phrase, regardless of more usual or less technically precise possible interpretations. He uses a stipulative definition when he gives a familiar work a new meaning or introduces a new term. For instance, Cattell (in Sahakian, 1965, p.398) defines 'sentiments' as 'major acquired dynamic trait structures which cause their possessors to pay attention to certain objects or classes of objects, and to feel and react in a certain way towards them'. The word 'sentiment' is thereby stipulated to have a special (although perhaps rather vague) meaning within Cattell's Theory of Personality. A descriptive definition of 'sentiment' might be quite different — e.g. 'mental feeling or emotion'. Of course, the stipulated and described (conventional) meanings of a word may not be totally inconsistent. But they may differ in precision, emphasis or scope. In this case it is important for the writer who adopts a term to be consistent in its use: alternating between using the term as stipulated and as it is more conventionally used can generate considerable confusion.

An instance of such confusion arises in Mitchell's book *Psychoanalysis and Feminism* (1974) in which the Freudian notion of hysteria (and hysterical neurosis) is discussed without explicit definition of what Freud meant by the term. To the contemporary reader who is unaware of Freud's stipulated meaning for 'hysteria', Mitchell's account might be quite misleading. Conventionally, hysteria refers to an extremely excited, agitated, even 'giggly' state (e.g. one laughs or cries hysterically). But to Freud the concept of hysteria had a more subtle meaning, referring to the somatic (bodily) manifestation of 'repressed' fears or wishes. Hence it would include frigidity and hypochondria, as well as various amnesic or paralysed states. Mitchell's failure to state explicitly how Freud (and she) use the word 'hysteria' undoubtedly confuses some of her readers. In particular, they would be confused about the function of 'anxiety' in hysteria. The Freudian hysteric is *not* overtly anxious, in contrast to the conventional meaning of the term for which overt anxiety is an essential characteristic. The issue is not whether Freud's (or Mitchell's, or our commonly accepted) definition is *true* or *false*, for the analytic statement which implicitly defines hysteria for each author is intended to be trivially true by that writer.

It is worthwhile adopting another term to refer to such implicitly definitional statements. We might say or stipulate that they are 'writer-analytic'. More fully, a statement is writer-analytic if it is, or is an obvious consequence of, a statement whose truth depends only on the way the writer intends to employ words. So, for Cattell, the statement expressing his definition of 'sentiment' (above) is writer-analytic. In contrast, as we have seen, a statement is generally analytic if it is true as a consequence of the way its words are conventionally used. Writer meaning determines whether or not a statement is writer-analytic. Conventional meaning determines its general analyticity. For Cattell, the statement 'Sentiments cause feelings' is writer-analytic, since, as may be checked above, it follows from his definition of 'sentiment'. The statement 'No maiden aunt is an only child' is analytic in the general sense. Its truth is an immediate consequence of the way the words of the sentence expressing it are conventionally used.

We have highlighted the difference between what a writer means by his words and what they would be conventionally taken to mean, and we have mentioned some of the difficulties this can cause. For example, sentences which conventionally express synthetic statements can be intended to express writer-analytic statements. Sometimes, however, the converse happens: sentences which conventionally express analytic truths are used by a writer to assert a synthetic statement. An amusing instance would be the statement 'All women are female' which was deemed *false* for the (admittedly rather controversial) purpose of classifying athletes as 'male' or 'female' at the 1972 Olympic Games. To understand what is meant in cases such as this, the reader is obliged to reinterpret the words used in the sentence. He cannot rely on their conventional meanings.

Finally it is worth emphasising that despite what has been said above, a writer's definitions are not sacrosanct. Sometimes he may be inconsistent or fail to justify his choice of definition. The latter point will be considered in detail in a later chapter, but, clearly, some definitions are more valuable than others, even if all are essentially analytic. The former point concerning inconsistency is particularly noticeable when an author purports to give a familiar word a new technical meaning. To a careful reader it sometimes becomes apparent that he has slipped back into using the word with its older conventional meaning.

This is particularly likely in psychology, where many words are *value-laden*. That is, they do not merely describe, but express judgements about, behaviour. Sometimes an author asserts what he assumes is a fact, and in doing so uses a word in a non-evaluative way. But this statement may then be used as the basis for an evaluative judgement which employs the same work and relies on its more usual, evaluative meaning. Good examples are 'intelligence', 'creativity' and 'femininity'. Clearly, whenever familiar terms like these are given novel interpretations which purport to ignore the words' conventional evaluative connotations, one should be careful not to revert to their original meanings.

1.2.3 Statements, Questions and Implications

We have suggested that the reader's ability to express in his own words an idea which someone else has stated is the mark of successful understanding. This is surely a minimal requirement. However even if the reader can paraphrase sentences in this way, it does not follow that he fully understands the original sentences as their author did, for there are degrees or depths of understanding beyond the essentially linguistic level discussed already. Ideally, it is some evidence of such 'deeper understanding' of psychological material that teachers strive to find in their students. How, then, is one to know if one understands psychological material at a level beyond the purely linguistic? Let us suggest an answer by discussing some relatively trivial examples which are not of an explicitly psychological nature.

We have all been asked to explain some matter to a friend or acquaintance.

It may be the theory of relativity or why we were late home. The explanation may require a number of statements each of which elicits a nod of comprehension. And yet a later event, possibly a question the listener cannot himself answer, shows his lack of understanding. Even though each statement seemed to be understood, some more global or conceptually abstract comprehension was lacking. Each statement may have been understood at the linguistic level, but the deeper 'conceptual' level, which requires the more active manipulation of ideas, has not been achieved. There are two important aspects of this ability: ideas understood at the linguistic level must be capable of being employed to solve problems beyond those covered by the original statements (i.e. one must be able to go 'beyond the information given'); second, the relationships *between* the statements must be understood. One needs to understand, not only what each individual statement means, but also what questions or problems the set of statements provides information about.

It may even be said that a statement can only acquire significance (and hence be fully understood) if one understands which questions or problems it answers. To illustrate, consider the statement 'Mary wore her red hat'. Viewed as an answer to the question 'Did Mary or June wear her red hat?', it differs from the same answer to the question 'Did Mary wear or carry her red hat?' Other questions which alter one's interpretation of the statement could be constructed. There is an important sense in which the different questions highlight different aspects of the statement. One moral that can be drawn from this example is that reading the same material with different questions in mind can give it very different significances. And to read material without seeing it as an answer to any questions at all is to read, in effect, uncomprehendingly.

Regarding statements as answers to questions not only helps resolve doubts about what an author means; it can also serve to deepen one's understanding of the total significance of a passage because it may relate that passage to the author's ideas advanced elsewhere. If one reads Freud's *Three Essays on the Theory of Sexuality* in isolation, ignorant of the questions to which Freud's general theory addresses itself, much of the essays' import may be lost. But if read after one has been introduced to the general issues which Freud addressed, the essays 'fall into place'. Sexual aberrations, for instance, are considered as part of the answer to questions about the origins and nature of neuroses, not merely as explorations of the nature of sexuality *per se*.

A second, related requirement for deeper understanding is that one sees the *implications* of what one reads. Put briefly, the more implications one is able to draw from a statement, the better one might be said to understand it. Since the idea of 'implication' is one which will recur frequently in subsequent chapters, we will attempt to make it precise.

To see the implications of a statement is to understand what difference or differences it would make if it were true. That is, assuming the statement is true, what else must also be true? A criminal suspect may say 'The victim took the glass off the table', which, to the detective, implies that the glass was on the table. If this is not consistent with other evidence, then the implication may incriminate the suspect. Part of the detective's understanding of the statement involved seeing one thing that it would mean or imply if it were true. We may say that one statement implies another if it is impossible for the first to be true while the second is false; or if the truth of the first statement guarantees that the second statement is true as well (e.g. the truth of the statement 'The victim took the glass off the table' would guarantee the truth of the statement 'The glass was on the table'). It is important to notice that implication is a relation between statements which holds irrespective of whether the statements are, in fact, true or false.

We may usefully broaden the idea of implication so that not just one, but a number of statements may imply another. Thus we may say that a group of statements implies another if it is impossible for all the statements in the group to be true while the other statement is false: that is, if the truth of each statement in the group would jointly guarantee the truth of the other statement. For example, it is impossible for the two statements 'All psychotics are disturbed people' and 'All disturbed people are unhappy' to be true without the statement 'All psychotics are unhappy' being true as well. Again, note that the actual truth of the statements is immaterial; what matters is that *if* they *were* true, the implied statement would also be true.

Implication, therefore, is an aspect of understanding that carries us beyond individual statements; a deeper understanding of statements is achieved if their implications are known. A number of statements made by an author may be combined to see what other statements are implied by them, or these may be combined with additional statements in order to examine their further implications. The statements implied may serve to answer some previously unanswered questions.

1.3 EVALUATING STATEMENTS

Psychology students are called upon not merely to understand the material that they read or hear, but also to evaluate it. Assuming that the material to be evaluated has been understood, we shall focus on evaluation in terms of the truth value of the statements being considered. This is not to deny that one can evaluate aspects of statements other than their truth or falsity, but only to emphasise that this is the critical aspect of any statement in an empirical discipline like psychology.

As we shall see below, statements vary widely in the ease with which they can be judged as true or false. Indeed for many statements one is reluctant to assert that the judgement can reasonably be made, and one is content with the 'weaker' evaluation in terms of plausibility. We sometimes content ourselves with judging, not whether a statement is true, but whether, in the light of available evidence, it is likely to be true. Sometimes we are even more cautious, comparing only the relative plausibility of two (usually incompatible) statements.

We have already mentioned that evaluation is part of the process of understanding a statement. In many cases it is fair to say that understanding a statement involved knowing how to evaluate it (i.e. test its truth or falsity). For example, someone who understood the statement 'Fred is taller than Bill' would know that one way to evaluate it would be to stand the two men back-to-back on a level surface. If one is considering a statement made by someone else, then disagreeing with him over the conditions under which it could be evaluated is a sign that one has not understood what he meant. One might then ask him to propose a test which would allow the statement to be evaluated. We shall have much to say about the provision of explicit criteria for evaluation of psychological statements in a later chapter on definition. Let us merely reiterate here that often to know what someone means at least involves knowing how he would evaluate his statement as true or false.

Not all statements can be judged true or false in a simple way. In fact some statements are such that, if they are false, then this may sometimes be readily shown, but, if they are true, there is no effective way of ascertaining that this is so. For example, consider the statement 'All dogs are carnivorous', where this is intended to mean that every dog – past, present and future – is naturally carnivorous. It can be contrasted with 'All the cats in the present experiment are male'. If it is true that all dogs are carnivorous, then there is no direct way of determining this (e.g. one cannot observe dogs of the future). If, however, the statement is false, one instance of a non-carnivorous dog is sufficient to establish this. On the other hand, there are statements where the converse holds. 'This object is breakable' can be known to be true (if the object has been broken), but there is no comparably direct way of knowing that it is false. (There may always be unanticipated tests which will prove the statement true.) Hence failure to break an object does not prove it unbreakable any more than the failure to find a non-carnivorous dog guarantees that none will ever be found. We mention these otherwise trivial examples to emphasise that not all statements can be conclusively evaluated as true or false, even though their truth or falsity is often mistakenly believed to have been established. A number of psychological statements fall into these two classes: most commonly held empirical generalisations ('All learning involves reinforcement', 'All biologically normal humans can acquire language') fall into the first, while statements such as 'Earthworms are capable of discrimination learning' exemplify the second.

Leaving aside these essentially logical features of general statements, let us now consider whether there is any general method of judging individual (and sets of) statements as true or false.

The key to the general evaluation of statements lies in their interconnect-

edness. Individual statements which seem difficult to evaluate can often be unambiguously evaluated because of their connections with other statements whose truth or falsity is more easily judged. The question that arises concerns the nature of these 'connections' or relations between statements. Although there are many possible relations, two stand out as important for the present task. The first is the case where one or more statements *implies* another. This is the relation given prominence at the end of the previous section. The second is that which holds between two statements when one is *evidence for the truth of the other.* Unlike implication, this deceptively simply relation is difficult to define and its exact nature is so controversial that some philosophers of science even deny that there are any statements which stand in this relation to each other.

1.3.1 Implication

Recall that one statement implies another if they are so related that the truth of the first would ensure the truth of the second: if the first were true, the second could not be false. This is sometimes expressed by saying that the second is a logical consequence of the first. Knowing that this relation holds between statements facilitates evaluation in two main ways: first, if when trying to decide whether a statement is true or false, one finds a true statement or group of statements that implies it, then one's difficulties are over. The statement is true. (Remember that all statements implied by true statements are themselves true.) This is the logic of the method constantly adopted by mathematicians. In geometry, for example, one uses this method whenever one constructs a proof of a statement (theorem). In this case, the proof establishes that the statement is implied by a number of statements (axioms), which are known, or taken to be, true.

The second way in which implication allows statements to be evaluated is of particular importance in empirical disciplines like psychology. If, in trying to evaluate a statement, one can find among the statements that *it implies* just one that is *false,* again the matter is settled: the statement itself must be false as well. It cannot be true since a true statement implies only statements which are true (see earlier definition), and the statement in question has been found to imply a false statement.

This second method also applies when not just a single statement but a group of statements implies a false statement. If such a group collectively implies a false statement, then *at least one* of that group must be false. Notice that this establishes only that at least one is false, not that all the statements in the group are false; nor does it identify which one is false. Hence to anticipate later discussion, if a theory is regarded as a group of related statements, and if that theory implies a falsehood, some part of the theory is false. Moreover should a single statement, in conjunction with a set of statements all of which are known to be true, imply a falsehood, then the original statement must be false. Thus individual statements (which may include psychological hypotheses) can be evaluated in conjunction with established statements by means of this second use of implication.

We have examined two methods of evaluating one statement in relation to others: first, any statement implied by a true statement is true; second, any statement that implies a false statement is false. Notice that these rules do *not* state that if a statement is implied by a false statement it must be false, nor that any statement which implies a true statement must itself be true. There is an important asymmetry in the logic of implication which is all too frequently misunderstood. People often mistakenly believe that a result predicted by a theory (or group of statements) will not occur because the theory is false, or they assume that they can evaluate as true any theory which makes true predictions. Yet both types of judgements violate the rules of implication, despite the fact that they *appear* to be the methods employed by the empirical sciences. We shall have more to say about these points in later chapters. Here let us emphasise that it is only when the statement being evaluated is implied by a true statement or implies a false one that the rules of implication allow a rigorous true/false decision. In other cases different criteria are required.

1.3.2 Evidence

The second connection between statements we previously termed the 'evidence relation'; although easy to illustrate, this is difficult to define. We all make assertions about the evidence for or against statements such as 'The rods of the retina respond to white light', 'Imprinting occurs in all mammal species', etc., yet we seldom analyse what statements constitute evidence for these claims. In Chapter 3 we examine the connection between evidence and explanation. Here we wish to make only some general, but quite important, remarks.

By comparison with implication, the evidence relation concerns not whether a statement is unquestionably true or false, but rather whether it is plausible or not; whether it is *likely to be true,* given the truth of other statements (evidence). It is a matter of degree: we may say of certain statements that they offer slight or good evidence for some other statements. There is considerable disagreement about the exact nature (or even the existence) of this relation, but it is frequently taken to hold where a theory has successfully predicted the outcome of an experiment or other observation, and where the theory seems best to explain that outcome. The statement describing this outcome is said to be evidence for the theory that predicted it. In this respect it is like the converse of the implication relation. As we have noted, however, it is an erroneous interpretation that the outcome implies the truth of the statements which predicted it. The most that can be concluded, and then with some caution, is that one statement provides evidence for the other. Unlike the implication relation, the degree of evidence is conditional on additional information. Further facts can alter judgements about the status of what initially appeared to be weak or strong evidence. Hence in saying that the evidence renders a statement plausible or likely, we leave open the possibility of changing our judgement. The statement is not *'proved'* although it may be *'supported'* by the evidence. This is an important distinction which will arise frequently in later chapters.

1.3.3 Observation Statements

We have considered some ways in which statements that are difficult to evaluate individually can be judged in relation to other statements that are more easily evaluated. For this comparative process not to continue indefinitely, for it to be 'anchored', some statements are required which can reasonably be judged as true or false on other grounds. What kinds of statements might these be?

To return to one example we mentioned when illustrating comparative evaluation, elementary mathematical truths are capable of unambiguous evaluation, as are reports of simple observations made in, say, experiments. Although these statements belong to quite different classes, they can be evaluated without recourse to further, related statements. The central difference between the two is in the role of *observations* which are irrelevant to the first class yet critical for the second. Of the two, the second is considerably more important for evaluating psychological statements, but we will briefly discuss the first for the sake of contrast.

The first class, to which elementary mathematical truths belong, is what we previously called simple *analytic statements* – statements like 'All human primates are primates', 'Bachelors are male', '2 x 3 = 6'. Put another way, they are those simple statements whose truth or falsity is due only to the meanings of the words involved, regardless of any observations or experiences of the person making such statements.

However, as mentioned previously, apart from definitions and statements they directly imply, few interesting psychological statements are of this type. Psychology is concerned with statements to which *observations* are relevant, knowledge of whose truth or falsity makes a direct difference to specific predictions. Not only do simple analytic statements by themselves say nothing about what will or will not happen, but statements they imply fail to do so also.

The second class of statements, those that report observations, are of more direct importance to psychology. Reports of experimental phenomena are generally regarded as *observation statements,* although even some of these may be controversial. This is because statements vary widely in their degree of 'observability'. Hence we shall begin by treating statements as though their truth or falsity is either verifiable or not, and define a fairly narrow class which shall later be expanded as we consider various functions of such statements. Just as simple analytic statements are those about which everyone who understood the language would agree, so observation statements are those about which there would be agreement from anyone who both understood the language *and* observed the circumstances to which the statements applied. Put loosely, they are statements which can be evaluated by being compared, not with other statements, but with observable phenomena.

For example, consider the statement 'The subject was seated in front of the T.V. monitor'. This is an observation statement in that everybody able to observe the subject (and able to understand the statement) would agree on its truth or falsity. Under ordinary circumstances this criterion would not lead to any ambiguity in such cases. By contrast, however, 'The subject was an only child' is not a statement whose truth could be determined by merely observing the subject. Being without siblings does not 'show on one's face', so to speak; it is a characteristic which is not directly observable in the sense that applies in the first example. Despite this, the truth or falsity of this type of statement can usually be confidently determined.

However if these examples suggest that the contrast is simple, others complicate the picture: deciding if a statement is observably verifiable can be quite difficult. Contrast the pairs 'The subject was smiling' and 'The subject was happy' with 'The subject's face was red' and 'The subject's face was sunburnt'. All four may be true, but in both pairs the second goes beyond what is immediately observable in any direct sense. Although someone who understood the language and saw the subject could agree that he was smiling or that his face was red, agreement could not be guaranteed concerning the reasons for these observable characteristics. People are more likely to disagree about the reasons for smiling or for having a red face than about those directly observable characteristics. Hence the second statement of each of the above pairs goes beyond the first and is less likely to be judged as 'observational'.

In these examples, the second statements express what could be *inferred* from the first of each pair. In this respect, they are rather like statements which are not admitted as legal testimony. Eyewitnesses are generally required not to draw inferences from what they have seen. They are asked not to 'read anything into' what they report they have observed. However this distinction is difficult to maintain, for what a person 'sees' may itself be influenced by factors such as his expectations and biases − in short, he may infer as part of the process of 'reporting' observations.

In view of this, it is possible that there may be no statement which literally everyone viewing the evidence would agree upon. But this does not mean that we should completely despair of specifying a class of observation statements. For there are certainly some statements which involve relatively few controversial inferences. Earlier we noticed that understanding a statement involved knowing how it might be tested, and there is clearly a class of statements for which general agreement can be found concerning appropriate methods of evaluation. Should someone disagree with one of these, he, not the proponent of the statement, would be called on to justify his disagreement.

Let us briefly expand on this point. As the examples we have discussed show, observation statements take less for granted, or rely on fewer inferences, than other statements. When a person questions the truth of an observation statement it is usual to expect him to justify his doubts. On the other hand, people are more likely to accept differing interpretations when statements more clearly involve inferences. Hence, if one questions a report that 'the rat turned left at the junction in the maze', one will probably need to justify this stand. However, it would not be so peculiar to question the truth of a statement such as 'The patient had a weak ego', as this involves terms about which there is less consensus than those in the rat example. In other words, a statement that is less likely to be questioned on observational grounds alone provides a greater onus to justify disagreement than a statement involving controversial inferences or assumptions.

Notice, however, that even observation statements can be questioned. To qualify our original definition, an observation statement is one whose truth in most circumstances is relatively easily and uncontroversially assessed; but there is no guaranteed infallibility. Sometimes when such statements clash with a widely held view, they are questioned. A recent, interesting case in point is presented by the apparently inexplicable feats of Uri Geller who has been 'observed' to bend metallic spoons by moving his hands over their surfaces without applying force. This apparent phenomenon clashes with modern physical theory. Despite the testimony of literally thousands of people that 'Geller bent a spoon by stroking it', there are good reasons for a sceptic to reply that what was observed was Geller stroking a spoon and the spoon bending. That is, there is some reason not to infer, or read into what was observed, a causal relationship between the two events.

Given this brief introduction to some of the subtleties of ostensibly simple observation statements, let us now make some points concerning the general issues these raise for understanding psychological argument. First, if we accept that many observation statements involve implicit inferences, then it follows that they are likely to reflect the conventionally accepted psychological theories of the day insofar as they would be accepted unquestioningly by most psychologists. But in psychology there is frequent disagreement over what are acceptable observation or 'fundamental' ('bottom-level') statements. It is in their criteria for accepting or rejecting various statements as observational that psychological 'schools of thought' differ from each other. For example, behaviourists, cognitive psychologists, psycho-analysts and existentialists allow different types of inferences to be implicit in the 'descriptive' statements on which they base their respective theoretical interpretations. Hence, some maintain that only physical movements, not 'behaviour' (and certainly not 'actions'), can be observed. To such theorists, behaviour which is described by statements like 'The rat ran the maze to the goal box' or 'The man climbed the stairs' carry the inference that the organism in question *intended* the described movement. They might argue that, since intentions cannot be observed, then such descriptions are inappropriate as the basis of an observational science. Therefore even the statement 'The rat in the Skinner box pressed the lever' might be regarded as a statement involving unwarranted inferences.

To avoid these inferences it might be necessary to describe only the muscular and other movements of the rat in a totally 'physical' manner. Otherwise, should the rat press the bar with his left paw or his nose, both will be classed as the same response, which, in a very strict observational sense, they are not. This example is not an extreme one. Many psychologists dispute whether subjects' verbal reports (e.g. of an after-image or dream) should be considered legitimate 'scientific' data for similar reasons. Hence, even putative observation statements may not merely reflect 'the facts' – they may be 'theory-laden', reflecting the general theoretical presuppositions of their proponent.

2

UNDERSTANDING AND EVALUATING ARGUMENTS

An argument isn't just contradiction.

Can be.

No it can't. An argument is a connected series of statements intended to establish a proposition.

No it isn't.

Yes it is.

ARGUMENT CLINIC
from Monty Python's Previous Record

2.1 UNDERSTANDING ARGUMENTS

EVEN IF one can understand and evaluate individual statements in the sense discussed in Chapter 1, there are still a number of different issues which need to be understood when arguments are presented, analysed and evaluated. As we shall see, an argument is not merely the assertion of an individual statement. In general, the difference between the two lies in the fact that an argument does more than merely tell us that something is the case – it *provides reasons* in support of one or more statements. It follows that an argument must involve at least two statements – one putting forward a particular view, and at least one other specifying reasons for that view. When someone argues sincerely, he does not merely say what he thinks; he also says why he thinks it. It is this that allows listeners and readers to make critical judgements as to whether they should agree with what was argued. This process is the essence of all intellectual activity. Let us therefore explicate what it involves.

Arguing, like speaking, is something we all do well enough in day-to-day life without any formal knowledge of logic. But when one moves to a less familiar, theoretically abstract domain like psychology, some more explicit analysis of argument is necessary if naive confusions are to be avoided. The purpose of this chapter, then, is to provide some of the means for becoming more aware of the nature and value of the arguments one finds in psychology. Accordingly, it is necessary to introduce a number of mildly technical concepts. We believe that a thorough grasp of these will better enable the student to analyse and construct sophisticated psychological arguments. We have already discussed different types of statements; below we introduce the concepts of 'premiss, 'conclusion', 'argument', 'induction', 'deduction', 'validity' (and soundness). In considering these, we will outline some of the argument forms on which scientific reasoning is based, pointing to some of the more common misconceptions and fallacies found in this area.

2.1.1 The Elements and Structure of Argument

An argument can be defined as that totality consisting of a number of statements advanced jointly in support of another statement. More generally, it is a connected series of statements, each of which is either advanced in support of one or more of the others or is presented as supported by one or more of the others, or both. It can be noted immediately from this definition that although arguments consist of statements, they are not themselves statements. Clearly, as was mentioned previously, an argument must consist of at least two statements, one put forward in support of the other. Hence, a news bulletin is not an argument, although it is a connected series of statements. What is lacking is the intention that some of its constituent statements support, or are supported by, others. In the news bulletin any statements which might be said to support others are usually rare and generally not explicitly intended to do so.

Another way of characterising the difference between arguing and merely stating or describing something can be seen with respect to understanding. To understand an argument one has both to understand its component statements, and to identify which of these are intended as support for which others. One must understand the intended relationships *between* the constituent statements of an argument. Perhaps the best way to make this point clear is through an example. Let us analyse the following simple argument into its component elements and express the way these relate to each other in the encompassing structure of the argument. (Of course, arguments rarely display their structure at a level which will permit such an immediate analysis; more often than not the elements must be abstracted from the general flow of written or spoken language in which they inhere.)

Furthermore, on this question of instincts, I want to make it clear that instinctual behaviour in humans is not supported — humans do not display instinctual behaviour. As we saw earlier, instincts involve rigidly stereotyped, unmodifiable behaviour, but all human behaviour is characterised by plasticity.

The preceding passage has provided the vehicle for a very simple argument, and it is now our task to analyse this argument into its basic elements. Clearly, there are some phrases in the passage which simply act as padding and add nothing to the real force of the argument. For example, phrases like 'Furthermore, on this question of instincts' and 'I want to make it clear that' merely serve to maintain continuity and cohesion in the prose passage. The elements of the argument which we hope to uncover in our analysis are statements, and it is usual to list the component statements of an argument in the form of a dictionary where each statement is represented by a letter. For example,

A: Instinctual behaviour in humans is not supported.
B: Humans do not display instinctual behaviour.
C: Instincts involve rigidly stereotyped, unmodifiable behaviour.
D: All human behaviour is characterized by plasticity.

Having analysed the argument into its component elements, we can proceed to distinguish between its *premisses* and *conclusions*. Every argument must contain both a conclusion and at least one premiss. The premisses of an argument are those statements which are advanced to support others, and the conclusions are those statements which are intended to be supported. In our example, using the above letters to represent the component statement and an arrow to reflect the relationship of 'support', with brackets to indicate that a conjunction of statements is considered as a whole, we have the following structure:

This is, the statements D and C are offered jointly in support of the conclusions A and B; or, in other words, it is intended that A and B be inferred from D and C. As the original argument stands, however, the intentions of the author are not entirely clear. From what he has written he could have intended to express the following argument:

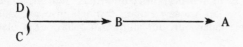

If this was so, then D and C jointly are intended to support B, which is then an *intermediate conclusion*. B, in turn, is intended to support A. Hence it is not always clear which of several alternative structures an author intends.

At this point we might distinguish *'unitary'* from *'extended'* arguments. The former have no intermediate conclusions — i.e. no component statement serves the dual role of being both a premiss and a conclusion. Consequently, their structure diagrams will contain only one arrow, linking premisses to conclusion. A common, alternative way of representing unitary arguments — one that we shall use later — is to indicate premisses and conclusion by writing the premisses, or letters that stand for them, in a vertical list. A line is then drawn beneath the list under which the conclusion is written, preceded by a triangle of dots, the conventional symbol for 'therefore'. Thus,

$$\begin{array}{c} A \\ B \\ \hline \therefore \quad C \end{array}$$

is an alternative representation of the unitary argument pattern:

Extended arguments contain intermediate conclusions and have a chain structure linking together a series of otherwise unitary arguments. Hence the structure diagram (or skeleton) of an extended argument must contain at least two arrows. An example of such an argument would be:

> Introspection must really always be retrospection, since it takes time to report on a state of consciousness. Forgetting is rapid, especially immediately after having an experience, so that some of the experience will perhaps be inadvertently lost.

Let us begin to analyse this verbally complex argument by setting out a dictionary of its component statements.

A: Introspection must really always be retrospection.
B: It takes time to report on a state of consciousness.
C: Forgetting is rapid, especially immediately after having an experience.
D: Some of the experience will be inadvertently lost.

In this argument, B is a premiss which directly supports the intermediate conclusion A. A and C then provide support for D. It can be seen that A, rather like B in the second interpretation of the previous argument, has the dual role of an intermediate conclusion and a premiss in that it is supported by B and provides support for D.

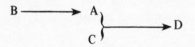

Even this example is not very complex when compared to the types of argument that one continually finds in advanced discussion in psychology and other scientific disciplines. However the basic structure of even the most complicated argument is amenable to analysis in essentially the way illustrated here.

As these examples illustrate, it is sometimes quite difficult to identify an argument. It is often unclear how the component statements are related, even though each is understood. Fortunately there are a number of key words and phrases which are conventionally used both to signal the presence of an argument and to identify its premisses and conclusions.

These include 'therefore', 'so', 'since', 'thus' and 'consequently', while common phrases to the same effect include 'hence it follows that', 'from this it may be seen', and 'from this it can be concluded that'. Such phrases not only alert us to the presence of an argument but also help reveal its structure.

If *A* and *B* represent statements, then the following are ways of expressing the same argument.

> A, therefore B;
> A, so B;
> Since A, B;
> A, hence it follows that B, etc.

Each has the structure:

$$ A \longrightarrow B; \ \text{or} \ \frac{A}{\therefore B} \quad \left(\frac{A}{\text{Therefore B}} \right) $$

As a general rule it is best to begin one's analysis by identifying the conclusion — what the argument is 'getting at' or 'trying to show'. As we have seen, this will usually be clear from the use of words such as 'therefore', 'so', 'thus', or phrases like 'it follows that' or 'it can be seen that' preceding the relevant statement. There may be more than one conclusion (i.e. more than one statement intended to be supported by relevant premisses). If so, then this should be clearly indicated in any analysis.

Given that one has identified the conclusions of the arguments being analysed, one asks what each is intended to be supported by, or on what grounds (of evidence, for instance) the arguer makes these statements. To answer this, the interrelationship between the relevant supporting premisses will need to be specified. Thus, are certain premisses to be taken conjointly, as alternatives, or as intermediate sequential steps in the argument? As our examples show, it is possible for a number of independent lines of evidence to support one conclusion:

Or for a number of premisses to form a chain of inference:

A $\longrightarrow$ B $\longrightarrow$ C $\longrightarrow$ D

Or for some combination of statements jointly to lead to an intermediate or final conclusion although neither statement is intended by itself to yield that conclusion:

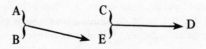

Clearly, therefore, the relationships that obtain *between* the premises of any argument must be understood if that argument is to be criticised in any way. For instance, in the example concerning introspection, *A* and *C* together are intended to lead to conclusion *D*. Neither *A* nor *C* by itself, provides strong reason for asserting *D*, but together they do. A very common structure in argument is that the conjunction of two (or more) premises often supports a third, otherwise unexpected, statement. This structure provides arguments with direction and leads to conclusions which might not have been anticipated by examining the premises in isolation from each other.

In discussing the above examples we have assumed that the form in which arguments are found in the literature is complete, containing all the premises which are intended to support the conclusion. However such complete detail is seldom explicitly specified. Nor is it always clear from the verbal form of an argument which, if any, statements are intended as premises or conclusions. For example, it is not clear in the following whether an argument is intended, and certainly, if one is intended, it is only incompletely presented:

Not all primates are monogamous. Humans are sometimes polygamous.

Presumably the second statement is intended as a reason for the first, although there is no obvious sign that this is so (e.g. no words like 'hence', 'therefore' or 'so'). Moreover the second statement would be intended as support for the first only if it is taken in conjunction with at least one tacit (unstated) premiss in the original presentation. (What is it?) This example raises an important problem in the identification and analysis of arguments. Authors frequently are content to leave, unstated, premises which they regard as obvious or generally assumed. Alternatively they may occasionally not formulate a conclusion, should it be otherwise clearly implied. Such incomplete arguments are called *enthymemes*. Most informally presented arguments are enthymemes; it is rare for someone to state explicitly all the components of a particular argument. Indeed it is often the most controversial or important premises which remain tacit. As we shall see when discussing evaluation, if one is to criticise an argument adequately, it is vital to spell out these assumed premises.

How can one tell what premises have been omitted? In general the best method to use is to assume that the proponent of the argument is arguing well — and to consequently read in any extra premises he needs if those he has offered explicitly are, in fact, to support the conclusion. Thus on this approach, in

Jones is a student, so he is likely to have an above average I.Q.

it is here assumed that 'Most students have an above average I.Q.'. Since it assumes the arguer is arguing well, this method is sometimes unduly sympathetic. However it does lead to a higher standard of criticism of arguments, for it saves a 'strawman' argument being set up and easily demolished.

2.1.2 Induction and Deduction

There are two main types of argument which it is important to distinguish because they are evaluated according to very different criteria. What distinguishes them is the different ways by which their premisses are intended to support their conclusions.

Therefore, before turning to the task of evaluating arguments it is necessary to distinguish these broad classes. The first — *deductive arguments* — are those in which the premisses purport to *guarantee the truth of the conclusion.* These are arguments in which it is the intention of the proponent that the conclusion be so related to the premisses that if the latter are true, the conclusion *must* also be true. The remaining class includes all those arguments whose premisses purport to *support* their respective conclusions, but not to guarantee the truth of those conclusions. These we shall call *inductive arguments.*

As can be seen by examining their definitions, the two classes exhaust the complete class of unitary arguments. In colloquial speech, the one term 'deduction' is employed indiscriminately to cover *both* types of argument. On the other hand, the term 'induction' is not often used colloquially in relation to arguments, and when it is used in technical contexts, some authors define it more narrowly than we have done. They usually reserve the term 'nondemonstrative' for the arguments we are calling 'inductive'. Hence Barker (1957, p.4) restricts the word 'induction' to those arguments '. . . which employ premisses containing information about some members of a class in order to support as conclusion a generalisation about the whole class (or a prediction about an unexamined member of a class)'. Our broader definition also includes these as inductive arguments, an example of which follows:

> There is reason to believe that the attachment of young children to their mothers is instinctive, since many other species (most notably mallard ducks and rhesus monkeys) show instinctive attachment behaviour.

In this example, the arguer does not intend his premiss to guarantee the truth of his conclusion; he merely intends that it lends support to it. In contrast, the following is a deductive argument:

> The neuroses are invariably the result of infantile sexual trauma, no matter how apparently non-sexual their symptoms. Necessarily, therefore, persons suffering from agoraphobia (a form of neurosis) must have suffered some emotional upset related to sexual experience.

In this case it is not intended that the premisses merely lend some support to the conclusion. Leaving aside the question of the truth of the premises, in this argument it is intended that if the premises were true, this would be sufficient to ensure or guarantee that the conclusion was true.

Since quite different criteria apply when one judges the worth of deductive and inductive arguments, it is imperative to know what type of argument one is analysing. Just as we have distinguished arguments from non-arguments with respect to the intentions of the proponent, so we use the same grounds for distinguishing deductive from inductive arguments. A number of words and phrases distinguish these intentions. For example, the occurrence of the word 'necessarily' in an argument of the form '*A, therefore necessarily B*' is a reliable sign that the argument is deductive, while the occurrence of qualifying phrases like 'so it seems plausible that . . .', 'it is likely that . . .', 'it is reasonable to conclude that . . .', or even, 'so, prob-ably . . .' regularly indicate that the arguer does not intend to guarantee the truth of the conclusion relative to his premises, but merely to lend it support.

If no stock phrase like 'plausibly', or 'necessarily' occurs, a simple test for distinguishing the two types of argument is to see if adding the word 'necessarily' prior to the conclusion alters the force of the argument. If it does not, then the argument can be interpreted as deductive. If it does, then it likely to be an inductive argument. An argument of the form '*A, so B*' would become '*A, so necessarily B*', which, if both are not considered to express the same intention, means that the original was not deductive. A con-verse test would be to prefix the conclusion by 'it is likely that'. Should this distort the argument, it can be taken to have been intended as deductive.

It is most important to know which of these two types of argument was intended, because almost all inductive arguments will be found to be very poor if judged by the criteria applicable to deductive arguments. Clearly, if someone merely intends his premises to lend some support to his conclusion, it would be surprising if they actually guaranteed its truth. This would clearly be judged a bad deductive argument although it might be quite acceptable as an inductive form of reasoning. Two important practical consequences follow: first, to assess someone else's argument fairly, one must determine whether or not it was intended as inductive or deductive; second, to have one's own arguments clearly understood and fairly evaluated, one must make clear whether or not one is arguing inductively or deductively.

2.2 EVALUATING ARGUMENTS

We have discussed three aspects of understanding arguments. The first was the need to understand the component statements; the second, identification of premises and conclusions; and the third was recognising whether an argu-ment was intended to be deductive or inductive. As we mentioned, the last issue is important because the standards for judging inductive arguments differ markedly from those applicable to the deductive variety. In this section we will consider only the evaluation of deductive argument for which criteria are relatively well defined, leaving the evaluation of inductive forms until the chapter on explanation (Chapter 3).

To argue is to propose a number of statements in support of one or more further statements. When the components have been understood and their functions as premises or conclusions identified, two questions arise: (1) Are the component statements true or false?; (2) Does the intended relation between premises and conclusion (or conclusions) actually obtain? Do the premises support the conclusion or not? We have considered ways in which we may try to evaluate the truth of statements, but how can we judge whether the argument succeeds in its intention? How can we determine if the premises (deductively) support the conclusion?

Let us begin by returning to our definition of deductive argument. Recall that in such cases the arguer intends his premises to guarantee the truth of his conclusion: assuming the truth of the former, the latter must also be true. But this is a relation we have already encountered − it is *implication*. We discussed it in relation to the evaluation of individual statements. Hence deductive arguments are those in which it is intended that, if the premises are true, the conclusion must also be true: the premises *imply* the conclusion. When implication obtains, the deductive argument is said to be *valid*. If, additionally, the premises are true, the argument is termed *sound*.

So the two important considerations in the evaluation of deductive arguments can be expressed by the questions:

(i)   Is the argument valid? (Do the statements which are the premises imply the statement that is the conclusion?)

(ii)   Are the component statements true?

Notice that the relation of implication is critical to the evaluation of both individual statements and the deductive arguments of which they are part. This is hardly surprising, for one of the main purposes of an argument is to express, and thereby show others, how a statement (the conclusion) can be evaluated. When one person presents another with an argument he is showing how the conclusion can be evaluated. He makes public his reasons for believing his conclusions to be true.

Although arguments consist of statements, as we have emphasised, they are not themselves statements, and although the statements of which they consist can be true or false, arguments themselves can be neither true nor false. Whereas the key feature of statements is their truth (or falsity), the key feature of arguments is their *validity* (or invalidity). Conversely, just as arguments cannot properly be described as being true or false, statements cannot properly be described as being valid or invalid. This is because what determines the validity of an argument is the relation that holds between premisses and conclusion. The argument is valid if that relation is one of implication, and is invalid otherwise. Yet whether this relation holds or not is almost entirely independent of the actual truth of the premisses and conclusion. For example, some valid arguments have true conclusions, whereas some do not; some have true premisses, whereas some do not. There is only one combination that is definitely ruled out: *no valid argument with true premisses can have a false conclusion.* All other combinations of true and false premisses and conclusions are compatible with an argument's being valid. Remember, an argument is valid if the premisses are so related to the conclusion that it is impossible for the premisses to be true and the conclusion false.

How can we tell if an argument is valid? That is, how can we judge if the premisses imply the conclusion. In general, ascertaining whether or not an argument is valid involves the careful application of one's knowledge of the subject matter of the argument and the use of one's imagination. In short, it involves asking of the argument in question whether there are any conceivable circumstances in which the premisses could be true while the conclusion was false. Consider the very simple argument

Schizophrenics all come from families with a history of psychotic disorder, and Jones's family has such a history, therefore Jones will exhibit schizophrenia.

That this conclusion is not implied by the premisses is clear, for it is possible to think of circumstances in which the premisses are true while the conclusion is false.

Sometimes, of course, one's inability to imagine circumstances in which the premisses are true but the conclusion false does not mean that there aren't any. There may be some conceivable, but not conceived, circumstances. The fault may lie in one's imagination. Are there any *other* guides to determining the validity of an argument? Fortunately there is a fact that greatly facilitates the determination of implication, and hence judgements concerning an argument's validity. This is the fact that there is a connection between the implication relation and some recognisable patterns in language.

Thus, for example, in general, any premisses having the patterns

All A's are B's, and
All B's are C's

will jointly imply a conclusion having the pattern

All A's are C's.

Thus if one's argument turns out to have premisses and conclusion that fit this pattern, then it will be formally valid. Indeed such patterns (or forms) are the subject matter of much of formal logic, and below we shall look at a couple of very elementary patterns. Unfortunately the patterns that most formal logicians study are patterns in artificial invented languages, and have limited immediate applicability to the wide variety of arguments presented in everyday English.

To apply the patterns of formal logic one needs to translate or symbolise ordinary English into these invented languages – a process often as hazardous as the aforementioned method of creative assessments of the possibility that the premisses can be true in certain circumstances in which the conclusion is false.

There is a more practical way of taking advantage of the link between implication and patterns in language. In general, if one can find an obviously invalid argument which has the same form as one that one wishes to criticise, then that suffices to show the latter is invalid. Thus one often hears a person reply to another's argument by saying, 'You might just as well argue that . . .' and give an argument with a similar pattern to the first, but with clearly true premisses and a clearly false conclusion. To adapt an example from Lewis Carroll, if the first person argues 'I mean what I say, therefore I say what I mean', a second person may reply, 'You might as well argue thus: 'I see what I eat, therefore I eat what I see'. What was not patently invalid is shown to be so by comparison with a formally similar, yet clearly invalid, argument. In its original linguistic form, the pattern of reasoning which underlies an argument may not be obvious and therefore some ability to compare arguments with forms that are well understood (e.g. various types of syllogism, *Modus Ponens, Modus Tollens*) can facilitate critical evaluation. One must be able to probe beneath the superficial linguistic aspects of arguments, seeking out the pattern (form) of reasoning that they exhibit.

2.2.1 *Modus Ponens* and *Modus Tollens*

We consider here two elementary argument patterns which underlie many common forms of scientific prediction and evaluation.

(a) **Modus Ponens**: Asserting the Antecedent. Consider the argument:

> If the ability to learn a language is largely innate, then children will all learn to speak at about the same age. P_1
>
> The ability to learn a language is largely innate. P_2
> _____
>
> Therefore, children will all learn to speak at about the same age. C

This is the simplest conditional form of argument and is so ubiquitous as scarcely to require formal presentation. It is conventionally represented as

If p then q
p
———————
∴ q

(Here the lower-case letters *p* and *q* mark places where an indicative sentence could be placed.)

Modus Ponens is often confused with a form of argument which is invalid, namely:

If p then q
Not p
———————
∴ not q

(Here, and in the following pages, 'not-*p*' stands for the negation of *p*, i.e. a sentence equivalent to 'It is not the case that p'.) The previous example is known as the *fallacy of denying the antecedent* and can be illustrated by altering the first example to yield:

If the ability to learn language is largely innate, then children will all learn to speak at about the same age.

The ability to learn a language is not largely innate.

———————————————————————————————————————

Therefore, children will not all learn to speak at about the same age.

Clearly, this conclusion does not follow. Actual matters of fact aside, if it were not the case that the ability to learn a language were largely innate, it could still be true that children learned to speak at about the same age (for other reasons). The denial of the second statement in a conditional (the consequent) is not necessitated by the denial of the first statement (the antecedent). This fallacy is surprisingly common and is probably due to mistakenly taking sentences of the form 'If *p* then *q*' to imply sentences of the form 'If *q* then *p*'.

These examples illustrate the important asymmetry between asserting and denying the antecedent in a simple conditional argument. The latter is not merely the logical opposite of the former. The reason that many people erroneously assume this to be the case is that, in practice, most instances of invalid conditional arguments do not lead to obviously implausible conclusions. Hence, rejecting the consequent on the basis of denying the antecedent is a very common practice. For example, if both the simple statements (*p, q*) in a conditional seem untrue, the denial of the antecedent is all too easily taken as grounds for the denial of the consequent. The following is a relevant case:

If computers can 'think' in a genuinely creative manner, they could be programmed to write a poem. Computers cannot 'think' in a genuinely creative manner, therefore it is ridiculous to think that they could write a poem.

Leaving aside the controversial questions concerning the meanings of words like 'think', 'creative' and 'poem', this argument is deceptively appealing because the relevant statements are widely believed (i.e. both the conclusion and the denial of the antecedent are widely believed). The same might be said of another (again grossly oversimplified) argument:

If the unconscious mind exists, people's dreams are capable of being analysed and understood. However the concept of unconscious mental processes is simply ridiculous, so there is no likelihood of ever comprehending people's dreams.

Both of these arguments are invalid as they stand. Both, suitably interpreted, would be valid of the conditional in each were of the form 'only if . . .', but without this modification each commits the fallacy of denying the antecedent.

It may be appreciated, therefore, that even a simple conditional argument such as *Modus Ponens* must be carefully analysed if one is to avoid a fallacy as patent (at least after it is brought to one's notice) as denying the antecedent. Similar caution is necessary with the equally common argument paradigm *Modus Tollens*.

(b)   **Modus Tollens**: Denying the Consequent. In a sense this form of argument is the converse of *Modus Ponens,* and may be illustrated by expanding our example concerning language acquisition:

If the ability to learn language is largely innate, then children will all learn to speak at about the same age.

Children do *not* all learn to speak at about the same age (or, It is not the case that children all learn to speak at about the same age).

Therefore, the ability to learn language is *not* largely innate (or, It is not the case that . . .).

Formally this can be represented simply as:

If p then q
Not q
———————
∴ Not p

Modus Tollens is a particularly common underlying form of argument in science, where, as shall be seen in later chapters, predictions from theories are often formulated in a manner which allows refutation of the theory by means of denying the consequent or consequents. Thus in the above example a theory of the biological foundation of language development predicts a phenomenon that is denied. Its deniâl is taken to be sufficient to refute the original (theoretical) statement. Although the issue of falsification of theories is extremely complex and will be discussed at length later, let us make some general points about the importance of *Modus Tollens*.

First, it might be said that this form of argument captures the spirit of the critical method of the sciences. One begins with a hypothesis or theory (p) to test which one formulates observationally testable statements which it implies (including, say, q). This is then empirically evaluated, and, if found to be false (Not-q) is used as the basis for concluding that p is false; that is as the basis for rejecting the original hypothesis or theory. This is exactly one of the methods we suggested could be used for evaluating individual statements. Hence *Modus Tollens* makes explicit, in the form of an argument, the reasoning that is implicit in that procedure of evaluation.

In contrast to *Modus Tollens* it is *not* valid to argue deductively:

$$\frac{\text{If p then q}}{\therefore \ p}$$

This is termed the *fallacy of asserting the consequent.* To continue our example, although it might appear valid to argue that if all children learn language at approximately the same age, then the ability is largely innate, this is not so. Another example which makes this point might be:

> If the Freudian theory of dreams is correct, then men will have dreams with accompanying sexual excitation. Men do have such dreams. Therefore the Freudian theory of dreams is correct.

Or, even more trivially,

> If all rats are white, then all the rats in this Skinner box will be white. All the rats in this box are white, so all rats are white.

Clearly, each of these arguments is fallacious. Yet, this form of argument is very frequently passed off as valid by being camouflaged in complicated language.

Another pattern of argument is often mistakenly thought to be valid. Consider:

> If p and q then r
> It is not true that r
> _____
>
> Therefore it is not true that p.

Although it resembles *Modus Tollens,* this argument is invalid; all that can be relevantly concluded is that either it is not true that *p* . . ., or it is not true that *q* . . . As we noted in the preceding chapter, if a number of statements (here *p* and *q*) imply a false statement, then it cannot be determined which of the former is false. In the absence of any other information (e.g. that *q* is true) it cannot be concluded that *p* is false. It is the whole set of antecedent statements which implies the consequent, not just one, as in *Modus Tollens.*

2.2.2 Evaluation and Understanding

A number of aspects of the evaluation of arguments go beyond the questions of the truth of premisses and the validity of the argument. For example, there are some arguments that are unsatisfactory even though they have true premisses and are valid. These essentially fail to show how to evaluate their conclusions as true or false because those conclusions are little more than *restatements* of the premisses of the 'argument', or of what is assumed by the premisses. Hence in evaluating the components of the argument, the same questions are raised by the premisses as by the conclusion. To take a blatant example, 'Monday follows Sunday, so Monday follows Sunday' is clearly valid, although uninformative or 'circular'. The premiss and conclusion are identical and although the argument is valid it provides no guides as to how its conclusion could be evaluated. It is a totally trivial 'argument' because it 'begs the question' — someone in need of help in evaluating the conclusion is equally ignorant when confronted by the premiss. In other words, such an argument assumes what it seeks to prove. Although not as blatant as our illustrative case, examples of these deficient arguments are quite common. We will further examine arguments like this from the psychological literature when we consider circular explanation in the next chapter.

It is important to distinguish between evaluating a person's argument and judging his motives for proposing it. Psychologists are particularly prone to attributing motives to their opponents rather than assessing the soundness of their arguments. But whether someone's argument is due to his 'peculiar' childhood, his 'distorted' beliefs, class background or empty stomach is irrelevant to the validity of what he writes or says. It is the argument, not the arguer, that must be evaluated.

Finally, it is worth mentioning the relation between evaluating and understanding an argument. As we argued with respect to statements in Chapter 1, should what someone states appear patently false, then one should re-examine one's interpretation of what he said. Similarly, in the case of arguments, one may make premature judgements unless one is certain which components are premisses and which conclusions (or both), and whether a particular argument is intended to be deductive at all. Moreover authors frequently omit statements that are particularly obvious. Consequently, if an otherwise reasonable author appears to argue in an invalid manner, this might best be taken as an indication that he is taking something (i.e. some statement) for granted, without stating it. He may be arguing enthymemically. Here the problem becomes one of explicating and evaluating the missing premisses. Similarly, if one finds that an argument is obviously invalid, it may be that one is expecting more from it than was intended. In particular, one may have judged an inductive argument to be deductive.

3

EXPLANATION

I don't understand you, Sir.

I have found you an argument.   I am not obliged to find you an understanding.

Samuel Johnson

3.1 INTRODUCTION

PSYCHOLOGY is generally defined as the *science* of behaviour — a definition which obscures as much as it reveals. In particular, it does not specify what a 'science' is — especially in relation to complex human behaviour. However it is conventionally assumed that psychology attempts to *explain* why animals (including, or especially, humans) behave as they do, and hence ideally allows the prediction of the conditions under which specific behaviour will occur. Although there are some who would argue that human behaviour is inherently inexplicable, and that psychology cannot, therefore, be a genuine science at all, it is clear that to understand complex, empirically significant arguments in psychology, some analysis of 'explanation' and 'prediction' is essential.

We take the view that science is continuous with 'common sense'. The activities of the scientist are extensions of, not essentially different from, the activities of the sensible layman, although they may be carried out with more care and thoroughness. Reasoning, we noticed in the previous chapter, is not the exclusive domain of the scientist. Argument, the public expression of reasoning, is similarly not peculiar to science. Indeed people present, identify and evaluate arguments well enough for everyday purposes without any special study. For scientific purposes, however, some explicit attention to the nature and evaluation of scientific arguments has proved valuable.

The case is similar with respect to explanation. Each of us is both familiar with, and readily able to provide, explanations for a wide variety of everyday matters. Yet despite this everyday familiarity and capacity it is necessary, for the purposes of scientific or disciplined thought, to become better acquainted with the nature of explanation and, in particular, with criteria for distinguishing better explanations from worse.

In the preceding chapters we discussed what is involved in understanding and evaluating statements and arguments. As we shall see, explanation has connections with each of these four concepts. In this chapter we shall present two of the most widely known views on the nature of scientific explanation. The first view relates explanations more to argument and evaluation, while the second relates them more to statements and understanding. Accordingly, we shall call the first the Argument-Model of explanation, and the second, the Statement-Model.

The Argument Model, as we have called it, is perhaps the most influential and widely accepted view of the nature of explanation and is associated with the work of Carl Hempel (1965, 1966). The Statement Model is sometimes known as the 'statistical-relevance' approach and is most closely associated with the work of Wesley Salmon (1971, 1975).

After presenting each of these views (giving more space to the more influential of the two) we shall examine ways in which explanations can be assessed, finally looking at the connection between explanation and induction. There will be an introductory discussion of a number of general features of explanations and then, since the concept is central to both the Argument and the Statement Models, we shall discuss the nature of scientific laws.

Let us begin by locating some of the general features of explanations. One can ask for an explanation by asking 'Why?'. For example, the questions 'Why does forgetting occur more rapidly at first?', 'Why is there a bigger standard deviation in I.Q. in the male population than in the female population?', 'Why do humans dream during sleep?', 'Why did Johnny fail his exams?', 'Why did he try to run away from home?', etc., all ask for explanations as answers. Another common way of requesting an explanation is to ask for the cause of a particular occurrence or phenomenon. Thus, 'What is the cause of schizophrenia?' also asks for an explanation. However not all 'why' questions ask for an explanation as an answer. Some such questions, in context, express doubt about the truth of a statement and ask for reasons for believing it to be true. They ask not for explanations but for justifications. In contrast, someone using a 'why' question to ask for an explanation accepts the truth of the statement describing the event or state of affairs he wants explained and expresses puzzlement as to why it is true.

Indeed explanations are generally required only of statements which have *already* been evaluated as true. For if they are false, there is nothing to explain (although sometimes we are not sure whether a statement is to be judged true or false and we may ask how it would be explained if it were true). Thus a request to explain why males are brighter than females could be completely answered by saying 'They're not'. That is to say, there is nothing to explain. Frequently, the statement to be explained has been found true as a result of some observation or experiment, and the explanation offered shows how the event it describes could have been expected (or could have been predicted). Although the explanation is not needed to show how to evaluate what it explains, for the statement is already held to be true, the explanation does serve to integrate what has happened into the belief structure of the (otherwise) puzzled person by showing how it could have been evaluated. It increases the coherence of his beliefs. Explanations systematise a body of knowledge.

Requests for explanations can be answered in a number of quite different ways. Some questions, like the one above about dreams, can be answered by showing what (if any) function dreaming serves. Others, like the one asking for an explanation of Johnny's running away from home can be answered by citing his motive or the purpose he had in running away — perhaps to hurt his parents. We shall look at aspects of these and other types of explanation in Chapter 7. In this chapter we shall examine explanations which include laws — deductive explanations and probabilistic explanations.

These requests for explanations can be put in the standard form: 'Why is it the case that p?' — where 'p' can be replaced by a declarative sentence characterising some event, phenomenon or state of affairs. Thus our first illustrative question can be put into this form — 'Why is it the case that forgetting occurs more rapidly at first? It is worth noting something that is not apparent when explanation-requests are written down rather than spoken: explanation-requests often have a contrastive force, which is signalled by the way a particular work or phrase is stressed in the request. Thus if the word 'more' is stressed in the above request, then one is being asked to explain specifically why forgetting occurs *more*, rather than *less* rapidly, at first. If the word 'first' is stressed, then one is being asked to explain specifically why it occurs more rapidly at *first* rather than later. Many explanation-requests do not ask simply why a particular state of affairs is the case: they ask more specifically why some particular aspect of it is 'this way' rather than 'that way'.

In everyday usage, the word 'explanation' is ambiguous. Sometimes it is used to refer to sentences, sometimes to statements and sometimes to the phenomena or states of affairs they describe. Sometimes it is used to refer only to the part that does the explaining; at other times it is used to refer to the composite of explainer and explained — what does the explaining, together with what it purports to explain.

In this chapter we will, in most cases, leave the first three different meanings for the context to determine. In context it will be easy enough to tell whether we are referring to sentences, statements or states of affairs. (Where it is not, we will say explicitly which we mean.) However it is worth introducing some special terminology to help with the second ambiguity. Since we are concerned in this chapter with the structure of explanation we will be constantly referring to the different parts of an explanation — the part that does the explaining and the part that is to be explained. To save a lot of words we call the first part the *explanans*. The second part — what is to be explained — we call the *explanandum*. These words, taken from Latin, are widely used with this meaning in the literature on explanation. The nearest single English word for the explanans is 'explainer', but this is usually used to refer to the person who does the explaining. Perhaps the closest in meaning to explanandum is 'explained', but this is more typically used to describe the process rather than to describe what is explained. (A better invented word would be 'explainee'.) Since we will be using them constantly in the rest of this chapter it is worth checking that you know what each means. The explanans is the part that does the explaining (or purports to), the explanandum is the part that is (purportedly) explained. We shall reserve the amgibuous word 'explanation' for the composite consisting of explanans and explanandum. Both the argument model of explanation and the statement models require laws to be included in the explanans. As a preliminary to presenting these models we turn to a brief discussion of the nature of laws.

3.2 LAWS

When a person studies high-school physics he often memorises a number of 'laws' (Newton's laws, Charles's laws, Boyle's laws, etc.). These are universal, apparently immutable principles which subsume widely diverse physical phenomena in a most parsimonious manner. It is therefore tempting to expect psychology (a science) to revolve around similar universal principles. It may come as a surprise to the student to discover that (a) psychology does not appear to include 'laws' of such general character, and (b) physical laws are themselves subject to much controversy. One of the controversies, which we will only mention in passing, is over whether or not laws are statements. The usual view is that they are not only statements, but true statements, correctly describing regularities in the universe. This is the position we shall adopt here. One of the opposing views is that laws, particularly theoretical laws, are not statements at all, but solely devices or instruments for ordering and organising experience. Their value is as instruments, making internally coherent a set of otherwise unrelated phenomena. This 'instrumentalist' position does not hold that laws are true.

As the divergence of the above views indicates, there is considerable difference of opinion as to the nature of laws. Since our concern here is with the place of laws in explanation, in this section we focus only on two aspects of a widely agreed-upon property laws must have — namely, generality.

Laws are true synthetic (Chapter 1) general statements, but not every true synthetic general statement is a law. For instance general statements like 'All the animals in the study show retardation in discrimination learning ability' and 'The cases of schizophrenia studied by Laing all come from repressive isolated families' are not law-like. Although they are generalisations, they are insufficiently general. They just summarise what could be expressed in a finite number of specific statements. Thus, 'Case 1 studied by Laing came from a repressive isolated family', 'Case 2 studied by Laing came from a repressive isolated family', etc.

There is a further property associated with generality which is taken to be characteristic of laws. A generalisation of the form 'All A are B' is a law only if it implies or supports the truth of certain statements of the form 'If x were an A, x would be a B'. This later statement is called a counterfactual conditional, and, put generally, the property required of a law is that it imply or support the truth of the corresponding counterfactual conditionals. That the generalisations in the preceding paragraph fail this condition can be illustrated as follows: the generalisation 'The cases of schizophrenia studied by Laing all come from repressive isolated families' does not imply or support the truth of the claim that if Smith were a case of schizophrenia studied by Laing, he would have come from a repressive isolated family. Loosely put, laws have to be so general that they apply not only to things with a certain property but to things lacking it: of things lacking the property A, they say that had they been *A* they would have been *B*. A law does not simply say all *actual A*'s are *B*'s; it says *any A* would be a *B*.

The great generality of law statements makes establishing their truth difficult. Consequently it is often difficult to tell if a statement that resembles a law in other ways really is a law, for one of the conditions for a statement to be a law is that it be true. Such candidates for law 'status' are called, naturally enough, *law-like* statements − a term we shall use later in this chapter.

3.3   THE ARGUMENT MODEL OF EXPLANATION

The nature and logic of scientific explanation is the subject of an extensive philosophical literature, so no pretence is made of considering all the alternatives or of covering the more technical details in this elementary discussion. However, the concept of explanation is central to nearly every theoretical controversy in psychology and requires some detailed analysis.

We follow Hempel (1966), with whom this model is most closely associated, in distinguishing two major classes of explanation:

Deductive-Nomological (D-N) and *Probabilistic* or *Inductive-Statistical* (I-S).

As the names suggest, these are closely related to deductive and inductive argument forms respectively. Arguments, we saw in Chapter 2, are a means of showing how statements can be evaluated, and, as we mentioned above, the argument model is linked with evaluation. Indeed Hempel takes, as the main requirement that scientific explanations must meet, the condition that 'the explanatory information adduced affords good grounds for believing that the phenomenon to be explained did, or does indeed occur' (1966, p.48). If we link the explanatory information (explanans statement) with the premises of an argument, and link the statement describing the phenomenon to be explained (i.e. the explanandum statement) with the conclusion, then the above condition is the condition that the premises should support the conclusion. This is the link the argument model makes between explanation and argument.

In our view, although explanations are not arguments as we have defined them, they are sufficiently like arguments for the argument model to be very illuminating. Like arguments, explanations show how a statement could be evaluated, but unlike arguments they are not typically offered with the main intention of supporting the statement which they show how to evaluate. To the extent that they are like arguments in showing how their conclusions (analagously − explananda) can be evaluated, they are only like a very restricted class of arguments. It is the special restrictions that throw most light on the nature of explanation.

3.3.1 Deductive-Nomological Explanation

The name of this model of explanation, 'Deductive-Nomological', is a helpful description of its main features. It represents an explanation as a special kind of *deductive* argument with the explanandum as conclusion and with premisses (explanans) including at least one law (for which the Greek word is *nomos*, hence the English adjective *nomological*).

Scientific explanation has generally been analysed as a process of sub-suming particular 'facts' under general 'laws' of nature. However one frequently attempts to explain, not only particular 'facts', but also other generalisations or laws or the general properties of certain classes of objects. So the D-N (Deductive-Nomological) model covers cases where some deduction from a more general law-like generalisation is present (i.e. a generalisa-tion of broader scope or range of application than the phenomena or regularity being explained). Consequently, D-N explanation might be briefly characterised as 'deduction' from a 'law', or 'subsumption under a law'.

For example, one might explain why humans suckle their young by stating that this practice is common to all mammals, adding if need be that human beings are mammals. If the request was not to find out what *causes* humans to suckle their young, this form of explanation might be quite adequate. Of course, it might be asked why mammals suckle their young, but that is a different question which does not effectively reduce the explanatory adequacy of the former account. An explanation can be evaluated only in terms of the phenomenon being explained; there is no universal, 'all-purpose' explanation, only explanations of particular phenomena or generalisations. This point is sometimes overlooked by people who persistently ask 'why', whenever a putative explanation is proposed (e.g. 'Why do people eat?' – 'Because they want to survive'; 'Why do people want to survive?', etc.). There can be no answer to such questions which may not itself lead to other questions. For that reason, explanations seek only to provide information about the phenomenon being explained, and insofar as they achieve this aim, can be regarded as adequate.

Hempel (1966, p.61) outlines the model thus:

The explanations . . . may be conceived, then, as deductive arguments whose conclusion is the explanandum sentence, E, and whose premiss set, the explanans, consists of general laws, L_1, L_2, . . . L_r and other state-ments, C_1, C_2, . . . C_k, which make assertions about particular facts. The form of such arguments . . . can be represented by the following scheme:

$$L_1, L_2, \ldots L_r \qquad \text{Explanans sentences}$$
$$C_1, C_2, \ldots C_k$$

$$E \qquad \text{Explanandum sentences}$$

The D-N model is sometimes called the Covering Law approach and L_1, $L_2 \ldots L_r$ are often called 'covering laws', $C_1, C_2, \ldots C_k$ would include all relevant antecedent conditions (called initial conditions) — particular conditions relevant to the possible application of the covering law (such factors as the species of animal referred to, relevant experimental conditions, etc.). To illustrate this pattern, the following explanation

Each member of an identical twin pair has eyes and hair which are the same colours as those of his co-twin. This is because eye and hair colour are genetically determined (develop from the same genetic material).

could be schematically represented thus:

L_1:   Eye and hair colour are genetically determined in humans.
L_2:   Each member of an identical twin pair develops from genetic material which is the same as that of his co-twin.
$C_1 \ldots C_k$: Although not included in the original, essentially incomplete explanation, antecedent conditions which might be assumed could include: no administration of artificial colouring agents to the hair or eyes; intra-uterine environments constant across twins within pairs, and so on.

E: Each member of an identical twin pair has eyes and hair which are the same colour as those of his co-twin.

This type of explanation is extremely common in the biological and behavioural sciences (although seldom would details be made as explicit as in this example). One might say that an event or state of affairs, etc., is explained on this approach (involving laws in a particular way and using the implication relation as discussed in Chapter 1) if one is in a position to evaluate as true the statement describing it.

The parallel drawn between deductive arguments and explanations by the D-N model of explanation gives a guide in the evaluation of explanations. On this model, the criteria we discussed in Chapter 2 for evaluating deductive arguments can be applied in assessing the worth of explanations. For deductive arguments two evaluative questions were raised: (1) Do the premises imply the conclusion? and (2) Are the premises true? In this model, these become (1) Does the explanans imply the explanandum? and (2) Is the explanans true? If the explanans does not imply the explanandum then the explanation is unsatisfactory, and if the explanans is not true the explanation is unsatisfactory. In section 5 we will look in more detail at ways of assessing the worth of explanations.

3.3.2 Inductive-Statistical Explanation

Not all generalisations are appropriate to deductive explanation, and consequently it must also be acknowledged that by no means all explanation is deductive in the strict sense outlined in the previous section. As anyone who has studied psychology might have quickly noticed, most of the arguments which assert a relationship (e.g. a causal one) between psychological phenomena are based on probabilistic statements, not universal generalisations. The certainty that appears to characterise laws in the physical sciences often seems lacking in the behavioural and social sciences. Most frequently, particular events in these sciences are explained by means of *probabilistic* or *statistical* generalisations which, for example, might assert that the likelihood of an event is high, given some other occurrence. Inductive-statistical explanation, as the name suggests, represents explanations as *inductive* arguments with a statistical law among the premises.

Hempel (1966) schematises such inductive explanations in a similar way to D-N explanations. For instance (p.59):

The probability for persons exposed to the measles to catch the disease is high.

Jim was exposed to measles.
_____   (makes highly probable)
Jim caught the measles.

A general scheme that this exemplifies is:

The probability of an event of kind A also being of kind B is high.
This is an event of kind A.
_____   (makes highly probable)
This is an event of kind B.

Such a scheme suggests the similarity with inductive arguments. In contrast to deduction arguments, the conclusion is not implied by the premises; although highly likely, in relation to them it does not follow from the premises. Just as inductive arguments do not guarantee the truth of their conclusions, so this type of explanation does not show why the explanandum phenomenon or event *must* have occurred.

In the light of this, some people argue that such explanations are not really explanatory. Yet it would seem difficult to deny that the argument is explanatory, because it brings forward 'good grounds for believing that the phenomenon to be explained did or does indeed occur' — (Hempel's main requirement for a scientific explanation (see earlier)). In line with this, one of Hempel's specific requirements for inductive-statistical explanations is that, in relation to the explanans (premises), the explanandum should be highly probable.

One unsatisfactory feature of inductive explanations not shared by D-N explanation is that even though the statements in the explanans may be true, further information may undercut their explanatory force. Thus in the measles example, if it is discovered that when Jim was exposed to the measles he had just recovered from the disease, the original explanation might not be regarded as adequate. In colloquial language, the following conversation might reflect the shifting confidence in inductive explanations:

A: Why did Jim catch the measles?
B: He was recently exposed to them.
A: But he has only just recovered from measles himself.
B: Well sometimes they can be caught twice in quick succession. This must have been one of those times.

In his second contribution to the conversation, *A* introduces information in the light of which it is highly unlikely that Jim would catch measles even if he has been recently exposed to them — information which undercuts the explanatory force of *B*'s explanation.

In a growing discipline like psychology it is not unusual to find preliminary I-S explanations undercut in this manner by new information. There is no sure way of avoiding this, but it is important to be aware of the possibility, and to try and anticipate information that may have this effect.

In conclusion it is worth stressing another difference between the D-N model and the I-S model. The D-N model can be used to explain both specific phenomena and general states of affairs (e.g. those described by laws). In contrast, the I-S model is only intended to apply to specific events or phenomena. Consequently, explaining in turn the statistical generalisations that are invoked in I-S explanations (e.g. 'There is a high probability of persons exposed to measles catching the disease') is often done in the deductive fashion of the D-N model, from more general laws.

3.4 THE STATEMENT MODEL OF EXPLANATION

In our introductory remarks for this chapter we distinguished two types of 'why-questions': those requesting an explanation and those requesting a justification. We noted that it was important to separate the two. Yet Hempel's main requirement for a scientific explanation was that the explanans should justify ('give good grounds for believing') the explanandum phenomenon. A major criticism that proponents of the statement model bring against the argument model is that it links explanation too closely with justification, for an argument, as we have noted, is a way of justifying one's evaluation that a statement is true. This criticism is particularly directed at the I-S model of explanation (see 3.3.2). Put in our terms, these critics hold that explanation has more to do with understanding than evaluation. This is not the only criticism. Another is that the argument model pays too little attention to the requirement that the explanans be (causally) relevant to the explanandum. We shall look at others below, In answer to these criticisms, the particular statement model we shall discuss both denies that explanations are arguments and utilises the concept of statistical relevance, whence it takes its name.

3.4.1 Statistical-Relevance Explanation

According to this view, an explanation of a particular event is a body of statements describing factors which are statistically relevant to that event. A factor is said to be *statistically relevant* to an event of a certain kind if it makes a difference to the probability of occurrence of such an event. To use an example taken from Salmon (1971, pp.10-11), consider someone's recovery from a neurotic symptom during psychotherapy. It may be that the rate of recovery of people undergoing psychotherapy is very high and so the treatment would seem to explain the recovery. But if the rate of spontaneous (i.e. untreated by psychotherapy) recovery is *as* high, we cannot claim in the light of these suppositions that the treatment explains the recovery. If the treatment makes no difference to the probability of recovery — if there is the same rate of recovery whether people are treated or not, then it is a statistically irrelevant factor, and, consequently, on this model it is not explanatory.

This approach to explanation differs most markedly from the inductive statistical model in not requiring that in relation to the explanans the explanandum is highly probable. It is in this sort of case that the link between explanation and evaluation (and hence prediction) is most clearly broken by this model. It allows an explanation to consist of explanatory facts in the light of which the explanandum may be very unlikely. This model also utilises a number of statistical conditions as a guide to which of the statistical relevance relations are causal. But we will not pursue the details here. As in the I-S model, care has to be taken to reduce the chance that omitted information might be relevant and so change the probability of the explanandum in relation to the explanans.

The provisional nature of this sort of explanation, the fact that, unlike deductive explanations, inductive or statistical explanations can be undercut in this way, raises the following questions. Does our current need to use inductive explanations reflect the nature of the world or just our ignorance of its nature? If we knew enough, could we replace every inductive explanation with one fitting the D-N model? Are all probabilistic laws ultimately reducible to deterministic ones? Are there in fact objectively random processes in nature?

We cannot hope to answer these questions here as they involve the philosophical doctrines of determinism and indeterminism. Although some of the best theories in science are still probabilistic, it is not clear whether this reflects on us or the world. Perhaps as a *working* hypothesis, the determinist position is better, in that it encourages us not to rest content with probabilistic laws but to search for underlying deterministic ones. Perhaps in some areas such a search is futile. One such area might be the study of human behaviour. This is not the place to explore these questions.

3.5 EVALUATING EXPLANATIONS

In the previous two sections we discussed three models of explanation — two argument models and one statement model. Being models, they were meant not only to describe what explanations are like but to specify what they ought to be like — to provide a model or ideal for scientific explanations. As a result the models provide criteria for evaluating explanations and we shall discuss these in this section. Despite this, purported explanations may appear to fit these models without really being good explanations, so we shall also discuss ways in which such apparent explanations can be distinguished from genuine explanations.

To evaluate an explanation we must have an explanation to evaluate — just as with the evaluation of statements and arguments, the evaluation of explanations first requires that the explanation be identified and understood. As with arguments, so with explanations. One needs not only to identify and understand the component statements but also to identify and understand the interrelationship (structure) of these statements — that is, which ones describe the explanans and which ones the explanandum. Again as with arguments, the exigencies of communication mean that there is often a large gap between what is verbally presented as the explanation and the intended explanation. If something is too obvious to be stated, it may be left unstated, or perhaps only implied but, nevertheless, be an essential part of the explanation.

What is omitted may be some particular claim or it may be a law that is required for the full explanation. Even citing a cause of a particular event by way of explaining it can be fitted to the D-N model of explanation. This is done by taking the causal claim to imply an unstated law connecting events and circumstances, which are relevantly like the claimed cause, with events and circumstances relevantly like the event to be explained (see Chapter 5, section 5.2). However as with enthymemes (elliptically presented arguments), so with elliptically presented explanations — what is left unstated may be very difficult to determine precisely.

Once the explanation has been filled out, if it is elliptical and identified, an important preliminary check to make is to ask whether the explanandum (statement) is really true. If not, as we noted earlier, there is nothing to explain. Beyond being an interesting intellectual exercise, further evaluation of the explanation would be pointless. Where what is being explained is a regularity or even a law, it may be difficult to tell with certainty if it is true, but we should at least have good reason to think it is. (For these considerations, see 3.5.2.)

When the explanation has been identified and checked, how is it to be evaluated? How are we to distinguish good explanations from bad? How are we to distinguish better from worse? How are we to distinguish genuine explanations from those only masquerading as such? There are two central criteria for judging explanations. They can be formulated as the following questions:

1. Would the explanans, if true, explain the explanandum?
2. Is the explanans true?

The first question concerns the relation between the explanans and the explanandum. What one accepts as an answer to it will depend upon the model of explanation one is using. Apart from questions excluding trivial explanations, for each model the basic question is:

For the D-N model:
Does the explanans logically imply the explanandum?
For the I-S model:
Does the explanans render the explanandum highly probable?
For the S-R model:
Does the explanans cite factors that are statistically relevant to the explanandum?

We take the first question to be asking if the proposed explanation has explanatory force. Is it a possible explanation? For both the I-S and the S-R models there will also be further questions, as we noticed. These concern the availability of further information that might undercut the apparent explanatory force of the explanans.

The second criterion is that the explanans should be true. It is easy to invent an explanans with explanatory force, e.g. one implying the explanandum, but unless it is true it does not explain it. We shall discuss this second criterion under the heading 'Acceptability of the Explanans'.

3.5.1 Explanatory Force

We take the force of an explanation to be the degree to which the explanans would, if it were or is true, explain the explanandum. It gives some means of assessing an explanation which is independent of the question of the truth of the explanans. Separating these two questions enables one to reject some purported explanations without showing or knowing that the explanans is false or unacceptable. An explanans known to be false can still be judged for explanatory value.

Although there are a number of conditions that an explanation must fulfil if it is to have explanatory force of a non-trivial nature (discussed below), the basic question is whether the explanans logically implies (D-N), makes highly probable (I-S), or is statistically (or causally) relevant to (S-R), the explanandum, according to which model of explanation is being used. Thus each of the three models gives a different account of the required relation between explanans and explanandum — implication, high probability and statistical relevance.

Despite the differences between the proponents of the various models, there is quite wide agreement about the explanatory force of a number of types of explanations. Deductive-nomological explanations in which the explanans logically implies the explanandum and in which the law appealed to is a causal law are held to have greater explanatory force than either the I-S or the S-R types of explanation. This might be loosely expressed by saying that explanations that explain why-necessarily something is the case, rather than why-probably or why-possibly, have greater explanatory force. In line with this judgement some people hold that only D-N explanations are fully explanatory. Because the D-N model is widely held to be the ideal form of explanation we frame most of the following discussion in terms of it. This refers to some common ways in which explanations can lack explanatory force. We conclude this section by discussing a more general notion of explanatory force.

Partial 'Explanations'. Explanations in which the explanans has nothing in common with the explanandum mislead no one. A more deceptive type of pseudo-explanation is one in which the explanans seems to imply the explanandum, but in which it, in fact, only implies part of the explanandum. Such explanations are called *partial explanations* and they are quite common in psychology and psychology essays. Instead of explaining the explanandum in full specificity, they only explain part of it. To illustrate this we will consider an example familiar to most students of psychology — the Muller-Lyer Illusion.

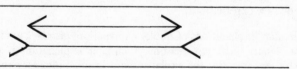

What needs explaining is the illusion. Why, given the associated lines at the end of each, does the top line look shorter than the bottom line, even though they are the same length. One purported explanation of this illusion can be dismissed without inquiring into the truth of the explanans. It is what Gregory (1966) calls the 'confusion' theory. Here it is held that the perceptual system is confused by the shapes and this yields the illusion. As Gregory comments, '[This] gives no hint as to why the perceptual system should be confused by these and not other shapes; or why the confusion should lead to distortions only in certain directions' (1966, a, p.143). Both parts of this sentence implicitly criticise the explanation for being partial. The first part points out that the attempted explanation does not explain why *these* rather than some other associated lines lead to the error of judgement. The second part shows that if this explanans explains at all, it only explains a *difference* in length. It does not explain the specific illusion which is that the top line looks shorter.

A useful practical check, to test whether or not a D-N explanation is partial, is to ask:

Given the explanans, could the explanandum have been predicted?

If the explanation is complete as required, the explanans will imply, and hence allow the prediction of the explanandum. The confusion 'theory' (it does not warrant the description) fails this test. It does not enable us to predict that the top line looks shorter.

It has frequently been argued that the logical properties of explanation and prediction are identical, and that the only difference between the two is 'pragmatic'. For instance, Hempel (1965, p.249) discusses the difference in terms of the temporal relationship between the explanandum and the proposal of the explanans:

> If the explanandum E is given, i.e. if we know that the phenomenon described by E has occurred, and a suitable set of statements . . . is provided afterwards, we speak of an explanation of the phenomenon in question. If the latter statements are given and E is derived prior to the occurrence of the phenomenon it describes, we speak of prediction.

This thesis is usually known as the *Symmetry Thesis* and has been the subject of an extensive philosophical debate, resulting in considerable refinement of the original proposal. For present purposes, the thesis serves to emphasise that explanation and prediction are alike in some respects. We are here recommending the prediction test only as a way of unmasking partial deductive explanations.

Circular 'Explanations'. Circular explanations also lack explanatory force, but for a very different reason. A circular explanation is one in which the explanans includes the explanandum. In most circular explanation the verbal formulations differ in a way which hides the fact that it is really the same statement expressed in different ways. The classical example of a circular explanation is explaining why opium is a sleep inducer by citing the fact that it has a dormitive virtue or quality. Since the statement 'Opium has a dormitive virtue' is effectively the same statement as 'Opium is a sleep inducer', the explanans is identical with the explanandum, and consequently the explanation is circular. In circular explanations, even though the explanans logically implies the explanandum, it does this so trivially that the explanation is not effective.

Analytic 'Explanations'. A related type of deficient explanation to look out for is one in which the apparent law statement, though true, is not an *empirical* law — explanations in which the 'law' statement is not a synthetic statement, but an analytic one. An obvious example of this would be attempting to explain why Smith is unmarried by citing the fact that he is a bachelor and all bachelors are unmarried. To illustrate with a more deceptive example: an author who has defined a reinforcer as 'anything which increases the probability of a response', when asked to explain why something increases the probability of a response, cannot explain it as follows: 'It is a reinforcer and all reinforcers increase the probability of a response.' For as he is using his words, the 'law' statement — 'All reinforcers increase the probability of a response' — is an analytic statement, and so is not law-like at all. Of course, as we noted in Chapter 1, exactly the same words might be used to express a genuine synthetic law-like statement, so when criticising an explanation it is important to have fully understood the kinds of statement it consists of. This type of failing is linked with circular explanations, in that if the generalisation in an explanation is an analytic truth, the explanans often amounts to very little more than a restatement of the explanandum.

The preceding discussion has been about deductive explanations. We now consider briefly a few points about the explanatory power of inductive (or probabilistic) explanations. Such explanations do not purport to show why the explanandum must be true. They merely purport to show how, in relation to the considerations introduced in the explanans, the explanandum is (highly) probable. Other things being equal, the higher this probability the greater the explanatory force.

We noticed earlier, in discussing the 'measles' example, that inductive explanations run the risk of being undercut by further information. This information, when added to the explanans, can radically reduce the explanatory power of these explanations. Consequently an important question to ask when assessing (or constructing) an inductive explanation is: How complete is the explanatory information? This question does not ask if the explanans is true; it is a question that seeks to ensure that all the available relevant information is being used, and that consequently the explanans does have, to the best of the available knowledge, the explanatory power it claims.

So far in this section we have considered the explanatory power of an explanation as the relation between an explanans and a *single* explanandum (either particular or general). A more general notion, particularly important in science, has to do with how well a certain type of explanans would explain a number of diverse phenomena. If the different law-like statements of a variety of such explanations go together to form a coherent theory, we can investigate the explanatory power of the theory.

That is, we can ask: how well would this theory (if true) explain these (diverse) phenomena? To answer this question we at least need to be able to judge individually of each phenomenon, how well the theory (together, where necessary, with the particular initial conditions) would explain it, and, of course, that is what we have just been examining. However, extra considerations are involved in this wider question. Here we just mention two of the most important – generality and simplicity.

Generality is a precondition if a theory is to be able to explain a diversity of phenomena. It has to be sufficiently general either to imply or to bear probabilistically on many different phenomena. Simplicity is an important related notion, connected with the coherence of the theory. Without the requirement that the theory be simple, any heterogeneous collection of law-like statements could be grouped together to form a 'theory' with the desired generality. But they would do so at the expense of simplicity.

As preconditions for the explanatory power of theories, generality and simplicity establish the main link between explanation and scientific understanding. In explaining a wide variety of apparently diverse phenomena, a theory having these properties increases our understanding of the world. Phenomena previously thought to be unconnected are related through the generality and coherence of the theory that explains them. This relationship reveals new similarities which, in turn, expose new differences, enhancing understanding.

3.5.2 Acceptability of the Explanans

In this Section we consider the other main criterion for evaluating explanations – the truth of the explanans. At first glance, the explanans should not only be true; it should also be known to be so. This accords with a common view of explanations – namely that they should explain the unfamiliar in terms of the familiar. For familiar truths are mostly ones that people claim to know are true. However, many good scientific explanations do absolutely the reverse. They explain quite familiar phenomena in terms of very unfamiliar phenomena. In physics, for example, subatomic particles with strange properties are used to explain a wide variety of everyday phenomena. Correspondingly, many of the explanans used in good explanations are not *known* to be true. So, although it would be a bonus if the explanans were not only true, but known to be true, as a requirement for a good explanans it is too strong.

The requirement is simply that the explanans be true. However requiring that a good explanans be true and telling in practice if it actually is are two quite distinct matters. Given that the explanans is required to contain law-like statements, and that because of their generality we cannot determine conclusively if law-like statements are true (whereas sometimes we can tell more conclusively if they are false), the second criterion, while expressing what is required of a good explanans, is impractical. A weaker, more practical criterion for a satisfactory explanans is that it should be (scientifically) acceptable: that there should be good reason to think it is true and no conclusive reason to think it is false.

Of course, that the explanans is acceptable does not mean that it is true. There can be good evidence for the truth of statements which are, in fact, false. Put another way, having good evidence at one time that a statement is true does not rule out having better evidence, at another time, that it is false or vice versa. But if one is interested in whether or not a statement is true, having good evidence that it is, is preferable to having no evidence at all.

Although (non-elliptical) explanans sentences consist of both general and particular statements, in this section we will be concerned largely with criteria for the acceptability of general (law-like) statements in the explanans. However much of what we say applies not only to general statements but to statements in general. We noted earlier that some explanations are given by citing a cause of the event to be explained. In Chapter 5 we examine more specifically criteria for the acceptability of causal claims.

A minimum requirement for acceptability of a statement is that there should not be conclusive evidence that it is false. If there is conclusive (not merely conclusive-looking) evidence that it is false, then it is false and consequently unacceptable. Putting this another way, the least one can ask is that the statement should not be incompatible with established facts. However this is a very weak condition for acceptability and many unacceptable statements satisfy it. Irrefutable statements form an important class of scientifically unacceptable statements which, nevertheless, meet this requirement. We shall discuss them later in this section.

A stronger requirement for acceptability of any statement is that there should be some evidence in its favour. If, however, the statement is being used in an explanation, we need to make the requirement stricter than this. For in general, if the explanation has explanatory force and the explanandum is true, there will be some evidence for the explanans – namely the event of phenomena it would explain if it were true. (We will discuss this important relation between explanation and evidence in the next section.) Consequently there will be *some* evidence for the explanans of all such explanations, and so the requirement just mentioned will not distinguish better from worse among those explanations which have satisfied our first criterion (i.e. those explanations having explanatory force). What is needed is not merely that there be some evidence for the explanans, but that there be *independent* evidence for the explanans: Evidence independent of the (evidence for the) explanandum.

The important question to ask is whether there is independent evidence for the truth of the explanans. If, in evaluating an explanation, we find no independent evidence for the explanans, then the explanation will, in general, be judged unsatisfactory, because of lack of evidence for the truth of the explanans. Explanations in which the only evidence for the explanans is the explanandum are sometimes called *'ad hoc'* explanations. The 'confusion' explanation, cited earlier as illustrating another common fault of explanations, is also a good example of an *ad hoc* explanation. If we ask what independent evidence there is for the claim that the perceptual system is confused, the answer is − none. The only evidence of confusion is (the evidence) that the illusion occurs. Many weak explanations can be uncovered by applying this test. If someone attempts to explain a suicide by saying that the dead man had a death wish he can be asked if there is any independent evidence for the death wish. (He can, of course, also be asked other questions concerning the explanatory force of the explanation; for instance, how would having a death wish explain this suicide?) If the suicide is the only evidence, then the explanans is insufficiently supported to be acceptable in an explanation.

The request for independent evidence can also help to uncover another, already mentioned, defect of explanations − circularity. If the explanation is circular, then the explanans will contain a sentence which is simply a different formulation of the explanandum sentence. Since, in such explanations, the explanans is identical with or includes the explanandum, there cannot be independent evidence for (part of) the explanans. Consequently, circular explanations are *ad hoc*. Even though there may be very good evidence that opium has a dormitive virtue, there can be no evidence that opium has a dormitive virtue which is independent of evidence that it is a sleep-inducer, for these two sentences make the same statement.

We have mentioned prediction as a practical test of explanatory power. As we saw, asking whether a given explanans would have enabled one to predict what it is meant to explain can show an explanation's failure to bear on its explanandum − perhaps through being a partial explanation, or being only an explanation sketch. The prediction test can also be used to indicate whether there is independent evidence for the explanans. If one could not have predicted that a particular result would have occurred before one knew it had, that could indicate not only that the right relationship between explanans and explanandum fails to hold, but also that, prior to the explanandum event, there was not sufficient evidence to warrant accepting that particular explanans, and, consequently, insufficient evidence to use it in a prediction. In explaining the Muller-Lyer illusion, the confusion 'theory' also fails the prediction test on these grounds, as well as on those due to lack of explanatory force. Before one knew that the Muller-Lyer illusion had occurred one could not have predicted, on the basis of the 'confusion theory', that it would. One reason was that the confusion theory does not predict the illusion in full detail (i.e. it lacks explanatory force). Another reason is that, prior to knowing that the illusion had occurred, there were insufficient grounds for holding the opinion that such lines would 'confuse' the perceptual system, and consequently insufficient grounds for using the statement to predict the illusion. Another name that is sometimes used for what we have called *ad hoc* explanations is *'post hoc'*. This name for these explanations highlights the fact that too often the explanans can be 'justified' only *after* the explanandum is known to have occurred.

The independent evidence test is important in psychology because the social and behavioural sciences are especially prone to such *post hoc* explanans sentences. Indeed there is a class of everyday explanations which, since they are arguably *post hoc,* we will not consider in this chapter. These are often known as teleological explanations. In psychology they include attempts to explain behaviour by citing purposes, goals, intentions, motives or desires of the agent. In many such explanations it is possible to be wise only *after* the event they purport to explain, and consequently they do not serve to predict any further behaviour. Hence they frequently are not readily *refutable,* and for this reason are often rejected as adequate scientific explanations, despite being very common in everyday discourse. We shall consider teleological explanations in a later chapter. Let us now elaborate on the important notion of refutability.

Refutability. Recall the confusion theory explanation of the Muller-Lyer illusion. We have been able to use it to illustrate several different faults from which explanations can suffer. Underlying these faults is its vagueness – a vagueness that makes it impossible to test – that renders it unrefutable. In science, despite the sound of its name, *refutability* is a highly desirable property for a statement to possess. Refutability is such an important property for the explanatory statements of an empirical science that some highly developed views on the nature of the science have taken it as their key concept.

Quine and Ullian (1970, p.50) who take a 'hypothesis' tc be (roughly) a statement used to explain describe refutability thus:

> It seems faint praise of a hypothesis to call it refutable. But ... some imaginable event, recognisable if it occurs, must suffice to refute the hypothesis. Otherwise the hypothesis predicts nothing, is confirmed by nothing and confers upon us no earthly good beyond perhaps a mistaken peace of mind.

Another word for this property is 'falsifiable'. A less misleading one is 'testable'. The terms 'refutable' and 'falsifiable' are misleading because they wrongly suggest that if a statement has this property it must be false, since any statement that can actually be refuted or falsified is false. However a closer look at the definition shows that it required only that some *imaginable* event would suffice to refute the statement. If the statement is true, such an event will never actually occur. For a statement to be refutable the event need not actually occur, but it must be imaginable. Of course, if such an event *does* occur then the statement will have been refuted.

A useful practical test of refutability, for someone who believes a statement, is to ask him under what circumstances he would give it up. Could he specify an event which, should it happen, would refute the statement and cause him to no longer believe it? Here it is important that the second of Quine and Ullians's conditions be met — that the event be recognisable if it occurs. Otherwise, any generalisation, however unrefutable, would seem to pass the test. Someone who believed that All *A* are *B* (or that No *A* are *B*) could say that he would count it as refuted if he ever ran across an *A* that was not a *B* (or, correspondingly, an *A* that *was* a *B*). In this respect compare the refutability of the two statements 'No cats dream' and 'No cats undergo rapid eye-movement sleep'. The former would be refuted by a dreaming cat and the latter by a cat undergoing rapid eye-movement sleep. But the two events are not equally clearly recognisable.

In this way, an advocate of the 'confusion theory' explanation of the Muller-Lyer illusion might claim that his 'theory' was refutable. He would be prepared to give it up, he might say, in the event that the perceptual system were not confused. But how would he recognise this event if it did occur? That's easy — he would recognise it if the illusion did not occur. If the 'theory' is simply a restatement of the illusion then he is right, for any statement that amounts to the claim that the illusion occurs would be refuted if it did not. (In this case, using this simple restatement in an explanation of the illusion would be circular.) However if claiming that confusion has occurred amounts to more than simply claiming that a specific error of judgement has occurred, then recognising an error of judgement (the illusion) is not the same thing as recognising the occurrence of confusion. In its vague state, the 'confusion theory' is unrefutable.

In general, refutability of the explanans is an important requirement for scientific explanations, both for the acceptability of the explanans and for the explanation to have full explanatory force. If the statement is refutable, then it can be tested, and may, as a result, acquire evidence in its favour — one of the requirements for an acceptable explanans. If it is not refutable, then it will not imply the specific event it has been called on to explain and consequently the explanation will lack full (i.e. deductive) explanatory force.

Not all statements are directly refutable on their own. Theoretical statements may need to be taken in conjunction with a number of other statements if they are to conflict with 'some imaginable event, recognisable if it occurs', and in this case if such an event does occur it is not always clear which of the statements one should count as refuted. Nevertheless the principle is important. If the truth of a statement (in combination with others) makes no difference to what circumstances or events to expect, if whatever could happen would not, however remotely, conflict with it, then it may, as Quine and Ullian say, 'confer upon us no earthly good beyond perhaps a mistaken peace of mind'.

3.6 INDUCTION AND EXPLANATION

When we distinguished inductive arguments from deductive arguments in Chapter 2 we noted that, unlike deductive arguments, there were no clear guidelines for evaluating inductive arguments. Recollect, that whereas deductive arguments purported to *guarantee* the truth of their conclusions, inductive arguments merely claimed to offer some sort of support and provide weaker non-conclusive evidence or grounds for believing their conclusions.

One very important class of such arguments includes those inductive arguments which express the reasons we have for accepting law-like statements and scientific theories, or for preferring one theory to another. Consequently any guidelines we offer for evaluating inductive arguments will help in the difficult but important task of evaluating theories in psychology. One guideline is an important link between induction and explanation and between the evaluation of inductive arguments and the comparative evaluation of explanations, to which we now turn.

We have seen that, typically, explanations are required only for statements which have already been evaluated as true. Although explanations are like arguments in that both show how a statement — the explanandum or the conclusion of the argument — could be evaluated (or what factors bear on it), they are different in purpose. The purpose of an argument is the evaluation of its conclusion, but since any explanandum is already evaluated (as true, and hence in need of explanation), the purpose of the explanans is to reduce puzzlement and increase understanding by showing how the explanandum statement could have been evaluated and by showing what factors bear on it. It is notable that, for many explanations, one is a good deal more confident of the truth of the explanandum than one is of the truth of the explanans, which includes law-like statements. Although the latter may be regarded as plausibly true, there is no way of being certain that they are not false. Indeed we are frequently so sure of the truth of the statement to be explained that we take its truth as support for the statements that are advanced to explain it. This is often the reasoning that lies behind the claim that certain evidence supports a theory. The theory, if true, would explain the evidence.

Thus, if a statement p explains why q is the case, then the truth of q can be offered in support of p. Here, therefore, is an important link between argument and explanation. We can take explanations of the form 'p explains q' and produce a corresponding inductive (i.e. non-demonstrative) argument of the form 'since q, (there is reason to believe that) p'. But we want to know more. We have seen that in this case q gives *some* support to p. What are the conditions under which q gives not just *some* support but *strong* support to p? An illuminating answer to this is: q can be taken to provide strong support for p when p is the *best of competing alternative explanations* of q. This condition provides a way of evaluating the worth of an important class of inductive arguments.

A special case of this occurs when there seems to be no other explanation. If this were true, p, being the only explanation, would trivially be the best. In these circumstances q will be taken to very strongly support p. The commonly used pattern of reasoning, 'p must be true: it is the only explanation!' illustrates this. An antecedently implausible statement can be strongly supported if it seems to be the only explanation of a particular event. Innocent men have been found guilty and hanged for lack, at the time, of any other explanation of events.

To illustrate more generally this important condition let us consider some simple examples. First, the fact that most observed A's are B's is often taken as a reason for holding that most A's are, in fact, B's. That is, one inductively generalises from the observed to non-observed instances. One's reasoning could be represented by an inductive argument of the form 'since most observed A's are B's', it is reasonable to conclude that, of all A's, most are B's'. Thus someone may argue from the evidence that most observed (or recorded) instances of suicide come from lower socio-economic groups to the conclusion that most suicides come from these groups. However, it may *not* be reasonable to draw this conclusion, and the requirement that the conclusion be the best of competing alternative explanations serves to distinguish when it is reasonable from when it is not. In this application, the principle yields: if, in the light of all the available evidence, the best explanation for the fact that most observed A's are B's is that most A's are, in fact B's, then the inductive conclusion is reasonable. In our present case, a better explanation for the fact that most recorded suicides come from lower socio-economic groups may be that the families (and doctors) of people who suicide from the higher socio-economic groups conceal the fact, and the deaths are not recorded as suicides. If this is a better explanation in the light of available evidence, then the earlier inductive conclusion is not justified by the evidence – it is not the best explanation of the evidence.

We have already examined some of the considerations that determine whether one explanation is better than another. One is worth emphasising here. Other things being equal, a D-N explanation is better than an inductive (I-S or S-R) explanation. Indeed a general principle is that, other things being equal, the explanation that renders the explanandum more probable is the better. This applies even if, on either explanation, the explanandum is highly improbable.

Another example of this type of reasoning can be perceived as a basis for use of the familiar 't' tests found in the inferential statistics armoury which serves the empirical psychologist so well. When an experimental psychologist concludes that the difference in performance between two groups of subjects is statistically significant, he is asserting that the hypothesis that there is, in fact, a particular difference between the parent populations from which the two groups are drawn, is a better explanation of the results than its competitor.

The competing hypothesis may be that there is no difference between the performance levels of the two parent populations. Given the observed results, the hypothesis that there is a difference is the better explanation of the two. For if it were true the observed result would be more probable than if its competitor were true.

Of course statistical inferences like this are always subject to various assumptions, e.g. concerning the nature of the distribution in the parent populations of the performance variable compared in the study. But, allowing for these assumptions and the adequacy of the methodology adopted, the direction of theoretical argument is frequently *from* the observation *to* the best supported explanans of the competing alternatives. To make this point in a more general way, good inductive arguments frequently involve reasoning to a conclusion which, if true, would best explain the premises. Hence the usual goal of an author in the discussion section of a psychological paper is to show that his theory or hypothesis best explains the results of his research (and, ideally, of other relevant research). He claims his theory has greater explanatory power than competing alternatives in the light of his research evidence. He may express this by claiming that the evidence best supports his theory.

However if his theory does not really explain the results, or if he is insufficiently knowledgeable to know of, or insufficiently inventive to think of, better competing alternative explanations, he would be wrong to claim good evidence for his theory. This highlights two important questions to be asked in evaluating such inductive arguments and the reasoning they express in favour of theories.

1.   Does the theory really explain the evidence cited in its favour?
2.   Is there a better alternative explanation for the evidence?

Considerations introduced earlier in this chapter will help in answering the first question. The second question is difficult to answer conclusively in the negative, for there may be a better explanation which no one has considered. That a statement provides the best of the *available* alternative explanations does not guarantee its truth. But this is to be expected. The inconclusiveness of answers to this question reflects the well-known inconclusiveness of induction.

4

DEFINITION AND CLARIFICATION OF TERMS

*'The question is' said Alice, 'whether you can make words
mean so many different things.'*

*'The question is', said Humpty Dumpty, 'which is to be
master - that's all.'*

Lewis Carroll

4.1 INTRODUCTION

ONE MAJOR difficulty with psychology is its terminology. A great deal of psychological literature, as well as informal debate, seems to consist of merely defining and redefining words, preparing for argument rather than actually engaging in more substantive discussion. This is reflected in the fact that antagonists in psychological debate seem to be continually calling on each other to clarify their definitions, or to justify the choice of a particular term. For instance, in the debate about hypothesised psychological differences between peoples of various 'races', it is common to hear opponents say things like 'It (the outcome of the debate) depends on what one means by 'intelligence',' or 'There are many ways of defining and distinguishing 'races' '. To the student of psychology it may appear that answers to the questions in which he is interested will never be forthcoming because it is impossible to provide and justify reliable, unambiguous definitions. That is; the criteria an author adopts for the use of a word may not be commonly accepted. Hence unless he explicitly states these criteria, his statements may be misunderstood by his readers who employ different criteria for the use of the same term.

One possible solution is simply to ignore the problem in the hope that definitional issues will resolve themselves as more research data are collected. We have probably all felt like saying, in exasperation, that definitions should be put to one side in order for the 'real' issues to be debated or researched. Indeed many text books and journal articles begin with this tactic: the author admits the possible ambiguity or controversial nature of an expression, and deliberately provides only a somewhat arbitrary, 'working' definition to facilitate discussion. In many cases such tentative definitions suffice. But in other, often quite important, cases, the definition of terms becomes a central focus of the psychological debate.

Put briefly, definitions and clarification of meanings are necessary only if there is some possibility of misunderstanding between a writer and some of his readers. In particular, the writer himself will be one such reader. If he re-uses the same word or phrase unwittingly with a different meaning the second time, this particular type of misunderstanding can lead to invalid reasoning. When this occurs in an argument it is known as the 'fallacy of equivocation'.

More generally, in many branches of psychology there is considerable risk of misunderstanding. In Chapter 1 we indicated how the same term could be used with different meanings by people working within the conventions and assumptions of different theories. This is the main reason for needing explicit concern for definition in psychology. Unlike physics, in many branches of psychology there is no settled framework or theory within which problems are posed and solved. For instance, psychological theorists concerned with studying language acquisition in young children will define the phenomena to be explained in different theoretical vocabularies depending on whether their approach derives from a behaviouristic background or one that stresses the more abstract 'cognitive' dimensions of infant language. Lacking agreement about the appropriate way to describe the phenomena being explained, theorists from these backgrounds may find it difficult to comprehend their opponents' arguments unless detailed, explicit definitions are provided.

A major cause of terminological diversity, and hence a factor which increases the need for defining and clarifying terms, is the strong impetus in psychology towards measurement and quantification. Not content with statements like 'bright people tend to be tall', psychologists seek to correlate intelligence with height in a mathematically precise way. Hence they need some way of measuring intelligence. There are already accepted procedures for comparing the heights of any two people, and even accepted procedures for linking these with numerical values. But, until recently, this has not been true for the concept of intelligence. The recently developed tests which allow fine-grained comparisons of peoples' intelligence, although widely used, do not ensure unanimous acceptance of their theoretical rationale. It is still a question of debate whether the proposed test actually does measure the concept it claims to measure, or at least whether it is the only or best way of measuring that concept.

It is worth noting that most everyday, general terms have a vague penumbra of meaning. There are always borderline entities for which it is difficult to decide if a term is applicable. For various scientific purposes one may stipulate some relatively sharp line in this grey area, thereby clarifying the meaning of the term. However prior to having any specific purpose in mind, it may be best to leave such terms undelineated, for it may later suit various theoretical ends to draw the line differently. Such apparent vagueness (or 'open-endedness') will be judged a fault only if it prevents the terms being used to answer, clearly, questions which later arise. In other words, rigid, premature delimitations of a concept may not be very useful, however precise the definition.

Given these general preliminary considerations, our discussion focuses on four major aspects of the problem of definition. First, we consider various types of definition, especially the 'operational' variety; second, we emphasise that many apparently simple psychological concepts may be employed in ways which implicitly make theoretically important assumptions. They cannot be coherently employed unless certain statements are assumed true. Failure to examine these assumptions may seriously weaken any critical appreciation of the argument in which they are made. Third, the technical use of psychological terms frequently needs to be distinguished from the use of similar terms in everyday speech. Finally, we shall emphasise the need to distinguish the definition of a term from the provision of criteria for its use. Given that the words found in psychological debate cannot simply be adopted with the naive expectation that they will be reliably understood, how do psychologists attempt to ensure that their terminology is adequately clear? Our brief answer to this question focuses on two major classes of definition (stipulative and operational) and then considers some of the most common inadequacies and misconceptions concerning psychological terms (circular definitions and reification).

4.2 STIPULATIVE (NOMINAL) AND DESCRIPTIVE DEFINITIONS

In Chapter 1 we distinguished two main classes of definition — stipulative (or nominal) and descriptive. When offering the latter a writer tries to spell out the usual or conventional meaning of a term, whereas in a stipulative definition the writer indicates how he proposes to use a word or phrase. Thus as we illustrated there, one could either try to specify the conventional meaning of 'sentiment' or, as Cattell did, stipulate a particular meaning for that term.

There is an important difference between descriptive definitions and stipulative definitions. Where a descriptive definition attempts to describe a convention (a conventional meaning of the term being defined), a stipulative definition attempts to set up or establish a convention. In using a stipulative definition an author attempts to establish a convention with his readers to use a term in a particular way. If he keeps to the convention to use the term in a particular way, say to take *A* to mean *B*, and if his readers interpret *A*, whenever it occurs, to mean *B*, then communication should be facilitated. A stipulative definition can be interpreted as a statement of intent. The intention is to use a word in a certain way.

The local convention set up by a stipulative definition between an author and his readers for their mutual convenience can, however, be a source of some misunderstandings. If any of the parties to the convention fail to follow it, misunderstandings can ensue. These are particularly likely where an author stipulates a new meaning for a term that already has a conventional (language-wide) meaning. If the author forgets that, as he is to use it, the word has a special meaning, and as a result he lapses back into using it with its usual meaning, confusion will result. As noted if this occurs in the course of an argument, we may have the fallacy of equivocation. Equally, if his reader forgets that for him the word has a special meaning and lapses into reading it as though it had its usual meaning, he will misunderstand the author.

Where literature is written for a technical audience the stipulative definitions are often omitted, as it is assumed that the convention is known. In these circumstances someone who is unwittingly not a party to the convention can easily be misled. Some of the mistakes purveyed by popularisers of science may result from this situation.

It is more obvious that stipulative definitions are used to establish a convention where new words are coined to suit a new theoretical need than where the words are already in use but are adopted for a more specific technical purpose. 'Proactive inhibition' is an instance of the former. This term would carry virtually no precise meaning outside its technical usage to refer to specific interference effects in memory. However other expressions carry informal or colloquial meaning despite being nominally defined in the context of a particular theory: an example might be 'habit strength', as used in Hull's learning theory. Although it is precisely stipulated within that theory, the meaning of 'habit strength' is a refinement of its more usual interpretation rather than a completely novel stipulation. Hence one's understanding of the concept relies to some extent on the prior use of the word or phrase outside its restricted theoretical context. Words 'borrowed' from ordinary language, but given precise technical interpretations, are quite common in psychology (e.g. 'anxiety', 'ego', 'reinforcement').

Because they serve to establish a convention, stipulative definitions cannot be criticised as being incorrect. They are not 'true or false'. This is not to say, however, that they cannot be criticised. Apart from the criticism that can be brought against both kinds of definition, namely that the words used to define the term do not themselves have a clear meaning, other special criticisms can be levelled against stipulative definitions. These centre on the way in which definitions can be misleading when an idiosyncratic or narrow stipulation is inadequately distinguished from conventional usage (e.g. 'I.Q.' – cf. 'Intelligence'; 'superego' – cf. 'conscience').

Unlike a stipulative definition, a descriptive definition can be either right or wrong. It can accurately describe the conventional meaning of the term being used or it can misdescribe it. In connection with the adequacy of a descriptive definition, it is also important to distinguish between the meaning, sometimes called the 'intension', of a term and its 'extension'. The extension of a term is the class of all those entities to which the term correctly applies. Thus the extension of the term 'schizophrenic' is the class of all schizophrenics, since they are the people to which the term applies. Terms that differ in meaning can, nevertheless, sometimes have the same extensions. Two such terms that come close to having the same extension are 'creature with a heart' and 'creature with a kidney'. The meaning or intension of a term determines, but is not determined by, its extension – the class of those things to which it correctly applies. A minimal constraint on the accuracy of descriptive definitions can now be specified: for a descriptive definition to be accurate, the extension of the term as described must coincide with the extension of the term as it is conventionally used. If the extension of the term as described is a more restricted class than the actual extension of the term when it is used with its usual meaning, the definition is said to be *too narrow*. If the term has been defined in such a way that it would apply to a wider class than the class the term is conventionally taken to apply to, then the definition is said to be *too wide*. To illustrate these distinctions, if an author writes, 'As is well known, the term 'behaviourist' means 'a person who studies behaviour', then his definition is too wide, as it could be used to apply to (and hence its extension would include) not only behaviourists but other psychologists as well, since non-behaviourists also study behaviour. Equally, an attempted definition of 'language' as 'a vocal system of communication' is a definition that fails to include in its extension the non-vocal sign languages used by the deaf. Consequently it is too narrow.

In psychology it is sometimes difficult to tell whether a definition is being offered as a stipulation or as a description. This is because (as was indicated previously) the words chosen to define a certain term or the word chosen to fit a particular definition are often used in other related ways within ordinary language. However, as we have stressed, the importance of definition is in helping to interpret other things the author says. So even if an author mistakenly takes himself to be describing the meaning of a term, one can treat his descriptive definition as though it is stipulative and use it to help understand what he says.

There are no reasons for proscribing stipulative or nominal definitions. One may employ words in whatever way one likes, given that one's terminology is made explicit and that one does so consistently. For example, one can nominate 'manifest anxiety' as the term to summarise scores on various pencil-and-paper tests concerning fear-arousing situations, etc. Here one uses an older, perhaps vague term ('anxiety') to relate to certain objective criteria.

Such a procedure is defensible on much the same grounds as 'operational' definitions which we will discuss in 4.3. Nevertheless the stipulative aspect of the proposed criteria should not be overlooked, for the criteria may be questioned by psychologists of different theoretical persuasions, or the author may himself overlook the restricted criteria for the application of the term he has chosen. Indeed this example indicates the possible abuse of definitions nominated in a particular theoretical framework. The word 'anxiety' has a more general, conventionally accepted usage than applies in the present case. That is, the nominated interpretation is more restricted than the original meaning of the term. Hence if one does not adhere strictly to the nominated definition, the term quickly acquires 'surplus meaning' — connotations and implications over and above its narrower interpretation. It is important to be aware of this when employing words such as 'anxiety', for there is the danger that the words will be used in their vague, original sense, however much one tries to alter their usage by stipulation.

To conclude, there can be no hard and fast rules against providing stipulative definitions, for one's argument must begin somewhere. It is therefore better to render one's terminology explicit than to leave it obscure. Moreover many expressions 'borrowed' from common language can quite legitimately be 'tidied up' or more narrowly specified in this way. However, nominal or stipulative definitions need to be carefully scrutinised. This is so whether they are obvious verbal tautologies or whether they involve observational operational criteria. It is important to realise that what are apparently precise, informative definitions may be, at best, quite preliminary, or at worst, quite restricted and arbitrary when further examined. But many types of definition are subject to similar criticism: theoretical and empirical justification is always required. However it is fair to emphasise that purely stipulative definitions are particularly prone to one form of abuse – circularity.

Circular definitions. Perhaps the most common abuse of definition is the use of essentially circular and hence non-informative criteria. In such cases the putative definition simply proposes verbal analysis or seemingly relevant operations which do not really clarify how the term being defined is to be employed. It is this type of circularity which is so blatant in the often-quoted definition of 'intelligence' as 'that which intelligence tests test'. It is frequently argued that such a definition is circular because the word 'intelligence' occurs on both 'sides' of the definition. To proponents of this criticism, the definition is analogous to defining 'tennis' as a 'game played by tennis players' or 'neurosis' as 'the illness suffered by people who are classified as neurotic'. In the case of 'intelligence, if an intelligence test is a test of intelligence, the question of what constitutes intelligent behaviour is left quite unspecified by the proposed definition. Similarly, without an independent account of 'tennis player', if one saw a game of tennis and had to rely solely on the definition given above, one could not readily recognise the game.

If one adopts circular, or otherwise vague, definitions of terms, one may preclude any genuine argument about substantive issues. For instance, the person who maintains that intelligence is what intelligence tests test may effectively allow no debate about the nature of intelligence (including the criteria by which we might judge behaviour as intelligent or otherwise). He presents, as the premiss to his argument, a definition which precludes alternatives, and, hence, certain possible conclusions.

The way in which the choice of definition may effectively beg a question can be illustrated by the following hypothetical dialogue on a topic of considerable controversy: the issue of whether non-humans can employ language.

A: There is no doubt that lower forms of life than man can use language.

B: I don't consider that possible. Only man can speak and create novel sentences at will.

A: Yes, but bees can communicate by means of dances. Their dances convey precise information about pollen sources by indicating both the direction and distance of these from the hive.

B: That is so; but merely being able to transmit and receive coded information in that way is not the same thing as using language.

A: Why not? Any organism which can communicate with others of its species must be able to use language – the transmission of coded information is what defines a language system.

B: How can I argue with you? Your definition of language completely begs the answer.

A: So does yours − but in the opposite direction: for you will only allow as language, systems of communication which are practically identical with human speech.

In this debate it is clear that *A* and *B* do not really disagree about the evidence before them and the debate results from two opposed and incompatible assumptions. In effect, the debate is exclusively concerned with the definition of 'language'. The antagonists can only 'agree to disagree' about what language 'really' is, or they can accept one definition for the sake of pursuing a related argument. In the latter case, *B* might accept that a language is a coded system of information transmission and proceed to argue for the existence of different types of languages in different animal species.

Whatever the outcome of our hypothetical debate, it is important for students of psychology to be aware of the issue it illustrates: although many discussions appear to be about 'evidence', they are, in fact, centred on questions of definition.

4.3 OPERATIONAL DEFINITIONS

Psychologists define terms in order to avoid having their statements misunderstood. If one cannot indicate how one is using a term, then it is unlikely that one's use of the term will be consistent, the result of which will be misinterpretations by one's readers. As we noted in Chapter 1 this is particularly likely in psychology, where everyday terms are often employed with slightly different interpretations in their more formal contexts. As mentioned previously, one set of examples of this is provided by concepts which have been given scientific quantification by contemporary psychology. Not content with saying that one person is more intelligent than another, the psychologist wishes to measure and describe, in numerical terms, the magnitude of such differences. To speak quantitatively of human intelligence, some measuring instrument and reliable procedures are presupposed. Although the word 'definition' may be something of a misnomer, psychology textbooks speak of providing 'operational definitions' in these and other cases. In order to understand the importance of the problem of definition in psychology, it is essential to be aware of the historical background to the controversy concerning operational definitions.

However before considering this historical background, let us clarify what we shall mean by a 'theoretical' term, for it is these theoretical terms whose clarification and definition are generally regarded as most controversial. This notion is itself controversial; but let us stipulate that a term is 'theoretical' if its use implies a body of statements which are necessary for it to be understood. This may be true in varying degrees of perhaps all terms, but some terms are clearly used for concepts which have significance only as part of a body of (non-observational) statements. If we consider some examples, degrees of theoreticity can be illustrated. The underlined terms in

    (i)   'There is a <u>human</u>.'
    (ii) 'There is a <u>bachelor</u>.'
    (iii) 'There is a <u>schizophrenic</u>.'

seem to reflect increasing degrees of theoreticity in that they demand increasingly more knowledge if they are to be correctly (conventionally) used. Recall that in Chapter 1, we distinguished observation statements from statements requiring more inferences, and argued that the latter may be theoretically 'loaded' to varying degrees. The terms of an observation statement are relatively uncontroversial and are at the opposite pole from theoretical terms, about which most definitional controversy centres. In the above examples the underlined terms are, in typical application, increasingly likely to be interpreted differently by people who adopt varying general theories. It would be unusual, although not impossible, for people to disagree whether or not something was 'human', although there may be much more (theoretically motivated) conflict about whether a person is 'schizophrenic'. It would not be unusual for one psychologist to ask another 'What are the criteria by which you classify someone as schizophrenic?', or, more conventionally, 'What do you mean by "schizophrenic"?' Later we shall see that these two questions may not be identical but let us return to the issue of operational definitions, for it is with the aim of providing reliable, uncontroversial meanings for psychological terms that this approach developed.

In the early decades of this century psychology was emerging as a 'science', relying on observations which were 'public' (as opposed to 'private' introspection). It was rather self-consciously adopting the models and methods of the natural sciences in place of philosophically pedantic speculations about the nature of the human mind. Its new-found pragmatism and methodological changes, however, did not solve the problem of the nature of psychological concepts. Whereas the theoretical terms of physics and biology appeared well-defined and unambiguous (at least to most psychologists), the ghost of mentalistic terminology still haunted the psychological laboratories. Attempts to exorcise this persistent spectre culminated in two (related) schools of thought – *behaviourism* and *operationism*.

To understand the methods and conventions of contemporary psychology one must know the basic tenets of these two important theoretical orientations. For their combined influence has been, and still is, quite profound in many areas of psychology.

As all students of psychology are aware, behaviourism rejected mentalistic concepts in favour of publicly observable data. For example, it replaced the nineteenth century concept of the 'association of ideas' with the concept of 'stimulus-response connections'. In so doing it implicitly ruled out the need to provide elaborate verbal definitions of apparently vague terms like 'image', 'idea', 'intensity of sensation', and so on. Many psychologists must have felt a sense of relief at being able to unselfconsciously ignore these seemingly intangible concepts without undue pangs of academic conscience. This security was considerably reinforced by the arguments of what has come to be known as *operationism*. This movement came prominently to the notice of psychologists in the 1930s and appeared to legitimise their radical rejection of mentalistic expressions in favour of behavioural data. Psychologists had not been the only scientists experiencing difficulty clarifying their theoretical constructs. It was the attempt to clarify the processes of definition in modern physics which gave direct impetus to a similar programme in psychology. In *The Logic of Modern Physics* (1927) Bridgeman proposed operational definitions for various physical concepts.

In Bridgeman's analysis, he argued that the meaning of a term depended on the operations employed to measure or indicate the presence of the phenomenon or quality under consideration. An example may clarify what this analysis involved: the meaning of the word 'velocity' in the context of a particular physical theory can only be precisely specified by detailing the methods (i.e. the *operations*) by which velocity is measured. This anchors the concept to observable processes and apparently obviates the need for further elaborate verbal definition.

In the original formulation, the meaning of a word was said to derive directly from the set of corresponding operations. That is to say, the word is completely defined by means of the set of so-called operations. This is an important point: operationism was not proposed merely as a methodological exercise or pragmatic recommendation, but as an analysis of the way in which adequate definitions could be provided for various theoretical terms which might otherwise be obscure. That is, it attempted to provide a complete analysis of the *meaning* of scientific terms.

Although it has been severely criticised by philosophers, operationism was quickly adopted by a psychology wishing to add rigour to its theoretical constructs and divest these of their mentalistic connotations. The appeal of operationism was very great, especially to behaviouristically oriented psychologists. Terms like 'drive', 'habit strength', 'expectancy', even 'cognitive map', were analysed in a manner termed 'operational'. The philosophical objections to Bridgeman's original formulation were largely overlooked by psychology, which saw in operationism a valuable tool for reducing or eliminating the elements of ambiguity inherent in the mentalistic legacy bequeathed to the new science from earlier speculations. Much of the influence of operationism is still apparent today, although many of the original tenets of behaviourism have been considerably eroded.

Let us examine the nature of operational definition in psychology and attempt to assess its value. (Again our treatment will be pragmatic rather than philosophically detailed.)

We have said that the original formulation of operationism equated the meaning of a term with a particular set of operational procedures. As critics were quick to point out, this is a very strong thesis concerning definition — one which may have unacceptable consequences. It would seem to imply that literally any variation in observational procedures for measuring a phenomenon or quality in effect redefines that phenomenon or quality. This conclusion seems clear from Bridgeman's (1927, p.5) formulation of operationism:

> We may illustrate by considering the concept of length: What do we mean by the length of an object? We evidently know what we mean by length if we can tell what the length of any and every object is, and for the physicist nothing more is required. To find the length of an object, we have to perform certain physical operations. The concept of length is therefore fixed when the operations by which length is measured are fixed: that is, the concept of length involves as much as and nothing more than a set of operations. *The concept is synonymous with the corresponding set of operations.*

But a consequence of this view would be that the 'length' of various objects measured by discrete physical matching procedures (using tape-measures or rulers) and the 'length' of interstellar distances are different concepts, for they involve different measuring operations. This raises the question of whether one is justified in using the one word ('length') for both of these (operationally distinct) concepts. Why not give each a different name to indicate the differences between the two? There are two possible replies to this question. First, the operationist might argue that some further set of 'higher-level', more general, or abstract operations could be invoked for relating the two original sets of operations in a manner which made the choice of one word appropriate to both. Alternatively, he might accept that different words should be used to indicate concepts defined in operationally distinct ways. This seems a more plausbile suggestion: it is quite common for 'scientific' definitions of words also employed in colloquial language to be quite unlike their informal interpretations.

These sorts of considerations held sway with many psychologists during the thirties and forties. Moreover the appeal of operationism was greatest amongst some historically very important theorists — especially those studying human learning (e.g. Hull, Tolman), which was the paradigm of objective, 'scientific' psychology until at least the late 1950s. However despite the frequency and apparent ease with which psychologists employ 'operational definitions' there are many criticisms and qualifications relating to both the general thesis of operationism and to the uses to which psychology may put so-called 'operational' definitions.

A typical criticism would point out that operationism fails as an account of how complete scientific definitions are, or could be, provided. For instance, one operational definition of 'hunger' which has been employed concerns the 'duration of food deprivation'. In some contexts this might be a useful, objective working definition. But it could be argued that it is by no means a complete definition of hunger. It is possible to be deprived of food without feeling hungry (e.g. by taking appetite suppressors). Hence the selection of one operation as the defining condition of a term like 'hunger' appears to be, at best, incomplete at worst, quite arbitrary. Ironically, the very goal of operational definitions which were proposed to allow objectivity and reliability of usage cannot be achieved by simply spelling out one or a few operational aspects of any, otherwise complex, concept. On the contrary, the choice of 'operations' may be just as arbitrary or restricted as the verbal definitions which they supposedly replace. Mandler and Kessen (1959) make this point in the following way:

> Unfortunately, it is neither particularly scientific nor useful to adopt a word and to define it in terms of some set of operations. This *alone* is obviously possible in the most tender-minded investigation; it is a trivial bow in the direction of scientific respectability and satisfies only the most primitive notions of scientific communication. However, the use of a term which is *already* functioning in a scientific framework imposes certain limitations on the investigator, and this imposition tends to be a function of the historical and theoretical use of the term. When a new set of operations is employed for a particular term, its definition is extended. At this point an operational analysis will be helpful in specifying new areas of application and new grammatical relationships (*Ibid.*, p.111).

In general, the more abstract a psychological concept is, the more variable will be its attempted definition, whether 'operational' or not. Hence a word like 'intelligence' creates many definitional problems. Indeed for a period of time some psychologists seriously supported the utility of defining intelligence as 'that which intelligence tests test'. Because such tests were widely used and the term 'intelligence' was already functioning when this analysis was advanced, there was a sense in which the slogan was not merely tautologous. But as a viable descriptive *definition* it is none the less somewhat circular or, at best, incomplete. For it merely leaves unspecified the operational criteria for judging something to be an 'intelligence' test (as opposed to, say, an 'aptitude' or 'personality' test). For instance, is speed of mental functioning a dimension of intelligence? Are clerical accuracy or artistic skills to be conceptualised as aspects of 'intelligence' according to some operational criteria? The answers to these questions are unresolved by the glib 'operational' formulation given above. They will depend on further theoretical analysis of the concept of intelligence to which empirical findings (e.g. intercorrelations between tests or test items) will probably be relevant.

'Operationism', therefore, offers no simple panacea to the problems of definition. The question that arises is how the student of psychology should regard operational definitions in view of these theoretical limitations. One very useful way of benefiting from this controversy is to see the requirement of operational objectivity from a more general perspective than psychologists originally viewed it. It might be more profitable to regard operational analyses as attempts to specify precise criteria for scientific *usage* of terms, rather than as offering complete, unambiguous and unalterable *definitions*. One can then restate the essential insight of operationism in the following manner: *operations can be profitably employed to determine if and when a term is applicable.* That is they serve as criteria for its application.

Thus the 'meaning' of a term is left partially 'open' and only the criteria for employing the term in a given context are specified. This is a much 'weaker', more pragmatic approach to the problem of definition than the stricter versions of operationism. But such an analysis still emphasises the need to achieve reliable, empirically viable interpretations of otherwise potentially ambiguous terms.

4.4   DEFINITIONS AND CRITERIA FOR THE USE OF THEORETICAL TERMS

The history of operationism shows that there is an important difference between providing a definition for a term and providing criteria for its application. To have criteria for the application of a term is to have some way of telling whether or not the term applies to any entity. An example from physics is the litmus paper test for the presence of an acid. Given that a substance is either an acid or an alkali, the test is: if it turns litmus paper red it is taken to be an acid; if it turns litmus paper blue it is taken to be an alkali. This criterion provides an observable means of classifying substances — at least in respect of alkalinity and acidity. However knowing the criterion does not mean being able to define what an alkali or acid is in the sense of being able to specify the essential attributes of each type of substance in a more general way. It would seem fair to say that a person could reliably judge to which of these two classes a substance belonged without knowing how the two differed from each other in general. That is, one may employ a term quite reliably by means of a criterion for deciding when it applies, without knowing what the term 'means' — i.e. without being able to provide a general definition which goes beyond that limited criterion. Paradoxically, this may be the case even when a term is very widely used in a discipline like psychology or medicine. It is relatively easy to specify, and gain consensus about, the criteria for calling someone 'schizophrenic' or 'diabetic', even though it may be difficult to gain general agreement concerning a definition of the term (this is certainly true of the term 'schizophrenic'). Indeed psychologists and doctors might be said not to know what a 'schizophrenic' or a 'diabetic' *is*, in this sense, at all!

Conversely, it is frequently argued that if one is to know the meaning of a term and be able to use it significantly, then one must be able to judge of any entity whether or not the term applies to it. Indeed this view is what appears to motivate psychologists' ready acceptance of operational definitions, for these specify routine observable procedures for deciding the application of a particular term. However it can be seen that this underlying view involves too strong a condition for many quite adequate definitions to meet. Although it would seem ideal to have some way of definitely determining whether an entity is or is not correctly described by a term, the lack of such a criterion does not imply that one does not know what the term means. For example, most laymen know what it means to have conceived a child, but only specially trained persons can spell out decisive criteria for deciding if this has occurred (at least during the early stages). This might also be said of a wide variety of medical and psychological concepts referring to physical conditions or behavioural dispositions. For instance, one may know the meaning of the term 'defensive', as this might be applied to an individual personality, without being able to offer any finite set of criteria for infallibly deciding whether a reaction is defensive. However, the term can be used in a meaningful and precise way within a particular set of theoretical assumptions (in this case, the psycho-analytic theory of defense mechanisms). Of course, the operationist might see this example in a different light. He regards observable criteria as essential for the scientifically precise application of a term, and could therefore deny that the person using the term 'defensive' could really be claimed to know its meaning at all if he cannot also provide criteria for its application. Without, at least, the possibility of such criteria the term is, for all 'scientific' purposes, meaningless. This strong thesis concerning the meaningfulness of terms seems to lie behind the view of many influential psychologists that theoretical terms cannot be employed unless they are capable of being unequivocally related to observable criteria analogous to the litmus paper test for distinguishing acids from alkalis. However, as we have argued in 4.3, this seems to be a very restrictive analysis of the meaningfulness of scientific terms.

Theoretical terms are one large and important class in the vocabulary of the sciences for which there are frequently no clear criteria to provide guidance concerning usage. Such terms generally refer to unobserved entities whose existence would systematically explain a number of observed phenomena. An example from physics is the term 'electron'; one from psychology is the term 'unconscious wish'. Their existence is taken to explain a variety of phenomena. However the links with the observed phenomena are

so diffuse that such terms generally lack any decisive criteria for their application, and yet, in the context of their respective theories, they do not lack
meaning.

One area where it is reasonable to ask for specific criteria for the application of a term is in the reporting of experimental results. For instance, readers
of a learning-experiment report must be provided with information
concerning criteria by means of which to infer, say, forgetting of material by
subjects, unless there is no doubt that the reader will otherwise understand
which commonly accepted criteria apply in that particular type of
experiment.

In conclusion, therefore, criteria which are sufficient to justify the application of a theoretical term are not identical to a definition of that term. Yet
many types of 'definition' offered within psychology are really more
accurately described as attempts to specify unambiguous criteria for adopting
a term in a particular context. Operational 'definitions' are essentially of this
type. Indeed to call them definitions at all may be mistakenly to assume that
they are complete specifications of a term's meaning in psychology. We have
suggested that many terms (e.g. 'libido', 'hysteria', 'proactive inhibition')
derive their meanings from sets of theoretical statements and their underlying
assumptions. (It is difficult to understand the concept of libido apart from a
general knowledge of Freud's theories, for instance.) Hence there are many
ways of *clarifying* the meanings of theoretical terms. The procedure which is
best called *definition* involves the specification of words or phrases which as
nearly as possible have the same meaning as the term defined. Other, perhaps
equally important, aspects of . clarification include indicating some of the
phenomena to which the term applies (exemplification) or to which it does
not apply, specifying some criteria for deciding if it is applicable, or even
simply ruling out some of the alternative meanings with which the term is
sometimes used. The method or methods adopted will depend on the degree
to which the term is dependent on its theoretical context, the availability of
operational criteria, and so on. There is no single, totally satisfactory
approach to clarifying what psychological terms mean.

4.5 REIFICATION

In psychology, perhaps more than in any other science, there is a strong
tendency for words to become 'reified'. Reification[1] consists of the
unwarranted assumption that a noun which labels an abstract concept
actually names, or applies to, an existing entity. This can most easily occur

1.   Another word frequently used to refer to this process is *hypostatisa-
tion* (verb: *hypostatise*) not to be confused with hypothesisation,
which does not imply any confusion of abstract concepts and concrete entities.

when abstract psychological adjectives ('intelligent', 'anxious', 'neurotic') are converted into their noun forms ('intelligence', 'anxiety', 'neurosis') and assumed to refer to specific objects or processes which people 'possess' to various degrees.

Reification is so prevalent in ordinary speech as to go largely unnoticed. For instance, the evaluative adjectives 'good' and 'bad' are often used to indicate that the objects or situations to which they are applied either satisfy, or fail to meet, certain criteria. Although there is often disagreement about such criteria in particular cases (what is a 'good' film, for instance) and even about the meaningfulness of evaluative adjectives in general, it is clear that when these adjectives are converted into nouns, reification frequently results. People often speak as though 'goodness' and 'evil' ('badness') were psychological qualities which a person possesses in the same way as he possesses, say, red hair or blue eyes. One hears it said that a person 'has a lot of goodness' or 'possesses great virtue'. Although it is easy to speak of such qualities in this way and in most cases no serious confusion results, it is but a short step to some very important sources of confusion concerning psychological language. This arises out of a failure to distinguish clearly between *evaluation* and *interpretation* on the one hand, and *description* on the other. Let us make some preliminary points about the distinction before relating it to the issue of reification.

First, at a superficial level, the grammatical form of evaluative and descriptive statements is the same, but this is no guide to their semantic roles. One can say '*x* is intelligent', '*x* is good', '*x* is neurotic', '*x* is male', '*x* is blue-eyed', using the same general grammatical form. But there are differences between some of these statements which may be quite important. Whether a particular example is regarded as a description or an interpretation of a phenomenon is open to debate, to which the following considerations are relevant. Consider '*x* is intelligent' and '*x* is male'. These two statements can be regarded as strictly descriptive (and hence devoid of evaluative overtones) only if it can be assumed that the criteria by which intelligent behaviour and biological gender can be ascertained are unambiguous and known to all parties to the debate about the issue. There will generally be consensus about criteria relating to gender identification and the statement '*x* is male' can be regarded as descriptive. On the other hand, '*x* is intelligent' need not be regarded as descriptive in this sense. For as we have seen, criteria for its application may be quite controversial. In everyday situations these criteria probably relate to academic achievement and some vaguely defined dimensions of social behaviour. But such criteria are not the only ones by which someone might be judged 'intelligent'. The choice of criteria will probably involve what must be termed a *value judgement* – either implicitly or explicitly. Such evaluation is also salient in the case of '*x* is neurotic' and, by definition, in '*x* is good'. Indeed it is not uncommon for one person to regard a certain person as 'neurotic' when another might regard him or her as morally very worthy.

These examples suggest that between evaluative predicates[2] (like 'good') and relatively neutral descriptive predicates (such as 'male') there is a range of terms (including 'intelligent' and 'neurotic') which require explicit consensus about relevant criteria if the biases of personal preferences are to be overcome.

The importance of the evaluation/description issue for what we have called *reification* should now be fairly clear. It is this: whenever evaluative predicates are erroneously interpreted as *descriptive* of some invariant characteristic of a person whose behaviour is being considered, then an abstraction has been reified. When we make the semantic leap from evaluation (however implicit this might sometimes be) to putative 'objective' description of 'what a person is like' we may confuse the criteria of evaluation with the person or the behaviour being judged. The next step in the process is the easy transition from adjective to noun, signifying the ultimate 'thingification' of the original term. Although it would be quite pedantic to suggest that terms which suggest the possibility of reification should always be avoided, reification may have far-reaching practical as well as 'academic' implications.

To return to our example of 'intelligence', people do commonly speak of a person's intelligence in much the same way as they discuss, say, his bank account. People have a certain amount of intelligence (in their heads) and a certain amount of money (in the bank).[3] The main danger of this metaphorical locution is that it may lead us to search for answers to questions which we might otherwise not be inclined to formulate. For instance, we might ask (as many introductory psychology texts still do) questions like 'How much (i.e. what percentage) of a person's intelligence is due to hereditary factors and what percentage is due to environment?'. Because the

2.   The analysis of the language of evaluation and moral judgements is a very complex area of philosophy. For the purpose of this elementary discussion we have had to oversimplify, concentrating on some of the most obvious abuses of evaluative terms.

3.   Psychological predicates like 'intelligent', 'honest', 'neurotic', etc., may also be interpreted as 'dispositions to behaviour' of various kinds. Just as we say that sugar is soluble, meaning that it will react in specific ways in liquids of certain kinds, so, when we say someone is 'intelligent' we imply a disposition towards certain types of behaviour in particular circumstances.

Apparent reification may sometimes be merely an abbreviated way of referring to such dispositional concepts. Nevertheless at other times there is genuine confusion of concepts and what they refer to.

question is posed in this apparently simple, quantitative way, it will probably be answered in a corresponding manner. For example, '80 per cent heredity, 20 per cent environment'. Taken in isolation, such an issue appears to be as simple as asking which financial interests contributed most to a company's profit – the bonds or the risk capital. If the question can be asked in simple quantitative terms, then, presumably, it can be answered in the same terms. However the analogy between an individual's intelligence and a commercial company's assets or income is by no means as simple as this example suggests. Although the grammatical form of the questions is similar, it does not follow that their meaningfulness and empirical validity are equally clear. If may only be by reifying 'intelligence' in a very crude way that the analogy appears to be valid at all.

It is examples such as this that have led some psychologists to argue that practically all common-language mentalistic abstractions involve implicit reification. The most radical proponent of this view is B.F. Skinner who, in his controversial book *Beyond Freedom and Dignity* (1973, pp.13-14), likens many of these putatively explanatory concepts to mythical 'pre-scientific' causes, akin to hypotheses about undefined 'essences' and magical 'forces' – even to possession by the gods. He states:

> Man's first experience with causes probably came from his own behaviour: things moved because he moved them. If other things moved, it was because someone else was moving them, and if the mover could not be seen, it was because he was invisible. The Greek gods served in this way as the causes of physical phenomena. They were usually outside the things they moved but they might enter into and 'possess' them. Physics and biology soon abandoned explanations of this sort and turned to more useful kinds of causes, but the step has not been decisively taken in the field of human behaviour. Intelligent people no longer believe that men are possessed by demons (although the exorcism of devils is occasionally practised, and the daimonic has reappeared in the writings of psychotherapists), but human behaviour is still commonly attributed to indwelling agents. A juvenile delinquent is said, for example, to be suffering from a disturbed personality: There would be no point in saying it if the personality were not somehow distinct from the body which has got itself into trouble. The distinction is clear when one body is said to contain several personalities which control it in different ways at different times. Psychoanalysts have identified three of these personalities – the ego, superego, and id – and interactions among them are said to be responsible for the behaviour of the man in whom they dwell.

The immediate problem with Skinner's rejection of internal causes of behaviour is that it allows no place at all for 'mental' qualities, capacities or dispositions. He rejects both the crudely reified concepts and many to which this label does not necessarily apply. Rather indiscriminately, he lumps all such postulates together, judging all as 'pre-scientific'. Therefore it may be fair for him to agree with Newton, who complained to his contemporaries that 'to tell us that every species of thing is endowed with an occult specific quality by which it acts and produces manifest effects is to tell us nothing'. But it does not follow that Skinner should reject all traditional psychological predicates as non-informative – a process he wishes to do (p.15) with the following, heterogeneous set of examples:

Almost everyone who is concerned with human affairs – as political scientist, philosopher, man of letters, economist, psychologist, linguist, sociologist, theologian, anthropologist, educator, or psychotherapist – continues to talk about human behaviour in this pre-scientific way. Every issue of a daily paper, every magazine, every professional journal, every book with any bearing whatsoever on human behaviour will supply examples. We are told that to control the number of people in the world we need to change attitudes towards children, overcome pride in size of family or in sexual potency, build some sense of responsibility towards offspring, and reduce the role played by a large family in allaying concern for old age. To work for peace we must deal with the will to power or the paranoid delusions of leaders; we must remember that wars begin in the minds of men, that there is something suicidal in man – a death instinct, perhaps – which leads to war, and that man is aggressive by nature. To solve the problems of the poor we must inspire self-respect, encourage initiative, and reduce frustration. To allay the disaffection of the young we must provide a sense of purpose and reduce feelings of alienation or hopelessness. Realizing that we have no effective means of doing any of this, we ourselves may experience a crisis of belief or a loss of confidence, which can be corrected only by returning to a faith in man's inner capacities. This is staple fare.

Not all of these psychological expressions are simple reifications of non-physical concepts. 'Instincts', 'attitudes' and 'frustration' may be terms which are capable of being made sufficiently clear to enable them to be employed in precise scientific study. Although they are sometimes abused in the way Skinner suggests, they need not be so abused. The issue is not simply that of whether a term refers to physical, observable processes (which, for Skinner, means 'behaviour'): it is rather a question of whether, in the context of psychological theory, they are essential for the explanation of behaviour. However this is a complex problem which raises important philosophical questions concerning the nature of science and scientific constructs which cannot be fully considered here. Suffice it to note that rejecting a concept because it is argued to involve reification may require more justification than that given in arguments like the one quoted above. Certainly we would advise taking each case on its individual merits within its general context.

Having made this point, it must be admitted that the temptation to reify psychological concepts is very great – especially when novel theoretical terminology is being introduced in elementary textbooks. Hence despite the cautionary statement that the Freudian id, ego, and superego 'do not exist as separate real entities and signify nothing in themselves', Lovell (1968, p.87) defines the first of these in the following way:

> The id which is almost wholly within the unconscious mind consists of instinctual drives; it knows neither values nor morality, it is non-rational and demands immediate satisfaction, and is essentially pleasure loving.

It is very difficult to avoid thinking of such constructs as mental agencies or forces, just as Skinner warns against. Hence when Lovell goes on to state 'When a child acts on impulse and throws a stone though a window he is under the control of the id' (*ibid.*), he is using the Freudian concept to *explain* (at least verbally) the behaviour in question. This is very obviously the type of expression at which objections such as Skinner's are directed.

In conclusion, although psychological terms are subject to two important abuses (circularity and reification), they can be employed in precise theoretical statements if their meanings are carefully clarified and made explicit. Psychological theoretical terms, like those from other disciplines, may be employed reliably and consistently by various authors provided that some explicit clarification or definition is proposed. This may consist of a stipulative, descriptive definition showing how an author intends to use a term, or it may involve the provision of explicit operational criteria. In either case vagueness and inconsistency should be avoided. However because theoretical terms derive their meanings from the respective theories of which they are part, their broad justification will normally involve questions which relate to the adequacy of the statements (and assumptions) of such theories. The problems of definition and usage of theoretical terms are not distinct from considerations of the general adequacy of theories.

4.6 EXERCISES

1. Concepts like intelligence are defined in terms of a general theoretical network, and within this network they are given operational definition in terms of some kind of measurement. Gravitation is a concept we arrive at by measuring certain properties in a network that includes falling apples and circling planets: this is its operational definition. The same is true of intelligence, and the often used answer 'intelligence is what intelligence tests measure' is neither an attempt to avoid the question nor a mere tautology. In a very real sense the question 'What is electricity?' can be answered by enumerating the experiments we use to measure electricity. Electricity is that which turns a magnetic needle when passing over it; it is that which makes iron magnetic when passing around it. (Eysenck, 1971, p.51).

(i) Is the analogy between intelligence and gravity or electricity as direct as Eysenck argues here? Why or why not?

(ii) Is it likely that intelligence will ever be other than operationally defined? Does this apply to electricity or to gravity?
(See also the questions relating to Eysenck's view of intelligence in the exercises for Chapter 6.)

2. Consider arguments for and against the following (possible) definition of 'femininity', questioning the sense in which the concept can be regarded as 'operationally' defined.

Femininity can be defined by reference to tests relating to the dimensions of behaviour ranging from masculine to feminine. These tests yield a score for each individual which, in effect, operationally distinguishes him/her along the relevant continuum. At the feminine end of this range is behaviour typical of females — passivity, maternal and domestic interest, concern with personal appearances.

3. Learning refers to increased frequency or speed of response omission as a result of practice. It excludes changes in response tendency due to maturation or other 'internal' physiological changes such as those due to lesions or general atrophy of the nervous system.

(i) Is this a good definition of learning? Why or why not?

(ii) Given that one can learn a skill or response 'tendency' without overtly performing it, would this preclude the possibility of defining learning solely in *operational* terms?

4. Siegler *et al* (in Boyers and Orrill, 1972, p.104) criticise R.D. Laing's contention that 'schizophrenia' is not 'really' a disease. They state:

First, Laing finds the practice of assigning diagnostic labels to patients unacceptable. He says: 'It is wrong to impute a hypothetical disease of unknown etiology and undiscovered pathology to someone unless he can prove otherwise' (R.D. Laing, The politics of experience, 1967, p.71). Laing is certainly entitled to believe that this is wrong, but it is only fair to note that the practice of medicine consists to a great extent of imputing hypothetical diseases of unknown etiology and undiscovered pathology to patients who are in no position to prove otherwise. *All diseases are hypothetical, all are labels.* Thre is no such thing as diabetes, there are only individuals who have certain experiences and physical symptoms which are said to have some relation to the hypothetical disease. Yet such a disease entity is an extremely powerful category, for all its philosophical inelegance [emphasis added].

(i) What is the authors' reason for claiming that *'all diseases are hypothetical, all are labels'?* What objections can be made to this claim?

(ii) How is the concept of *reification* relevant to both Laing's original statement (quoted) and to Siegler *et al*'s objection?

5. (a) Aggression is behaviour intended to harm (physically or psychologically) another living organism.

(b) Aggression is a 'response that delivers noxious stimuli to another organism' (Buss, 1961, p.1).

(c) Aggression research deals with 'collective or individual fighting behaviour in man and animals and with all those emotional states which accompany it' (Maple and Matheson, 1973, p.3).

(d) Aggression is a global concept which embraces behaviours deliberately or intentionally delivering noxious stimuli to other organisms.

(e) Aggression refers to any type of energetic, highly aroused potentially physically harmful behaviour.

Compare these definitions of aggression, and ask yourself the following questions:

(i) Is each too narrow? Too broad? Why?

(ii) Does each allow behaviour to be unambiguously labelled as aggressive or not? (e.g. How, if at all, could each encompass the concept of 'unconscious' aggression, or ritualistic, 'instinctive' fighting in lower organisms?)

(iii) In the light of your answer to (ii), can you suggest any 'operational' criteria for judging behaviour as aggressive?

6. The following are possible definitions of 'intelligence':

(a) The ability to educe relations and correlates.

(b) The ability to benefit from formal education.

(c) An all-round, inborn ability which remains relatively constant throughout a person's life, and is reflected in educational achievement.

(d) That which is measured by intelligence tests.

(e) The ability to adapt to one's physical and social environment.

(f) The ability to solve intellectual problems quickly and efficiently.

Taking each definition in turn,

(i) What type of definition is it?

(ii)   What are its strengths, weaknesses? (e.g. Is it too broad, vague, narrow, circular?).

7. There is a tendency among psychologists, as well as their students, to disregard theoretical issues concerning definitions of terms in the belief that these will disappear as more research findings accumulate. This may, of course, be quite justifiable. But it may perpetuate confusions.

   The following passages are taken from McClelland's paper 'Some Social Consequences of Achievement Motivation' (1955). He states 'Today . . . we have begun to study motivation in its own right . . .' and, later, 'It is becoming increasingly clear that we must pay attention to the type of motive we are measuring, its particular origins, and its particular consequences for human behaviour and society'. Yet, discussing the achievement motive, 'The human motive about which we know the most at the present time', he concedes:

   It will have to suffice here to say that we have developed what appears to be a promising method of measuring the achievement motive . . . There are those who argue that what we are identifying . . . are not really motives at all but something else, perhaps habits. I don't want to seem too light-hearted about psychological theory, but I should hate to see too much energy expended in debating the point. If someone can plan and execute a better research by calling these measures habits, so much the better . . . The fact of the matter is that we know too little about either motives or habits to get into a very useful discussion as to which is which. The important thing is that we accumulate data as rapidly and systematically as we can. Then I believe these theoretical issues will have a way of boiling themselves down to a meaningful level at which they can be settled (King, 1961, p.80).

(i)   Comment on the relationship between definition and data expressed here. Is McClelland consistent in his viewpoint in the sections quoted?

(ii)   Are the explanatory (including predictive) consequences of an achievement motive similar to those implied by calling it a 'habit'? If not, can one avoid some attempt at precise definition?

8. By the term 'thinking' we mean a connected flow of ideas or mental actions directed towards some clear end or purpose. Such a definition distinguishes between true thinking on the one hand and dreams and daydreams on the other. In fantasy, for example, our thoughts wander, are often unconnected and are not consciously checked (Lovell, 1968, p.21).

(i)   What type of definition is this?

(ii)   What assumptions does it make?

(iii) Given this definition of thinking, what mental processes other than fantasy, dreams and day-dreams would be excluded?

(iv) Could the definition cover the activity of

    (a)   species other than humans?

    (b)   pre-verbal infants?

    (c)   computers?

(v) Given your answers to (iii), (iv), would you regard the definition as either too broad or too narrow?

5

INTERPRETING PSYCHOLOGICAL EVIDENCE

'In scientific investigations it is permitted to invent any hypothesis, and if it explains various large and independent classes of facts it rises to the rank of a well-grounded theory.

Charles Darwin

PSYCHOLOGY, one often hears people say, is just 'common sense'. If this were true the following chapter would be unnecessary, for it deals with three aspects of the interpretation of evidence which, although very sensible, are not commonly understood by newcomers to the study of human behaviour. Each section emphasises the need for care in the interpretation of misleadingly simple evidence — the type of evidence that non-psychologists all too readily invoke to support their generalisations. First, we consider the comparative nature of evidence — stressing the need for appropriate 'control' conditions, the problems of confounded variables, and demand characteristics in psychological research. Second, the concept of 'cause' is analysed and distinguished from correlation; emphasis is placed on the difficulty of making causal inferences, given many types of psychological research evidence; third, evidence based on man-animal and man-machine analogies is critically considered.

In considering claims about the results of experimental research there is relatively little room for disagreement. The statements describing the outcomes will mostly be uncontroversial reports of what happened — either what we have called 'observation statements' or statements readily obtained from them such as descriptions of average performance levels on some task. In contrast, the discussion section of a paper (see Chapter 10) will contain many more controversial statements, for it is here than an author interprets the evidence provided in his research. He draws conclusions from the data, attempting to give his findings wider significance. In short, he will offer some *explanation* of them. Indeed interpreting evidence *is* offering an explanation of it.

To achieve this it is critical to look for, and compare, alternative explanations. Generally, the evidence will consist of observed phenomena, correlations, statistically based descriptions of group differences, inferred experimental effects, etc., and the interpretation will consist of some hypothesis (or hypotheses) intended to explain these phenomena. The question that always arises is: *Is this particular hypothesis the best explanation?* As we saw in the chapter on explanation, sometimes what purports to be an explanation cannot be independently tested and so is of little interest. Other possible hypotheses may be testable, but shown to be false and therefore unsatisfactory; and sometimes the proferred explanation, although not conclusively ruled out on such grounds, is not judged to be as good as another explanation. The alternative may be simpler, less *ad hoc*, of wider generality, etc. (recall the criteria mentioned in Chapter 3). The ability to evaluate psychological evidence, to make reasoned judgements between alternative hypotheses, is demanded of students at all levels of study, so let us turn to some important aspects of this task.

5.1   THE COMPARATIVE NATURE OF EVIDENCE

In everyday conversations, as well as in more formal psychological discussion, one often makes statements about the effects of some set of environmental conditions on some form of behaviour. For instance, people may claim that anti-social behaviour results from the exposure of young children to violent television programmes, or that female sex roles are imposed by the child's early family environment. However the evidence on which assertions about such factors are based is seldom made explicit or critically evaluated. Most people simply rely on their own informal observations of a limited number of examples to support such claims. For the psychologist, however, this is not good enough. Without being merely pedantic, the psychologist will frequently question the conclusion of another person's argument by examining the evidence (or lack of it) which relates to that conclusion. Very frequently, assertions can be shown to go beyond what is justified by the available evidence without detailed technical argument. To do this one needs only to understand some fairly general principles about the nature of psychological evidence. We shall try to illustrate these principles by the discussion of a number of examples.

The first example concerns the interpretation of many unusual, dramatic forms of behaviour as being caused by a 'state' called 'hypnosis'. Most people have seen stage hypnotists apparently wielding inexplicable power over helpless individuals. There is a temptation to seek some explanation of this apparent 'power' in either the hypnotist or the person being 'controlled'. Usually various abnormal psychic powers are attributed to the hypnotist, for he is in control of the stiuation.

Naturally, the phenomenon has interested psychologists; indeed it has perplexed them for well over a century. Subjects 'under the influence' of hypnotic suggestion have exhibited dramatic, seemingly inexplicable actions under carefully controlled laboratory conditions. These actions range from apparently 're-living' early 'unremembered' childhood experiences, to committing dangerous acts (e.g. handling ostensibly dangerous snakes) or acts which apparently conflict with the subject's moral beliefs (e.g..stealing).

In the light of these demonstrations it was also tempting for psychologists to attribute some causal role to the state of hypnotic trance, for the evidence on which this interpretation rested seemed unambiguous. However it has recently been emphasised that the numerous examples of hypnotically induced behaviour are, of *themselves*, insufficient to allow one to attribute a causal role to the hypothetical hypnotic state. It has been pointed out that many of the dramatic forms of behaviour apparently elicited by hypnosis can also be produced by subjects who are instructed to *pretend* they are hypnotised. That is the *comparison* of groups of 'hypnotised' and 'unhypnotised' subjects given otherwise similar instructions, does not always show the dramatic *differences* that might have been expected. Subjects told to pretend they are hypnotised will also frequently perform ostensibly dangerous acts. For example T.X. Barber, in an article entitled 'Who Believes in Hypnosis?' (Maas, 1974), points out that a variety of phenomena, which were long assumed to be unique to hypnotised subjects, can be observed in non-hypnotised persons as well. Some of these are like the very dramatic demonstrations of stage hypnotists, including inducing subjects to make their bodies rigid enough to be stretched out like a plank, head on one chair, feet on another; the disappearance of warts; and apparent insensitivity to pain!

Without going further into details of this argument it is clear that the original interpretation of both the nature and importance of the hypnotic 'trance', and the dramatic power attributed to hypnosis, depended on inadequate evidence. It had been wrongly assumed that the various feats just mentioned could be performed *only* by hypnotised subjects.

The failure to *compare* groups of subjects given instructions to simulate hypnotic behaviour with those actually hypnotised rendered the apparent effects of hypnosis more unusual than they might otherwise have appeared. In short, the moral of this example is that demonstration of a phenomenon, *in isolation*, may be quite misleading. The *differences between* individuals and groups, not the particular characteristics of any one example or group of subjects, particularly interest psychologists.

5.1.1 Control Groups

Normally, comparison conditions are incorporated into experimental designs in the form of what are called 'control groups'. There may be one or more of these in a particular experiment. A control group usually consists of a number of subjects exposed to the same conditions as those of the experimental group or groups except for one variable in which the experimenter is primarily interested. In most simple experiments it constitutes a 'base rate' comparison condition against which experimental effects can be gauged. Therefore in studies of the effects of practice on learning, at least two groups are necessary: one group practices a task for a certain period and is then assessed; the other spends an equivalent period on some irrelevant task and is then assessed. Assuming the groups are comparable at the outset, different performances are taken to reflect the effects of the intervening practice.

To return to the hypnosis example, appropriate control or comparison conditions were not regarded as necessary by early researchers in the area. This was probably because the dramatic phenomenon of hypnosis appeared to be so obviously different from the normal range of human behaviour that the need for comparison groups was never even considered. In many non-experimental contexts comparison conditions are either considered unnecessary or are not studied owing to practical difficulties. For example, samples of black children in the United States of America, on average, score lower on I.Q. tests than do 'comparable' white children. How these data are to be interpreted, however, is a matter of great controversy. It depends on whether one accepts the validity of comparisons between the samples actually tested. The obvious question which one might immediately ask is: In what respects are the black and white samples comparable? What factors (e.g. motivational, educational, nutritional) might distinguish the groups? Can one ever really isolate samples of children who are alike in all relevant respects except for skin colour (if this is the basis for classifying children as 'black' or 'white')? Obviously, these questions are crucial for the interpretation of what might otherwise be unambiguous data.

A further example which demonstrates the need for carefully chosen comparison groups is as follows: a common question debated by psychotherapists concerns the effectiveness of various types of therapy. In this context, statements like the following might be made: (1) '55 per cent of patients diagnosed as neurotic who have been treated by method A for a period of ten one-hour therapy sessions have recovered to a certain criterion'. Despite its superficial precision, and the use of quantitative terms, this statement is not really very informative if considered in isolation. It becomes significantly more informative when we add statements about appropriate comparison groups. These might include: (2) 'Only 10 per cent of similarly diagnosed patients given equal exposure to treatment B recover to the same criterion'; and/or (3) 'Only 10 per cent of similarly diagnosed patients *given no treatment* recover to the same criterion'. Statements about the *relative* benefit of various treatment procedures are now possible, at least within the range of methods actually discussed. But when statements (2), (3) are not made, the possibility is left open that *more than* 55 per cent of patients will recover, even if they are given *no therapy*. Obviously, if this were the case, the apparent effectiveness of A would be quite illusory. This is not a purely hypothetical example. Some authors have argued that the 'spontaneous remission' rate for neurosis is very high over a relatively short period. These examples remind one of those clever advertising slogans which use words like 'more' or 'improved' without specifying any comparison for the claim being made: 'These tyres give 50 per cent more grip . . .' 'More grip than what?' one might well ask. (These slogans are referred to as 'dangling comparatives').

5.1.2 Placebo Effects; Demand Characteristics

The example of the relative effectiveness of various methods of psychotherapy leads us to a discussion of what are often called 'placebo' effects. In medical and pharmacological research it is usual to provide one experimental comparison or control group with no actual medication or effective drug. This group is administered a 'placebo' — say a sugar or salt solution or tablet which subjects are led to believe is an effective medicinal agent. This group is then compared with those groups given quantities of the drug being evaluated. An effective drug needs to be shown to be more beneficial than the placebo, rather than being compared with the absence of any form of medication. Similarly, in research into psychotherapy or education, a number of conditions analogous to placebo treatments may be necessary.

An interesting recent illustration of this point concerns what is known as the 'self-fulfilling prophecy' discovered in educational research. There is considerable evidence that, when teachers are given false information that certain students are likely to improve noticably in academic performance, such children do, in fact, improve when compared with students of initially equivalent ability about whom different, pessimistic expectations are provided (Rosenthal and Jacobson, 1968). The former group of students improve when assessed by independent assessors on such indices as abstract reasoning ability. It is not simply that the students' own teachers judge them more favourably on purely subjective grounds. It seems that the teachers' expectations of success are the reason for the (quite arbitrary) predictions being fulfilled. This is rather similar to the effects of placebos in medical situations, except that the self-fulfilling prophecy affects a second person who interacts with the person whose expectations are artificially altered. If self-fulfilling prophecies are as ubiquitous as current research suggests they may be, then there is clearly a need for carefully selected control groups analogous to those given placebos in medical research to allow informative comparisons.

Expectancy effects are instances of what have come to be generally known as *demand characteristics* when they influence the outcome of psychological research. Specifically, demand characteristics are the entire array of cues and information (whether accurate or misleading) about the experiment which the subject may rely on to aid his comprehension of the experimental situation. This information may consist of cues from the experimenter (e.g. subtle, non-verbal feedback), inferences – even rumours – circulating on campus about the research project, or hunches based on the subject's prior knowledge of what he thinks are similar studies because most experimental subjects are keen to 'do the right thing' in the interests of 'science'; they may conform to the demands of the experimental situation (as they experience it) in very subtle ways.

Cues which inadvertently facilitate such conformity may be unconsciously provided by the experimenter. Greenspoon (1955) required subjects to produce as many different kinds of words as they could, reinforcing plural nouns with the response 'uh huh'. This significantly increased the incidence of plural nouns relative to a control period when no such cues were provided, although subjects did not report any awareness of the reinforcement or its effect.

In a similar way, the experimenter himself may be subject to the influence of demand characteristics. His expectations may be covertly communicated to the experimental subject, even if the subject is non-human. Or he may interpret evidence or perceive the experimental phenomena in accordance with his own wishes, especially if the evidence consists of relatively ambiguous responses such as dream reports or T.A.T. card stories. The best known instance of experimenter-provided cues of which the experimenter was himself unaware is the case of the horse Clever Hans (Rosenthal, 1964). Hans could apparently add or multiply simple numbers, giving the answer by tapping his hoof the appropriate number of times. The experts of the day were baffled because even when his owner was not present, Hans still solved the mathematical problems. But the horse was not as clever as a gentleman named Pfungst who demonstrated that whenever people proposed problems for the horse, they inadvertently gave the animal the answer by tilting their heads when the requisite number of taps had been given. The horse had learned to tap until that cue was provided, and he was reinforced for stopping at that point.

Rosenthal (1966, in Sampson, 1971, p.81) also shows how experimenters (in this case student-experimenters) were influenced by their expectations in determining the outcomes of experimental procedures. Half of the 'experimenters' were told that their subjects were inclined to view a series of photographs in terms of 'success', while half were led to expect subjects to see 'failure' in the photographs of faces which they judged. Naturally, subjects were assigned at random to the two types of 'experimenters', yet their judgements conformed to the latters' expectations in how they rated the photographs. Apparently the 'experimenters' had communicated their expectations to the subjects in some subtle way.

5.1.3 Confounded Variables

Demand characteristics cannot easily be disentangled from experimental variables, which are explicitly considered in the research design. Insofar as they co-vary with the latter, they are examples of *confounded variables.* There are many other examples of the latter which occur in research whenever potentially effective variables are not adequately separated but are overlaid on the specified independent variables. When this occurs, it is impossible to draw unambiguous conclusions from the evidence the research provides. That is to say, competing alternative explanations will not have been excluded.

Consider the following (fictitious, simplified) example of the hypothesis that a certain drug ('panacea 007') has the effect of inhibiting aggression in children in direct proportion to their age. That is, the older the child the more potent is the drug's inhibitory effect. To establish this would involve a very complex research design if the most patent types of confounding were to be eliminated. It would require much more than merely administering equal quantities of the drug to equal-sized random samples of, say 3, 5, 7, 9 and 11-year-olds. Assuming that some acceptable index of aggression (and hence its inhibition) is available that is reliable and generally accepted, there is a large number of independent variables that require control if confounding is to be minimised. To take just a few examples: First, the body weight of subjects would vary (systematically) with age. Yet body weight, *as such*, is presumably not the variable responsible for the different effects of 'panacea 007'. Hence some account of this variable must be taken. Second, knowledge (or expectations) about the possible nature of the experiment (i.e. demand characteristics) may vary with age, older subjects being more likely to understand the nature of the study and perhaps to act on their assumed knowledge. Thus in the absence of subtle instructions or additional placebo groups, 'panacea 007' might be effective in direct proportion to the intellectual maturity of the persons to whom it is administered! Third, there may be a whole range of subtle factors such as dietary variables which are confounded with age. These factors may *interact* with the drug to give what appear to be trends due to age alone. In fact, the list of variables which are possibly confounded with a very general variable such as age is potentially infinite.

As this fictitious example suggests, the essence of experimental design, and hence the interpretation of research generally, consists of *isolating* and *controlling* those variables which might otherwise be confounded with the variable or variables of primary interest. Although this can be achieved only imperfectly, that is no reason to ignore such an important practice. In effect, practically every time one criticises the conclusions drawn from research, one is pointing to the possibility of confounding: one shows that some other explanation of the results is possible. When one denies that the reason Negroes perform more poorly on I.Q. tests than whites is 'racial' (i.e. genetic),[1] one is saying that other (environmental) factors are confounded with race. Of course, as this example illustrates, some variables cannot be separately manipulated; by their natures they co-vary. In practice it is not possible to vary racial characteristics whilst holding the social effects of skin colour constant, for instance. In all but unrealistically 'ideal' circumstances, psychological variables are often inextricable. Hence differences of opinion may exist concerning the one piece of evidence insofar as confounding leaves a number of plausible explanations still open.

5.1.4 Case Studies

Despite the impossibility of disentangling all the potentially confounded variables, some of the most suggestive and theoretically influential psychological evidence does not come from carefully controlled laboratory

---

1. In discussing the evidence for racial or other large population differences on some psychológical dimension, the research data actually concern *samples* drawn from the respective populations. Obviously, all members of these populations are not tested.

   However inferential statistics provide estimates of the probability that one's sample data can be 'safely' assumed to reflect population characteristics.

studies or large-scale research projects at all. Rather, it comes in the form of case studies of individual persons (e.g. psychiatric patients), families, or social groups and institutions (e.g. radically unconventional schools like A.E. Neill's famous 'Summer Hill'). In these cases there is, by definition, no possibility of precise comparisions between individuals or groups which differ in only one or a few specific respects. In view of our previous discussion, this would seem to preclude case studies from having much psychological interest. In fact, however, they are widely cited and discussed. The reason for this is not hard to find. Case studies frequently exemplify complex forms of behaviour and extreme environmental situations which may not be replicable in an 'artificial' laboratory situation. For this reason alone they may be invaluable.

For instance, consider the case studies discussed by R.D. Laing and A. Esterson in their book *Sanity, Madness and the Family* (1970). These authors discuss eleven families from each of which one member has been hospitalised owing to what has been diagnosed as 'schizophrenia'. Each family is presented in terms of its internal dynamics — especially the patterns of interpersonal communication. After reading these cases one begins to appreciate what it might be like to be enmeshed in such families: one begins to understand the experience of the family group, although no attempt is made to 'explain' the phenomenon of schizophrenia in the sense that we have discussed explanation in previous chapters.

Yet to deny that detailed reports such as these may provide genuine and important psychological insight would seem to be unduly narrow-minded. How, therefore, can one reconcile the obvious methodological weaknesses of discussing isolated, selected examples with the requirement of comparison groups? This is a very important issue. Rachman (1973, pp.184-85), for example, criticises Laing and Esterson's case study reports on precisely the methodological grounds discussed in this chapter: he argues that their cases lack the necessary comparison or control groups and that the authors therefore may have confused correlation and cause due to their failure to distinguish confounded variables:

Do the families described by Laing behave differently from those in which one member is a delinquent? Do they behave differently from those in which one member is brain-damaged or obsessional or asthmatic or just normal? Even if differences can be demonstrated, further research would be needed before concluding that the observed differences have a special significance in relation to schizophrenic behaviour ... The transcripts presented by Laing and Esterson provide evidence of disturbed behaviour and attitudes in most of the eleven families. Many other research groups have also shown that the families of schizophrenic patients display disturbed behaviour and attitudes. This could support the theory that schizophrenia is caused by the patient's family.[2] Four other possible interpreta-

2.   The concepts of cause and correlation are considered in the following section of this chapter.

tions are: the family disturbance is a result of the patient's serious disorder: the patient's disorder is caused by extra-familial factors, but is exacerbated by disturbance in the family; the family disturbance is initially caused by coping with the patient's disorder, but then exacerbates the disorder; the family disturbance is a visible sign of genetically determined disorders of behaviour in the relatives of a person who is genetically vulnerable, as seen by his schizophrenic disorder.

Clearly, Laing's case studies raise as many problems as they were considered to clarify. Certainly Rachman has shown that they are inconclusive, and, by themselves do not constitute methodologically rigorous evidence. For very similar reasons there are many psychologists who reject much of the theory of Freudian psychology on the grounds that no compelling evidence, only isolated case material, is offered in its support (at least in the theory's original formulation).

In addition, psychologists sceptical about the value of case studies frequently make the following points:

(i) Case studies are subject to selective, biased or distorted reporting. For example, Freud wrote notes on cases after, not during, the actual interview period. Might he not have selectively recalled or emphasised those aspects most consistent with his preconceived ideas?

(ii) Case studies at best merely *exemplify* a range of phenomena. One, or even a number of apparently similar instances, does not indicate a general rule (the problem of induction). To take a Freudian illustration, the fact that one little boy, 'Little Hans.' showed ambivalent emotions towards his mother and father at the time that he was discovering sexual gratification through masturbation, does not indicate that these conflicts and pleasures are universal, or even common, in a particular society.

(iii) The absence of relevant comparison phenomena means that there are no statistical procedures appropriate to evaluating case study evidence in a way that would allow confident conclusions concerning the precise role of psychological variables.

(iv) The interpretation of case material is *post hoc* – i.e. it occurs 'after the event'. It is often possible to discover events in peoples' lives which may, in retrospect, appear plausibly related to subsequent behaviour, but which might not have been adequate to predict such behaviour in advance. Unless this information is used to make predictions about further cases, the 'evidence' is, at best, suggestive; at worst, misleading. This is because the precise conditions of a particular case are not replicable. It is a desirable feature of scientific method that the conditions of an experiment should be replicable in detail in order to allow others to retest hypotheses. But, by definition, case studies fail to meet this requirement.

In answer to these criticisms two points might be made. First, it must be admitted that biases are possible and need to be carefully guarded against.

Tape-recordings, (especially video-tape-recordings) of interviews may over-come this problem, although there are often difficult ethical dilemmas involved in such practices.

Second, it must be admitted that case studies are suggestive, rather than conclusive. They need to be supplemented by more controlled, comparative observations in which particular variables are isolated. But these restrictions should not be taken to mean that case studies are of no value. After all, many scientific hypotheses begin as hunches based on one or a few cases which may have been only accidentally observed. One cannot prohibit these sources of information merely because, by themselves, they are inconclusive.

5.2 CORRELATION AND CAUSE

Whether or not we are trained in psychology, our view of the world involves many generalisations about psychological causes and effects. Few of us pause to examine the evidence on which such generalisations are based, although that evidence may be very weak support for our beliefs. Perhaps a good instance of these beliefs might be the (widely held) statement that 'broken homes *cause* juvenile delinquency'. Let us consider this in some detail.

Assuming that precise definitions of the terms 'broken home' and 'juvenile delinquency' have been agreed upon for the sake of argument, and accepting that there are data which show that significantly more juvenile delinquents come from broken homes than would be expected by chance, is this sufficient to justify the stated belief about the *cause* of delinquency? Or are other interpretations not only possible, but even, perhaps, more plausible? To answer these questions we must understand the distinction between the concepts of 'cause' and 'correlation'.

First, it must be remembered that two factors may vary together in systematic ways without being causally related. That is correlation is *not* causation. For instance, people's heights and weights are positively correlated. Yet it would be quite unusual to say that a person's height was the cause of his weight. It is even more unlikely that we would interpret a person's weight as the cause of his height. Second, events which occur close together in time or are contiguous are not necessarily causally related, even if one invariably follows the other: night invariably follows day, but it is surely not 'caused by' day; neither is the red traffic light caused by the amber light which invariably precedes it. Such examples suggest that the use of the word 'cause' in the statement linking juvenile delinquency and broken homes may be quite unwarranted. In the example as presented the only evidence relating the two was correlational. That is the two factors were said to be statistically associated and no more. Hence it is logically possible to interpret *either* factor as the/a cause (or a component of a cause) of the other. For instance, the data are quite consistent with the assertion that juvenile delinquency causes homes to break up! The meagre correlational evidence is also consistent with a third, perhaps more plausible, interpretation: It can be argued that delinquency and broken homes are correlated owing to some third factor or set of factors which has yet to be specified. Thus the evidence on which the original generalisation was based may be consistent with at least two other interpretations.

Far from being obvious, causal relationships are difficult to determine. Frequently, they can be *inferred* only after a careful examination of the evidence. 'Causes' are *not* 'directly observed', although ordinary language does seem to give that impression. This apparently pedantic point has at least one important practical consequence. It is because the causal relationship between two events is seldom obvious that psychologists employ the terms 'independent' and 'dependent variable'. Despite their names, these expressions are relatively neutral with respect to cause-and-effect inferences. They refer to the manner in which variables are manipulated and studied rather than to their status as causes or effects. Briefly, we can define these as follows:

The Independent Variable is that which is manipulated (i.e. systematically varied) by the experimenter. For example, one might study the short term memory performance of subjects under differing degrees of distraction by extraneous noise. The independent variable would be the level of distracting noise which is varied by the experimenter.

The Dependent Variable is that which is observed to vary as a function of differences in the independent variable. In the above example it would be short-term memory performance.

Although, in this example, a cause-effect inference would be quite justified, this is not always the case. Sometimes the choice of which variable is the independent one is somewhat arbitrary, or, at best, a reflection of the expectations of the experimenter. In our juvenile delinquency example, one could conceptualise 'home environment' as either the dependent or independent variable, depending on the particular research hypothesis being investigated. In whatever manner we chose to name the variables, it would not determine the status of either as a 'cause' or 'effect'. Despite its name, 'dependent' need not be interpreted as meaning 'caused'; it is a more general term than that.

It is advisable for students to try to think in terms of such variables, despite their apparent artificiality. This may reduce the tendency to jump hastily to conclusions about 'causes' and 'effects' whenever psychological evidence is discussed.

Having illustrated the difficulties of inferring causal relationships from correlational data, we have not yet said anything positive about the concept of 'cause'. What does the word mean, and when is its use justified in psychology? Before trying to answer these questions it should be emphasised that the analysis of the concept of cause is quite a difficult and controversial philosophical problem. There are some philosophers (indeed some psychologists as well) who would dispense with the word altogether. But we cannot enter into this argument here. What follows is therefore a brief discussion which is intended to facilitate the interpretation of typical psychological evidence.

One way of trying to analyse the meaning of a word is to substitute an alternative in various contexts. Therefore let us try to replace the word 'cause' by some other phrases. This can be achieved by means of some simple examples. Some events are impossible without the occurrence of certain other events or the presence of certain conditions. There cannot be fire without oxygen, for instance. Another way of putting this is to say that the presence of oxygen is a *necessary condition* for the occurrence of fire. There are, of course, a number of other conditions necessary for this event. But we would not normally say that any one of these 'caused' the fire, although we might acknowledge that it was 'part of the cause', or 'one of a set of causal factors'.

On the other hand, some events are such that they always give rise to certain other events – they are said to be *sufficient* for a particular event to occur. These conditions, although sufficient, may not be necessary for the event. For example, being shot in the heart is a sufficient condition for one's death, but it is not a necessary condition – there are many other conditions sufficient for death to occur (i.e. other ways of dying).

Using this terminology, we might argue that the word 'cause', as used in science, most often refers to *sufficient conditions* for the occurrence of a certain event. Necessary conditions are not what is usually meant by the word 'cause'. But that does not mean that the isolation of necessary conditions is of no interest to psychology or any other science. This may be an important task in its own right. For instance, if an animal is to speak English, a necessary condition may be that the animal is a member of the species *homo sapiens*. This would be an important scientific hypothesis, although it does not specify causal conditions for speaking a particular natural language, like English. Such a causal account would require the specification of additional factors, such as whether the person had been exposed to examples of the language for a certain duration, at certain ages, etc.

The major task involved in the interpretation of psychological evidence might therefore be seen as deciding whether one has isolated necessary and/or sufficient conditions in one's research. This is seldom a simple matter. To return to our previous example concerning broken homes (A) and delinquency (B), it can be seen that the following types of questions may be formulated:

(i)   Is *A* a sufficient condition for *B*?
(Translated, this would read: Is the break-up of a family a sufficient condition for the occurrence of juvenile delinquency in one or more of the family's members?)

(ii) Is *B* a sufficient condition for *A*?
(Is the presence of a delinquent enough to break up a home?)

(iii) Is *A* a necessary condition for *B*?
(Is a broken home a necessary condition for juvenile delinquency?; *or* Can a juvenile delinquent not come from a broken home?)

(iv) Is *B* a necessary condition for *A*?
(Is it possible for a broken home not to include one or more juvenile delinquents as members?)

Without delving into the logic of the situation, it is clear that questions (i) and (iv), and (ii) and (iii) are related very closely. For if *A* is a sufficient condition for *B*, then *B* is a necessary condition for *A*. A simple example of this might be the relationship between a class of objects and a wholly contained class. Being an apple is sufficient for being a piece of fruit, but it is not a *necessary* condition. Being a piece of fruit is a necessary condition for being an apple, but it is not *sufficient*. In this example, it should be noted, it would be rather unusual to use the word 'cause', despite the use of 'necessary and sufficient conditions'. This observation raises some interesting questions about the concept of causality, and its relationship to the logic of classification. We cannot pursue the matter further in this elementary discussion, however. Instead, let us return to the immediate implications of our digression into these logical questions for our discussion of the interpretation of evidence.

The point that emerges from our discussion is that it is frequently not clear if one has isolated conditions which one could term sufficient for the occurrence of some specific phenomenon. At the risk of sounding ultra-cautious, it is probably fair to conclude that one is typically justified only in asserting that significant relationships between specific variables have been established. One might then go on to make tentative interpretations concerning cause and effect. Of course, the confidence with which one does this depends on the individual case, but one seldom finds the words 'cause' in psychological literature. What one does often find are conclusions which might be translated to read '*A* (the independent variable studied) is one of a set of conditons which are jointly sufficient for the occurrence of *B* (the so-called 'dependent variable' studied)'.

In our example one could expect to find research indicating that (certain types of) broken homes, in conjunction with certain other interacting factors, are sufficient to produce delinquency. Such a conclusion would leave many other questions unanswered, and would not be the only possible answer one could give to the question 'What causes juvenile delinquency?'. This suggests another point: the question 'What causes juvenile delinquency?' is really a very simplistic one, and is impossible to answer by means of one single statement. It is like asking a psychologist 'What causes crime?' or 'Why do people go mad?'. Anyone prepared to give what they thought was an adequate answer to such general questions would either be very naive or in possession of evidence that is unknown to psychology. Unfortunately, many students undertake the study of psychology with such oversimplified questions in mind.

In the light of these considerations some psychologists have tried to replace all cause-effect language by other expressions. They may therefore speak of 'functional relationships' between particular variables, leaving the question of cause and effect deliberately quite open. Whether this is ultimately a satisfactory method of avoiding the problems we have mentioned does not matter at this stage. What is important is that students should carefully consider all the possible interpretations of psychological evidence. They should then attempt to *justify* (i.e. argue in favour of) the particular interpretation which they support. If no particular interpretation (causal or other) seems more reasonable than others, it is obviously best to leave the causal inference open. The evidence may not be definitive, and any attempt to impose an interpretation may misrepresent the evidence, suggesting causes where none has been found.

5.2.1   Fictitious Causes

Psychology is particularly prone to the postulation of all manner of 'internal', 'mental' causes which are inferred solely on the basis of people's behaviour. In colloquial speech these generally pass unnoticed. In more formal discussions, however, they are frequently quite misleading or may prove virtually meaningless when closely analysed. Hence the title of this section refers to verbal labels which purport to indicate specific psychological causes, but, in fact, do not.

For example, if it is known that a certain person is good at mathematics, the 'cause' of this skill may be sought 'inside the person's head', so to speak. Of course, what is inside a person's head is related to how well he can do mathematics. That is not the issue. But to 'explain' the behaviour by saying, for example, that the person in question has a high level of mathematical ability or a 'well developed faculty for dealing with mathematical concepts' is not particularly informative. It is not very different from simply asserting that someone is good at mathematics because he is good at mathematics! In other words the hypothetical ability might be said merely to 'shift the problem, not solve it' – i.e. the behaviour is reinterpreted in terms of a mental predisposition which itself requires explanation. Another way of putting this criticism is to say that the proposal 'makes the problem into a postulate'. In our example the behaviour still needs to be explained, despite the hypothetical 'faculty' or skill which is said to 'underlie' it.

It is important to be aware of the ease with which this type of hypothetical 'cause' can be invoked. It must be remembered that behaviour does not explain itself: describing actions as aggressive, intelligent, gregarious, etc., is quite legitimate. But postulating inner causes for such actions by merely naming some ill-defined mental faculty or instinct to correspond to the observed behaviour is not, by itself, genuinely informative. Having made this point, however, the case against such postulates should not be overstated. Should the hypothesised faculty or instinct be supported by independent evidence, then its status may be quite different. That is should its existence explain a number of otherwise unexplained facts, it may not be a circular postulate. In our earlier discussion of explanation, the notion of independent evidence was introduced. Briefly, it was argued that evidence for the postulate which is independent of (or additional to) the behaviour being explained needs to be provided. That is to say there is nothing vacuous about proposing (to continue our example) an instinct of gregariousness, *provided* that there are reasons for postulating it *apart from* the particular gregarious behaviour it is intended to explain.

To conclude, although psychologists generally assume that every event has a cause (a view known as determinism), it does not follow that every time these causes are attributed to mental faculties, forces (dispositions) or capacities, genuine information has been provided. The verbal label 'cause' is not, in itself, an indication that a genuine causal factor has been isolated.

5.3 EVIDENCE FROM ANALOGIES

The interpretation of psychological evidence is further complicated by the prevalence of analogical arguments. An analogy is an argument based on assumed or demonstrable similarities or parallels between two objects or events. What is known about one set of phenomena is employed in an attempt to explain the other. That is analogies seek to relate unfamiliar (or unexplained) psychological phenomena to familiar, explicable phenomena, by asserting that the two are alike in relevant respects. In psychology, analogies generally fall into two classes: those that assert similarities between the behaviour of humans and other animal species, and those that seek models for human behaviour, or cognitive processes in the functions of mechanical devices — especially electronic computers. Thus defined, analogies include a number of quite 'weak' or tenuous assertions of similarities, as well as 'stronger', more rigorous attempts to 'model' psychological processes. It is, therefore, necessary to evaluate each proposed analogy on its merits: analogies *as such* cannot be excluded from psychology; nor is every proposed analogy of genuine interest.

5.3.1   Anthropomorphic Metaphors

Let us look briefly at some relatively 'weak' analogies, before discussing criteria for evaluating more rigorous instances. Weak analogies are essentially 'metaphorical' interpretations of psychological phenomena, frequently reflecting figures of speech which are ingrained in colloquial language. For example, the behaviour of animals is sometimes interpreted as being metaphorically similar to that of humans: we speak of humans' displaying 'pecking orders' (status or dominance hierarchies), or of their being part of a 'rat race' (being unduly competitive) and so on. The assumption underlying these figures of speech appears to be that humans are like animals in respect of these characteristics, presumably for similar (biological) reasons. However in these cases there is little interest in detailed explanation. The metaphor merely labels (and/or passes judgement on) the behaviour in a manner that is of literary rather than of psychological significance.

Similarly human motives and intentions are often attributed to animals: we say that dogs are 'brave' or 'loyal', or that lemmings 'commit suicide', describing these animals as though their behaviour were consciously intended or were motivated by human values. This practice is termed *anthropomorphism*. It is frequently found in discussions of animal behaviour by writers of popular books on controversial topics (e.g. Robert Ardrey's entertaining, although suspect, analysis of the origins and nature of human territorial behaviour in *The Territorial Imperative*). The tendency to anthropomorphise is very great when apparently inexplicable biological phenomena appear to be like those of human society: hence the widely held interpretation of the mass migration of lemmings which culminates in their death as an act of 'suicide' — an interpretation which a moment's reflection will show to be very difficult to sustain. For example, does each lemming (a small rodent) consciously 'decide' that its life is not worth living? Clearly these considerations are quite inappropriate in understanding the behaviour of rodents. In fact, there is no evidence that the mass deaths are analogous to human suicide in any way. As Dubos (in Proshansky *et al.*, 1970, p.204) points out (unfortunately adopting the anthropomorphic term 'mass psychosis' himself):

Although the nature of the initial stimulus that prompts the lemmings to migrate is not understood, crowding is almost certainly one of its aspects. As the rodents become more and more crowded they fall victims to a kind of mass psychosis. The result is a wild scrambling about that, contrary to legend, is not necessarily a march toward the sea but merely random movement. The animals die, not be drowning, but by metabolic derangements associated with stress; lesions are commonly found in the brains and the adrenals.

The metaphorical interpretation of human suicide as lemming-like, and —

its converse – of lemmings committing mass suicide, are therefore quite unjustified. But like many anthropomorphic metaphors, because it is part of our language, it is difficult to avoid. The principal argument against such figures of speech is that they are seldom of genuine explanatory value: describing animals as though they were humans makes their behaviour *more*, not less, difficult to explain because it introduces additional factors into the description of the explanandum: In the lemmings example, one has to explain not only why the rodents migrate periodically, but also why they (consciously?) seek to end their lives.

If these examples of metaphorical language seem relatively innocuous, it must be stressed that there are many important 'models' of human behaviour which are essentially extended analogies. With recent advances in the biological study of animal behaviour, and with the rapidly accelerating sophistication of electronic computing devices, psychological literature is replete with animal and machine analogies. The fertilisation of psychology by the disciplines of ethology (studying instinctive animal behaviour) and automata theory (formal discussions of computation and computers) has made it essential for students to be aware of the advantages and limitations of advanced forms of analogical argument. It could reasonably be claimed that many of the significant psychological questions currently being debated rely very heavily on this type of argument. To begin discussing the issues raised by such analogies, let us return to a distinction we made in Chapter 3.

5.3.2 Description *v.*s Explanation

It will be recalled that our discussion of the problems of explanation considered the issue of analytic 'explanations' based on an author's choice of definitions. It was pointed out that merely stipulating a new term as a replacement for some other descriptive expression was not, by itself, explanatory. Similarly, in considering analogies, the similarities asserted between the two sets of phenomena, and their inclusion under the one general descriptive term, may require detailed justification. It is, at best, a preliminary step to assert that two events or objects are *similar in certain respects* and to label them with the one term. For example, if it is observed that humans, as well as some species of birds, adopt status-defining hierarchies around which much of their respective social organisation revolves, it is tempting to speak of each species exhibiting 'pecking orders'. The common name reflects the observed (or inferred) similarities. The difficulties with extended analogical argument begin at the next step. Here, one attempts not only to describe the respective behaviours as similar, but to use this putative similarity as the basis for explanation. Thus having described both avian and human 'pecking orders', one may then seek to assert that both have the same cause (or type of cause). Hence if it is known that avian pecking orders are 'instinctive', it is tempting to argue that a similar cause operates in humans: that their 'pecking orders' are also instinctive. Clearly, this is an *inference* which may or may not be justified, as the following example illustrates. Discussing human territorial behaviour, Ardrey (1969, p.116) states:

> The parallel between human marriage and animal pairing requires no lecturer with a long pointed wand. The parallel between human desire for a place that is one's own and animal instinct to stake out such a private domain requires even less demonstration ... Are we then, confronted by parallels of such a conspicuous order, to dismiss the possibility that man is a territorial species and that evolution, with its territorial imperative has perfected an innate behavioural mechanism commanding precisely the morality we seek?

This passage points to two parallels between animal and human behaviour. It then suggests, by means of a rhetorical question, that in both cases ('marriage' and 'territoriality') there are biological causes in animals and man alike. This is, in effect, an analogical jump from the description of similar behaviour in different species to the inference of its common instinctive cause. But merely interpreting animal pair formation and territorial behaviour as similar to human marriage and home ownership does not, *by itself*, justify such an inference. It does not follow that because two phenomena are described in similar terms (however appropriate that description may seem), their causes are similar or identical.

The trouble with analogies is that, although they are easy to find, they are difficult to justify. If analogies are to be of theoretical interest, it is necessary for their proponent to do the following: (1) show that the two species or phenomena being compared are alike in more than name only: that is that the choice of a similar descriptive term is not largely an arbitrary one which suits the proponent's preconceptions (cf. Ardrey's use of 'territorial' to describe home ownership); (2) to avoid this, detailed specification is needed of *how* the two phenomena are alike: That is, an (operational) objectively testable formulation of what *dimensions of behaviour* are hypothetically similar; and (3) some predictions are necessary concerning *independent evidence* which would support (or possibly refute) the inferred causal account of the phenomenon being explained. These criteria are like those discussed previously for evaluating other forms of explanation. Let us now consider them in relation to more detailed animal and machine analogies.

5.3.3   Animal Analogies

The principal difficulty with animal-man analogies is that there are literally thousands of animal, bird and insect species. Each has some peculiar behavioural characteristics: some birds mate for life, some are 'territorial', some hoard objects, some eat the young of their own species under some conditions, others make ritualised, stereotyped mating displays and so on. Amongst mammals, even amongst primates, some of these behaviours can also be found. Therefore anyone wishing to assert an analogy between human monogamy, territoriality, hoarding, cannibalism, or mating practices, and the activities of some other animal species will probably be able to do so if he selects his examples carefully. But this is quite a facile, purely *arbitrary* use of analogy, which fails to satisfy any of the three criteria proposed above. For example, discussing maternal love, Harlow (1971, p.6) states:

> Girls will respond to babies — all babies — long before they approach adolescence. Attitude differences that are apparently inherent were demonstrated in the responses of preadolescent female and male macaque monkeys to rhesus monkey babies (Chamove *et al.*, 1967). Since the pre-adolescent macaques had never seen infants younger than themselves and had not been raised by real monkey mothers who could have imparted their own attitudes towards babies, we may assume that the differences in response pattern were primarily innately determined. When they were confronted with a baby monkey, almost all the responses made by the female monkeys were positive and pleasant, including contact, caressing and cuddling. These maternal-type baby responses were conspicuously absent in the males.

He goes on:

> Some years ago a photograph (which showed a baby monkey wrapped in a white blanket, eyes wide open and lips pursed) . . . was projected on a screen at a women's college in Virginia. All 500 girls in the audience gave simultaneous gasps of ecstasy. The same test has since been conducted with many college audiences. Not only are all males completely unresponsive but the presence of males in co-educational audiences inhibits the feminine ecstasy response. Evidently nature has not only constructed women to produce babies, but has also prepared them from the outset to be mothers.

This argument invites criticism on a number of grounds. As an instance of analogy it fails to meet the three criteria presented above: (1) it is essentially a very selective use of one primate species, (2) it fails to specify how the macaque and human maternal responses and ecstasy response are comparable (i.e. in what ways these are similar, or are part of more general sets of analogous behaviour); (3) there is no evidence advanced, independent of the response itself, to show that the human 'ecstasy response' is inherent.

To put the problem of analogies in other terms, one could say that they frequently allow their proponent to 'have it both ways' — i.e. to accept what is really inconsistent evidence while maintaining the original hypothesis. As Weisstein (Brown, 1973, p.412) points out:

One strategy that has been used is to extrapolate from primate behaviour to 'innate' human preference by noticing certain trends in primate behaviour as one moves phylogenetically closer to humans. But there are great difficulties with this approach. When behaviours of lower primates are directly opposite to those of higher primates, or to those one expects of humans, they can be dismissed on evolutionary grounds — higher primates and/or humans grew out of that old stuff. On the other hand, if the behaviour of higher primates is counter to the behaviour considered natural for humans, while the behaviour of some lower primate is considered the natural one for humans, the higher primate behaviour can be dismissed also, on the grounds that it has diverged from an older, proto-typical pattern. So either way, one can select those behaviours one wants to prove as innate for humans.

What Weisstein objects to in this passage is the *post hoc* interpretation of evidence to suit one's preconceived theory. It follows that one important method of overcoming the arbitrariness of these interpretations is to require that analogical arguments be evaluated by their *predictive* power, just as other explanations are usually judged. This requirement is particularly important if it is asserted that similar phenomena (in different species) have a similar cause (as Harlow asserts regarding the 'ecstasy' response in female macaques and female Virginians). What is required to substantiate Harlow's claim is evidence (employing appropriate controls and comparison conditions) that the human response is unlearned, as it is in macaques. In other words, as with all viable explanations, analogies require the support of what we previously called independent evidence (Chapter 3) concerning hypothesised causes of behaviour. If one is to argue that the female ecstasy response to babies is instinctive, one needs to provide more evidence than that it occurs in humans and is instinctive in some other species.

But let us not unduly stress the negative aspects of animal analogies. There are many examples of quite precise and heuristically important analogical arguments in psychology. Some of Harlow's own work on social deprivation in monkeys might fall into this category, if cautiously interpreted (see Harlow, 1959; Harlow and Harlow, 1962). Harlow deprived infant monkeys of various types of social, physical or maternal stimulation during the first two years of life. The onset and duration of deprivation were varied. The results suggested the need for certain social experiences within critical periods if the monkeys were to develop into 'normal' mature members of the species. Without infant social play, for instance, the monkeys were unable to groom, mate or care for their own offspring in the manner typical of their species. If results such as these are extrapolated to humans, they suggest that until about four years of age the child is particularly vulnerable to social deprivation which may have long-term detrimental effects. (This takes into account the different rates of physical development of the two species.) Although the resulting hypotheses may not be confirmed in all details when tested for the human case, the example does, at least, illustrate the possibility of deriving empirical predictions from animal analogies.

Moreover the animal case does, at least, indicate *possible* mechanisms for a particular type of behaviour. It is circumstantial evidence for the existence of such mechanisms in humans. Observations of primates help to show what range of behaviour exists in nature, and therefore to *suggest* causes for human behaviour. If one primate species exhibits certain well-defined behaviour, the causes of which are known for that species, this, at least, leaves open the possibility that similar human behaviour *may* have similar causes.

So although this section has warned against the arbitrary adoption of analogies, it is important to realise that they may be quite useful if carefully formulated. Analogies are a legitimate aspect of psychological argument insofar as they generate hypotheses capable of empirical evaluation.

5.3.4 Machine Analogies

As well as making comparisons across species of animals, psychologists have also sought to understand human behaviour through knowledge of the structure and/or function of man-made machines. As machine technology develops, so does the putative analogy vary. In a general sense, the human body and nervous system are 'mechanical', although not in the way that this might be said of an internal combustion engine or a hydraulic lift. In a more precise sense, however, some analogy might be asserted between the structure of an artificial device and that of a natural system.[3] It might be hypothesised that there is a one-to-one correspondence between the physical components (and hence their respective functions) in the two systems. For instance, the gross anatomy of the human eye is often compared to the structure of a simple camera, each component of the former (cornea, lens, retina) being analogous to a component of the latter (lens cover, lens, film). However in those examples of man-machine analogies of interest to psychologists, such structural equivalences are seldom postulated. More frequently, comparisons are aimed at elucidating or exemplifying certain aspects of 'thought' or brain *function*.

Clearly, the structure and function of any system are interdependent, as the camera example readily testifies. However it is possible to study the functions of a system in relative isolation from its precise physical structure. Hence psychologists are usually less concerned about the physical components of a system chosen to model human functions (e.g. problem-solving or pattern recognition) than they are about the functional equiva-

3.   Strictly speaking, it is usual to call such structural correspondences *homologous* rather than using the term *analagous*.

lences between the behaviour of the former system (e.g. computer) and that of the human being. Machine-man analogies are not necessarily intended to imply an identical physical cause for the functions of the two systems said to be analogous.

During the last fifteen years, the concepts and vocabulary of 'information processing' and 'control' devices such as electronic computers and self-regulating machines have infiltrated much of the territory of traditional psychology. By readily adopting the terminology of information processing and storage technology, 'cognitive' psychologists have attempted to 'model' human thought along lines exhibited by artificial devices. Because this has sometimes been misinterpreted as suggesting that psychologists uncritically accept an almost complete analogy between computers and man, it is necessary to examine what functions such models serve.

Mechanical computation devices are relevant to psychology in two general ways. First, they are studied in order to answer questions about the nature and limitations of particular descriptions of complex 'thought'. Here psychologists are interested in what has come to be known as *'artificial intelligence'*; that is in whether the machine can solve problems of a type usually regarded as peculiar to humans. For instance, playing chess, translating colloquial French into English, composing a fugue. Artificial intelligence research is directed at *what* machines can do with little emphasis on *how* they operate, and, consequently, little interest in whether the machine 'models' human 'thought' in precise detail.

Second, and of more direct relevance to psychology, is research referred to as *'computer simulation'* of human cognitive processes. In this research the emphasis is on programming the machine to display, in as much detail as possible, the processes by which humans hypothetically solve a particular type of problem, or 'encode input'. The researcher deliberately 'models' (reflects the structure and sequence of) human cognition in the processes performed by the machine. Clearly, this procedure assumes that a *precise* description (or hypothetical account) of the human processes is available on which to 'model' each step in the computer programme. The psychologist's interest in the machine (or more accurately, in its programme) is to ask if the initial psychological description is a viable or *realistic* (in programming terms) account of the processes in question.

Perhaps the most famous and ambitious attempt to simulate the problem-solving behaviour of humans is the work of Newell, Shaw and Simon (1960). They called their programme the General Problem Solver (G.P.S.):

G.P.S. grew out of an earlier computer program . . . which discovered proofs to theorems in the sentential calculus of Whitehead and Russell . . . The effectiveness of the Logic Theorist led to revised programs aimed at simulating in detail the problem-solving behaviour of humans in the psychological laboratory. The human data were obtained by asking college sophomores to solve problems in symbolic logic, 'thinking aloud' as much as possible while they worked. G.P.S. is the program constructed to describe as closely as possible the behaviour of the laboratory subjects as revealed in their oral comments and the steps they wrote down in working the problem (pp.257-58).

A successful simulation such as G.P.S., effected for a number of problem solutions, demonstrates at the very least that certain information-processing strategies are *sufficient* to solve the respective problems. This does *not* show that humans *necessarily* adopt such strategies, but is consistent with that hypothesis (especially if the computer programme derives from human protocols). The description on which the programme is based is therefore 'testable' by means of the simulation − at least in the sense that failure to simulate would suggest the inadequacy of the original description.

However care is necessary in the interpretation of mechanical analogies, whether these purport to be examples of 'artificial intelligence' or simulations. Just as the arbitrary, *ad hoc* adoption of animal analogies may lead to trivial, purely descriptive accounts of behaviour, so also is it possible to employ computer metaphors in a vague, relatively uninformative manner. It is all too easy simply to replace words like 'problem solving' by 'goal-directed information processing'; or 'perception of cues' by expressions such as 'analysis of stimulus features'; or to refer to abstract (often ill-defined) concepts like 'thinking' as 'information transformation'. But this jargon, *by itself*, may not generate valid insights into the nature of the processes involved. A computer simulation is a detailed attempt to model (realise in some other medium) the essence of human 'thought' or behaviour; it is not merely a metaphorical word-game. After all, both birds and helicopters 'fly', but the latter are not very useful 'models' of the former, despite our use of the one word for the behaviour of both.

It should also be remembered that the use of analogies is a continuing two-way process. The model used for comparison with the explanandum is itself constantly being redescribed or even discarded in the light of new information about both itself and the explanandum. As new 'machine languages' develop, for example, models such as G.P.S. have been superseded; new information about human thought will affect the detailed model also. It is therefore best to regard analogies, especially machine analogies, as tentative 'heuristic' aids to psychological inquiry: their value lies in suggesting hypotheses by explicating the details of psychological phenomena.

Strictly speaking, all analogies or models are incomplete. Nobody would assert that the eye was like a camera in all respects. However even allowing for this, it may be most illuminating to know exactly how the two differ − especially if they have been *assumed* to function in similar ways. When an analogy is shown unexpectedly to break down, a new conception of the phenomenon being modelled may arise. That is, negative evidence may be very important by showing how a possible model (which may have been widely assumed to be valid) is not a detailed analogue of a particular phenomenon (e.g. people, because of the memory and time limitations which restrict humans, do not play chess as in some of the early computer programmes).

To reiterate, our language is replete with metaphorical expressions which assume that behaviour or thought is analogous to phenomena which are more fully understood (e.g. 'simple' animals or man-made machines). But analogies require detailed specification of the dimensions of such assumed similarities if they are to be of potential explanatory value. The requirements of predictive power and of independent evidence apply to hypothesised analogies as to other forms of putative explanation. Failure to meet these criteria may result in arbitrary, *ad hoc* interpretations which may merely replace one unexplained phenomenon by another that is asserted to be analogous to it.

5.3.5   Reification and Analogy: An Example

Confusion of a metaphor or 'model' with the reality to which it is hypothetically analogous is one form of *reification*. This concept was introduced in Chapter 4 where it was defined as the process of interpreting abstractions as concrete realities, of 'confusing words with things'. Not only have particular words (like 'intelligence' or 'creativity') frequently been subject to reification; complex sets of interrelated assumptions have sometimes been interpreted in this way because analogues or models of psychological processes have been accepted as 'real': The 'as if' quality of analogies has been overlooked. A controversial, yet quite informative example of this process concerns the so-called 'medical model' in abnormal psychology and psychiatry.

For a variety of complex historical and sociological reasons, psychiatry has adopted many non-psychological concepts to categorise and explain 'abnormal' behaviour. Hence people who are 'anxious', 'depressed', 'confused', 'unable to cope with life's demands', suicidal, or 'criminal', may all be labelled 'mentally ill'. Once they are so diagnosed, it follows that mental hospitals and physical or psychological therapy are assumed to be appropriate solutions to their problems: that just as people who are physically ill require medical treatment to recover normal functioning, so do people who are mentally ill.

In the eyes of contemporary critics of this approach, medical jargon and the assumptions which this embodies (i.e. the 'medical model') have been given the status of descriptions of psychological phenomena rather than being merely an elaborate analogue which exhibits limited similarities with those psychological phenomena. That is the metaphor has been mistaken for 'reality'. Instead of saying that a person is acting *as though* he were (physically) ill, we say he *is* ill – although we deem this illness 'mental'. Hence although there may be no evidence of physical *disease* in many psychological disturbances such as 'neuroses' or 'perversions', the medical model designates them as *illnesses*. The whole terminology of 'abnormal psychology' is pseudo-medical, although, as many authors have recently emphasised, this vocabulary is not the only one possible. The medical model may not be essential to the description (nor, therefore, to the explanation) of 'strange' behaviour.

A pertinent example which illustrates this concerns homosexuality. It is possible to discuss homosexual behaviour without regarding it as a 'sympton' of some 'illness' which a person 'suffers from' or 'carries around inside himself' (like diabetes, T.B. or cancer) which requires cure by appropriate treatment. One could argue that homosexuality is no more a 'disease' which is responsible for particular 'symptoms' (i.e. behaviour) than are heterosexuality, maturity, femininity or masculinity, for example. To assume that there is a disease entity underlying homosexuality is to follow the (reified) medical model, although such an assumption may not be necessary for understanding homosexual behaviour.

It is instructive to recall that not very long ago some abnormal behaviour was regarded as 'sin' and taken to have metaphysical causes. Replacing the 'religious model' by the 'medical model' involved a great many social, as well as scientific, changes. Exorcising the demonological jargon from psychology has been achieved, but have we replaced one ghostly cause by another, merely through employing a medical approach to behaviour which the community deems 'sick' in a metaphorical sense?

5.4 EXERCISES

1. It is quite clear that one of the effects of living under crowded conditions is that the likelihood of suicide is greatly increased. There is evidence that the rate of suicide is significantly greater in those urban areas which have been developed for high-density living. What more evidence could be required?

(i) In what other ways could the evidence (as presented) be interpreted? What are some competing explanations of it?

(ii) What type of evidence would be required to support convincingly the conclusion asserted in the argument?

(iii) In view of your answers to (i), (ii), is the causal relationship postulated in the quoted passage justified?

2. Consider the following passages. In each case, rewrite by adding premises which would yield the conclusion more convincing support. (Recall our discussion of the comparative nature of evidence and of correlation *v.* cause.)

(i)   65 per cent of all prostitutes come from families from which one parent has been absent since the child's infancy, so prostitution is probably caused by parental neglect.

(ii) The evidence shows that marijuana smoking leads to other forms of drug taking which may be of an addictive nature. Virtually all drug addicts report having smoked marijuana before taking up other, 'harder' drugs.

(iii) There is little doubt that aspirin is an effective agent for the relief of headaches. People who take aspirin almost invariably report a reduction or cessation of pain.

3. The following data might be used to argue that attendance at a privately conducted secondary school caused students to perform better than they would have if they had attended 'public' schools.

	Public Schools	*Private Schools*
% Students Matriculating	38	86
% Students Not Matriculating	62	14

(These results are statistically significant)

(i)   Do these data alone offer strong support for the original contention? If not, what additional evidence would be necessary to allow one to accept that conclusion? (Think of possible confounded variables, i.e. possible alternative explanations for statistics like these.)

4. The following is an excerpt from Desmond Morris's discussion of 'exploration' in Weisz, P. (ed.), *The Contemporary Scene* (1970). It is from Morris's book *'The Naked Ape'* (1967).

Luckily we have evolved a powerful antidote to (the) weakness which is inherent in the imitative learning process. We have a sharpened curiosity, an intensified urge to explore which works against the other tendency and produces a balance that has the potential of fantastic success. Only if a culture becomes too rigid as a result of its slavery to imitative repetition, or too daring and rashly exploratory, will it flounder. Those with a good balance between the two urges will thrive . . . In all exploratory behaviour . . . there is the ever present battle between the neophilic[1] and neophobic[2]

1. Neophilic: attracted towards novelty.
2. Neophobic: fearful of novelty.

urges ... this state of conflict does not merely *account for* the more obvious fluctuations in fashions and fads, in hair style and clothing, in furniture and cars; it is also the *very basis* of our whole cultural progression (p.146; [emphasis added]).

(i)   Are the biological 'urges' postulated by Morris genuinely explanatory?

(ii) Is it really possible to 'account for' (explain) large-scale cultural differences by postulating biological urges in various states of balance or imbalance? Why or why not?

(iii) Can you think of any other postulates in psychology of which the same criticisms might be made?

5. The postulation of 'instincts' to 'explain' many aspects of social behaviour is common in the written work of psychology students. The following is an excerpt from one essay which concerned the 'mirror-image phenomenon' in international relations. This is the hypothesised tendency for opposing national groups (e.g. U.S.A. and U.S.S.R.) to hold very similar (distorted) images of each other.

The first factor to be considered is that man is inherently suspicious of anyone he does not know well. This characteristic may be observed in animals too, so it may be assumed that it exists in most creatures. There is a struggle for survival which instils caution in each creature be it passive or aggressive. There is a territorial boundary surrounding the creature and the intrusion of another causes a reaction which depends on whether the intruder is friend or foe. Quite often, in the case of man, those from other countries are unknown and therefore treated with suspicion or prejudice.

(i)   What is anthropomorphism? Where does it occur in this passage?

(ii) Discuss the logic of the argument from analogy advanced here. Granted that analogies are never strictly valid, is this a strong or a weak instance of this form of argument?

(iii) Comment on the phrase 'instils caution'. What view of evolution does this suggest?

(iv) In what sense might it be claimed that the author's use of the term 'inherent suspicion', coupled with his admission that reactions depend on 'whether the intruder is friend or foe', allows *any* reaction to be explained *post hoc*? Is this a strength or weakness of the argument?

6. Prostitution (the offering of sexual favours in return for material benefits) exists in the animal world among primates. Since man is a primate, we must therefore recognise that prostitution is a part of our over-all inheritance from our furry ancestors. As such it can never be discarded as long as our species survives, no matter how much wishful thinking we indulge

in. When a modern girl marries for wealth and/or status . . . she is simply obeying a powerful female instinct shared by our cousins the gibbons and monkeys and baboons for many millions of years. We can no more suppress prostitution than we can any of our other inherited instincts (R. Ardrey, letter to *Playboy*, March 1967).

N.B.   The argument presented here exhibits so many of the fallacies which we have discussed as to constitute an excellent example for sharpening one's critical skills. Indeed Alan C. Elms mounts a strong attack on arguments from analogy in social psychology in his book *Social Psychology and Social Relevance* (1972), which cites this example. The reader is referred to that chapter should he or she wish to study further the possible abuses of analogical argument. First, though, consider the following questions.

(i)   What logical errors are obvious in Ardrey's argument?

(ii)   What evidence does Ardrey offer for 'prostitution' being 'instinctive' (in *either* animals *or* man?)

(iii) What sort of evidence would be sufficient to refute the contention that prostitution is an 'instinct' in Ardrey's sense of the word? If no evidence would suffice, is this a strength or weakness of his argument?

(iv)   If one allows that prostitution is 'part of our over-all inheritance from our furry ancestors' on the basis of Ardrey's arguments, what other forms of social behaviour would need to be called 'instinctive'? What does this suggest about the original argument?

7. With reference . . . to the higher vertebrates, we shall maintain and defend the two following theses: I. Fundamentally, among animals, fighting is not sought nor valued for its own sake; it is resorted to rather as an unwelcome necessity, a means of defending the agent's interests. II. Even when an animal does fight, he aims, not to destroy the enemy, but only to get rid of his presence and his interference . . . Animals do not enjoy fighting for its own sake. Unless his anger is aroused, the agent's behaviour indicates that he has no appetence for the fighting situation; he does not seek it; when he is in it he does not endeavour to prolong it; and he reveals by his expressions that he does not enjoy it (Craig, in Maple and Matheson, 1973; pp.67-68).

(i)   List all the anthropomorphic expressions in the passage.

(ii)   Could the passage be rewritten without this anthropomorphic emphasis? Attempt to do this.

(iii) Does the change in terminology alter the theoretical assumptions of the passage? If so, how?

6

SOME COMMON WEAKNESSES IN PSYCHOLOGICAL ARGUMENT

A man who has committed a mistake and does not correct it is committing another mistake.

Confucius

THE DISCUSSION of psychological issues is complicated by a number of subtle (and not-so-subtle) fallacies which demand our attention. Many of these are difficult to classify, for they are not necessarily logical errors in the narrow sense defined in Chapter 2. They are more general inadequacies which involve inconsistencies, over-simplifications and conceptual confusions of various kinds. As such, each of the five considered in this chapter involves some abuse or omission of the canons of good argument. Specifically, they concern the use of illegitimate appeals to 'win' arguments; the tendency to force opposing explanations into over-simplifying, mutually exclusive categories; arguments in which there is insufficient detail to relate precisely the proposed explanans to the explanandum; and, finally, the failure to distinguish between matters of fact and matters of evaluation.

6.1   ILLEGITIMATE APPEALS

In Chapter 2 we highlighted the importance of argument and its superiority to mere assertion. We saw that arguments do not merely state their conclusions; they also give reasons in support of them: they show ways in which their respective conclusions can be evaluated. We noted that in many arguments (even extended ones) some of the supporting statements are not made explicit, but are left unstated. However, if the argument is to be useful, its premises should initially be less controversial than the conclusion. (If this is not so, the argument, in a sense, does not progress — its premises will be disputed, regardless of the conclusion they are advanced to support.) We previously noted two main types of relatively uncontroversial statements — the class of analytic statements and the class of observation statements. We saw how useful these statements could be in refuting scientific theories by means of the argument form *Modus Tollens*. Indeed *Modus Tollens* is an argument form which often involves an analytic statement ('If p then q') and an observation statement ('Not q') which together imply the falsity of an (otherwise more controversial) theory (represented here as p). In these cases an appeal to observational and analytic truths is made to evaluate a theoretical statement.

In contrast to this paradigm, there are two commonly used, but less legitimate, appeals which are assumed to justify acceptance of a particular statement. These are perhaps best described as ways of *persuading* rather than of *showing* others that a statement should be judged true. One of them is a type of argument; the other is not really an argument at all. Both involve some kind of appeal to authority, but make the appeal in different ways. We shall call the first 'argument from authority', and the second 'appeals to fact', and examine them in turn.

Argument from authority. To argue from authority is to propose the statement that a particular 'expert' holds a certain view as sufficient, or as significant support for that view. It may even be supposed that an argument is better insofar as more experts can be cited who agree with the conclusion. Sometimes the argument includes premises which purport to justify the expert's claim to relevant expertise. This type of argument is apparent in the following examples:

> (i)   The general consensus among the *experts* who have studied this question as *objectively* and *scientifically* as possible is that there is no proof of innate racial differences in intellectual ability. (This is a close paraphrase of a statement in Klineberg, 1964; each of the italicised words appears in the original.)

On the other hand, prior to arguing that there is considerable evidence to support the proposition that such innate racial differences *do* exist, Eysenck (1971) states:

> (ii)   I would be prepared to assert that experts (real experts that is) would agree with at least 90% of what I am going to say . . . (p.15).

It is tempting to try to settle which of the authors is correct by trying to ascertain which is more 'expert'. But this really has nothing to do with the value of the arguments which each advances or the truth of the conclusions they reach. As Eysenck himself comments, 'experts' abound in psychology whenever public interest in controversial issues is high. But arguments are not valid, nor statements true, because they are presented by experts (whether 'real' or not). It is the arguments and statements themselves, not their proponents that must be evaluated; appeals to expertise or status are often merely 'window dressing' — rhetorical techniques aimed at achieving *uncritical* support for the point of view advanced. Criticism of a person rather than of his arguments is known as an argument *ad hominem* and is to be avoided for the same reasons as arguing from authority. It is therefore quite irrelevant to refute or confirm the status or credentials of a proponent of a particular conclusion in the hope of discrediting or supporting his argument. This may be acceptable (or at least accepted) in political debate, but it has no place in academic discussion.

For instance, an argument sometimes suggests the inexpertness or even the immorality of a supporter of a view that one wishes to criticise. A variation of this consists of labelling a statement, argument or its proponent with an expression that carries negative connotations in order to denigrate that statement, argument or person. Although fashions change in this regard, one often hears arguments dismissed as 'racist', 'sexist', 'behaviouristic' or 'Freudian', without any attempt at refutation. Such pejorative labels are totally irrelevant to the evaluation of the arguments to which they are gratuitously attached. Clearly the important point is that, in general, someone's stating that something is the case is no guarantee that it is the case. Despite this, however, we do rely to a great extent on what others claim – we trust that their statements are true. Of course, the degree of trust will depend on the particular context in which the statement is advanced.

The varying deference given to authority can be seen from the different general approaches to the 'results' section and the 'discussion' section when one is critically evaluating a psychological paper or article. The usual practice is to take the 'results' as read, while being more critical or evaluative of the 'discussion' section. Usually the results section contains either simple observation statements or statements readily obtained from them, like statistical summaries, percentages, standard deviations, means, etc. Most authors of papers are taken to be 'authorities' on these matters. If they write that there was a certain outcome to the experiment, then most readers take it that there was that outcome. In contrast, they are not viewed as authorities when readers consider possible explanations and interpetations of the results of the 'discussion' section of papers. As a result, they need to *argue*, as opposed to merely *state*, their position. Then their readers can critically assess their reasoning, and try to think of alternative explanations and results that confirm or conflict with those explanations.

Of course, although it is not always done, one should also be critical of the 'results' section of the paper. It is not uncommon for an author to uncritically assume that one situation he observes guarantees that another holds, and for him to report only the latter. For example, an author may report 'None of the subjects surveyed had read *Playboy*', when a more accurate report would have been 'None of the subjects surveyed admitted having read *Playboy*'. To take the first report as read could be to have uncritically accepted a false statement (perhaps through misplaced reliance on another's critical skills – on his authority).

Hence the question is not whether one is to accept statements made by other authorities or experts, but whether one is prepared to accept a statement, even a theoretically controversial one, simply because it has authoritative support.

Appeals to 'fact'. Psychology is frequently condemned for its lack of factual information. Despite this, there is a tendency for authors to claim that the evidence supporting their viewpoint is 'established' or 'widely accepted' fact. This may be no more than a rhetorical device, similar to appeals to the authority or the status of a source of information. Whenever psychologists claim to be simply presenting the facts, it is advisable to read what they say with care. This is not because there are no 'facts' in psychology, but because the presentation and interpretation of what are claimed to be facts may be controversial.

The error of appealing to 'the facts' is the error of simply asserting a statement instead of presenting an argument of which it is the conclusion. People use phrases such as 'It is obvious that . . .' and 'The simple fact is that . . .'

when they are not going to present an argument but simply assert a statement. As we mentioned earlier, in every argument some statements must be left without argued support (i.e. the initial premises), so there will always be some statements that are simply stated, not argued. (Ideally, these should be less controversial than the conclusion they support.) The mistake of appealing to the 'facts' occurs when a *controversial* statement is simply asserted. To claim that a statement presents a 'fact' does not alter its truth or falsity.

Statements must be either true or false, but there are often many ways of expressing the same statement which involve different words or phrases. Hence what appears to be a 'fact' to one author may not be accepted as a fact by another author because it is couched in the language of a controversial theory.

To illustrate this, consider the observation that people sometimes attack others when frustrated by some person who is himself relatively immune to attack. This can be described in a number of slightly different ways, each of which is in some sense consistent with the fact expressed here in informal colloquial language. However close examination of each possible description reveals that the words adopted give the 'fact' a rather different status in each theoretical context. First, it might be said that it is a fact that 'humans displace their aggression on to others'. Second, one could merely claim that 'humans seek scapegoats for their frustrated aggressive tendencies'. A third formulation might be 'In humans, the stimuli associated with interference to ongoing goal-directed behaviour increase the probability of vigorous physical reactions to all subsequent stimuli'. (Doubtless there are other possible descriptions.)

The first (Freudian) and the last (behaviouristic) interpretation may each be judged true. Each may be a 'fact'. But it must also be emphasised that each sentence uses words having quite different meanings within their usual theoretical context — the terms of the respective statements are not theoretically 'neutral'. Indeed their theoretical backgrounds may be incompatible in many respects. Certainly the word 'displacement' would not be accepted without redefinition by a behaviourist. He might question whether the phenomenon of 'displacement' ever occurred in the sense specified by strictly Freudian theory. 'Displacement' is a theory-laden term in that it assumes that there exists some 'energy' or 'drive' which is capable of being 'released' and 'redirected' if 'blocked'. So one psychologist's fact may be another's fiction, even though both theorists may purport to be describing the same phenomenon. The appeal to 'fact' may be rhetorical strategy aimed at encouraging uncritical acceptance of a particular (covertly theoretical) argument.

6.2 MISLEADING DICHOTOMIES

When psychological issues are debated, the participants frequently resort to over-simplified points of view owing to the adoption of what we shall call 'misleading dichotomies'. By this we mean that alternative arguments are seen as reflecting either one set of factors or an alternative, incompatible set, even when these alternatives may be seen to be compatible with one another if analysed more carefully. This tendency to see psychological explanations as 'black *or* white' (not as black *and* white, or shades of grey) is exemplified by the numerous controversies concering the hypothesised effects of hereditary and environmental factors on many different psychological phenomena (e.g. 'intelligence', sex role behaviour).

While the distinction between 'nature' and 'nurture', or 'innate' and 'learned' characteristics, may be useful in many contexts, it may also create a misleadingly crude dichotomy which encourages the over-simplification of important psychological issues. This result is particularly likely if a further tendency is present, namely the practice of searching for single, clearly distinguishable causes of a phenomenon when a complex set of causal factors may be operative. For instance, psychologists often speak of 'the cause of schizophrenia' or 'the cause of stuttering' in a manner which suggests that only one factor is responsible for each of the respective phenomena. Of course, there are many alternatives to this. For example, it is possible that 'schizophrenia' results from a genetically determined biochemical abnormality alone; or from one of a number of such abnormalities; or from one or more of those in the presence of certain traumatic life experiences; or from a complex series of life experiences regardless of any biochemical abnormality. Indeed each of these alternatives has been proposed at various times in the history of research into 'schizophrenia'.

To illustrate the ease with which one may propose questions (and also interpret explanations) in terms of over-simplifying dichotomies and single independent causal factors, we shall discuss an example from a discipline other than psychology. This case sheds considerable light on some major psychological issues, however. It concerns the factors responsible for the height to which humans grow. Let us first consider this in the light of the 'genetic' *v.* 'environmental' factors dichotomy, for this is an instance where common sense suggests that the dichotomy is quite valid. People are assumed to inherit either their stature, or, at least, the potential to develop a certain stature. Informal observation shows that tall parents have tall offspring and shorter parents children of smaller stature.

From this it is generally concluded that a person's height is genetically determined. However, one's height is not determined solely by genetic factors; nor is the relationship between genetic factors and non-genetic factors (e.g. nutritional intake) at all simple in respect of their relative or interacting contributions to stature. For example, quite rapid increases in the average height of a population may occur when dietary habits are altered, even though it had previously been assumed that the population was of short stature as a result of genetic factors. The most dramatic illustration of this is the Japanese population, whose height has increased noticeably since World War II, possibly as a result of increased amounts of red meat in its diet (as a result of American influence).

As Hunt (1969) points out, Europeans, and Americans themselves, may have undergone a similar transformation over the past few hundred years. Discussing the possibility of greatly increased intellectual development through new forms of early education, he states:

> In connection with this possibility of a general increase in intelligence, we should consider also what has happened to the stature of human beings. It appears to have increased by nearly a foot without benefit of selective breeding or natural selection. While visiting Festival Port in Jamestown, Virginia recently, we examined the reproduction of the ships which brought the settlers from England. They were astoundingly small. The guide reported that the average height of those immigrants was less than 5 feet, and that the still famous Captain John Smith was considered to be unusually tall at 5 feet 2 inches. The guide's 'instruction book' puts the authority for these statements in the Sween Library at William and Mary. I have been unable to check the evidence, but scrutiny of the armor on display in various museums in England implies that the stature of the aristocrats who wore it must typically have been about the reported size of those immigrants to Jamestown. Also, the guide for the U.S. Constitution includes in his spiel the statement that the headroom between decks needed to be no more than 5 feet and 6 inches because the average stature of sailors in the War of 1812 was about 5 feet and 2 inches. This increase in height can occur within a single generation . . . Inasmuch as Professor Jensen resorts repeatedly to the analogy between intelligence and stature, such evidence of an increase in the average height for human beings, the reasons for which are still a matter largely of conjecture, should have some force in increasing the credibility for the genetic potentiality for a general increase in intelligence (pp.144-45).

The example of human stature (and its possible analogy with intelligence) indicates the dangers of assuming a simple dichotomy between hereditary and environmental factors, even in the case of a well-defined biological trait.

Yet psychologists continue to make assertions about causal factors which all too frequently presume a rigid dichotomy between such factors. In addition to the debate about the determinants of intelligence, another controversial issue is the origins of sex roles in young children. In this case, what begins as a difference of emphasis between proponents of the views that sex roles are substantially biologically 'given', and that they are learned, can too easily be reduced to a debate couched in dogmatically held dichotomies. But in a debate concerning such complex interacting factors as those responsible for sexual gender identity and role development, no exclusive concentration on 'innate' *or* environmental factors is likely to do justice to the range of phenomena to be explained. The subtlety and complexity of this topic can readily be appreciated by reference to Money and Ehrhardt (1972). Discussing different sexual 'orientations', they conclude:

> The most likely explanation of the origins of homosexuality, bisexuality, and heterosexuality of gender identify is that certain sexually dimorphic traits or dispositions are laid down in the brain before birth which may facilitate the establishment of either of the three conditions but are too strongly bivalent to be exclusive and invariant determinants of either homo- or heterosexuality, or of their shared bisexual state. The primary origins of the three conditions lie in the developmental period of a child's life after birth, particularly during the years of late infancy and early childhood, when gender identity differentiation is being established. The state of knowledge as of the present does not permit any hypotheses (many psychodynamic claims to the contrary) that will predict with certainty which biographical conditions will ensure that an anatomically normal boy or girl will become erotically homosexual, bisexual, or heterosexual. Once the pattern is established in the early development years, however, it is remarkably tenacious. The hormones of puberty bring it into full expression (p.235).

Clearly, any causal account of such complex behaviour must be carefully formulated if it is not to imply an over-simplified dichotomisation of alternatives. This conclusion requires some qualification, however. Frequently, to claim that sex roles are learned, not determined biologically, is not intended to deny entirely the relevance of biological factors. Rather, it is meant to suggest that, even given the range of biological predispositions, environmental factors may be sufficient to override these in the determination of relevant behaviour. This claim does not rely so crudely on the nature-nurture dichotomy, although it also needs to be stated very carefully if it is to avoid that oversimplifying tendency.

6.3   RELATIVE CONCEPTS

We have discussed in a previous chapter some of the problems involved in defining and consistently using psychological concepts. Here we shall consider some further subtleties of terms which are frequently sources of confusion. It will be emphasised that many psychological terms are capable of definition only in a *relative* rather than an *absolute* way, although this is not to say that such concepts are totally arbitrary or of no scientific value. This seems an important issue because it is often argued that words such as 'intelligent', 'normal', 'introverted', 'masculine' (and their respective opposites) are incapable of precise definition owing to their being 'purely relative' (although what this means is seldom explicated). Such alleged relativity is then held to imply that each is totally or largely 'arbitrary' — i.e. that each is capable of no systematic justification.

Asserting that a term is a relative one may be merely a rhetorical tactic, unless it is specified *how* it is relative. This point requires emphasis because, in a sense, practically every adjective applicable to behaviour might be said to be relative. Ordinary terms like 'quick', 'slow', 'complex', 'simple', etc. can be precisely understood only if a certain context is assumed. Their interpretation is relative to their context in much the same way as the terms we shall consider in detail in this section. What distinguishes terms like the latter, and makes them important in formal psychology, is the lack of agreement about the ways in which the use of such terms is 'relative' to specific contexts and criteria. Therefore let us first consider some possible interpretations of saying that a psychological predicate is 'relative'; we shall use the examples of 'intelligent' and 'masculine', both of which can be argued to be so in at least three respects. We shall then ask whether these terms are necessarily 'arbitrary' in any significant sense. First, let us clarify a possible confusion. Rather than speaking of a term or concept as being 'relative', it might be more accurate to say that the *use* of a term, or the *criteria* for applying a term or concept, are 'relative' — not the concept itself. However it is conventional to use the short expression and we shall follow this practice.

6.3.1 'Intelligent'

The adjective 'intelligent' is a relative term in three important respects. First, the concept refers to (or, more accurately, *evaluates*) dimensions of behaviour along an assumed *continuum*. Persons are not simply classified as either 'intelligent' or 'unintelligent', but as relatively so — i.e. relative to the range of behaviour of the population with whom they are compared. Although the conventional distinction between 'intelligent' and 'unintelligent' behaviour (or persons) seems to imply a dichotomy rather than a continuum, the potential range of judgements concerning human intelligence is not restricted to two or any other finite number. Clearly there can be no single, precise demarcation of intelligent from unintelligent behaviour. One practical result of this is the difficulty of classifying degrees of mental subnormality — the criteria adopted being subject to considerable debate. For instance, the differences between persons with measured I.Q.'s of 65 and 75 ('mentally subnormal' and 'borderline' respectively) may be rather difficult to specify unequivocally. Still greater uncertainty pertains when one person has an I.Q. of 69 and another a score of 71. Here the resulting difference in psychiatric classification might be seen more as a matter of rigid adherence to a numerical criterion than as a reflection of significant psychological characteristics. In such circumstances it would be fair to call the classification (or its decision point: I.Q. = 70) an *arbitrary* one, although that is not to suggest that it is either meaningless or easily avoided.

The second sense in which 'intelligent' is relative is rather more subtle. It concerns the fact that the continuum of behaviour considered to exemplify degrees of intelligence is based on a culturally relative judgement. Although it need not be argued that 'intelligent' changes its *meaning* when applied to different cultures,[1] the criteria for judging behaviour as relatively intelligent are themsleves relative to specific cultural norms and values, at least to some extent. There are different criteria to which judgements of intelligence relate in different cultures. Although it would seem fair to claim, for example, that one ethnic group lived longer on average than another, without spelling out the criteria for this judgement (these being uncontroversial), this would not be so when judgements are made about the comparative intelligence of two ethnic groups. In this case criteria to which the comparisons relate may well be controversial. In particular, it is likely to be argued that they would be different from one culture to another and hence quite unlike those on which judgements about relative longevity are based. If this point is accepted, it may be concluded that judgements about the relative intelligence of different cultural groups may be difficult, if not impossible, to make.

Third, 'intelligent' is a relative term in a somewhat more technical sense. When psychologists assess peoples' I.Q. they assign numerical values on which are based qualitative descriptions ('superior intellect', 'educationally subnormal', etc.) by comparing an individual against the range of scores obtained from a normative population (called the *standardisation* population). Hence if a seven-year-old English child has an I.Q. of 105 points, this is meaningful data only in the light of the standardisation group with which he or she is most appropriately comparable; in this case a statistically adequate, representative sample of English seven-year-olds. Statements about a person's I.Q. implicitly compare that person to a set of statistical norms.

Furthermore, to be of maximum value, these quantitative statements also need to specify the exact type of psychological test on which the assessment is based. Quantitative I.Q. values as absolute scores are not as meaningful as their numerical precision might suggest. For instance, it is possible that an I.Q. of 115 on one test (relative to specified norms) may be strictly equivalent to an I.Q. of 110 or 120 on another test, owing to peculiarities of standardisation. Although conventional psychometric practice attempts to minimise such anomalies, they are possible, given the nature of concepts like intelligence and their methods of assessment.

6.3.2 'Masculine'

Although psychologists are less concerned to measure and assign numbers to peoples' 'masculinity' (to yield, perhaps, an M.Q.?), the predicates 'masculine'

1.   See 4.4 – Definitions and Criteria for the Use of Theoretical Terms.

and 'feminine' are very common in psychological debate. The layman's lack of knowledge about the scientific validity of the *assumed* dimension or dimensions of behaviour labelled as being 'masculine', to various degrees, has not reduced the tendency to judge a diverse range of behaviour according to this concept. Despite this, both the layman and the expert generally fail to analyse what 'masculine' means, ignoring that, like 'intelligent', the adjective is 'relative' in a number of subtle respects. Anthony Storr, a prolific writer on 'popular' psychology, exemplifies this uncritical approach in the following segment of his book *Human Aggression* (1968, p.94). Discussing the role of aggression in the relation between the sexes, he makes the following points:

> As Jung used to point out, it is characteristic that the woman who appears in the unrelated man and the man who manifests himself in the unrelated woman are of inferior quality (to the 'related' woman and man). The man whose *feminine* side does not find itself projected upon a woman will be subject to unpredictable moods and an inferior emotionalism which can be pejoratively termed *effeminate*. The woman whose *masculine* aspect is not contained in the lover or husband becomes opinionated and dogmatic, and shows that insecure assertiveness which men find tiresome when they have to work for female executives [italics added].

One does not need to be a radical feminist to find much to question in this set of unsubstantiated assertions. But let us concentrate only on the author's use of the predicates which we have italicised. The first thing to notice is that Storr both accepts and denies that the masculinity-femininity dichotomy is an oversimplification which fails to appreciate the continuous range and continuing variability of behaviour to which the adjectives might be said to apply. He assumes (with Jung) that all people have a masculine and a feminine 'side' (i.e. that everyone is, to some degree, *both* masculine and feminine). However, at the same time, acceptance of both aspects of one's self is claimed to produce an inferior man or woman. That is Storr argues that a man is normal only when he 'projects' his feminine qualities. (Does this really mean when he *rejects* those qualities?) Similarly a woman must allow her so-called masculine aspects to be 'contained' in a lover or husband. But this seems a peculiar way to speak about the concepts of masculinity/femininity. What Storr effectively does is to *reify* the concepts by ignoring the *relative* nature of the masculinity-femininity continuum (if there is such a continuum). Although he had previously stated that '. . . we all have within us potentialities of being both masculine and feminine', his use of the concrete expressions 'feminine side' and 'masculine aspect' suggests that these potentialities are discrete, biological entities, or at least biologically based characteristics which each person possesses. Storr confirms this impression when he later speaks of the male's 'fully masculine role' (which incidentally involves 'dominance' of women!) and of females being (potentially at least) 'fully feminine'. In other words, there are *absolute* criteria for calling a person or his/her role, fully (completely) masculine or feminine, despite the fact that we are all both to some extent.

To see more clearly how Storr is committed to an inconsistent or an absurd interpretation of masculinity, let us ask what sense can be made of his notion of complete masculinity (or its opposite) by returning to the example of intelligence. It would surely be peculiar to assert that some people are fully (completely or totally) intelligent, for the same reason that it would be so to say that someone was, for example, tall or heavy in any absolute sense. Clearly, everyone is intelligent to some degree; there is no absolute zero point on such dimensions and no absolute upper limit. Yet Storr would have us believe that some people are fully masculine, although he never really defines this term. This is reminiscent of advertisements which claim that the smoker of a particular brand of cigarette is 'all man'. It seems fair to conclude that Storr's apparently expert argument is as conceptually crude as such sexist advertising.

But surely, it will be objected, the word 'masculine' is not meaningless, even if people like Storr do use it rather thoughtlessly. Let us therefore discuss how, as a relative concept, it can be employed in technically more sophisticated contexts if carefully qualified. As indicated above, the predicate is relative in much the same way as the term 'intelligent'. First, if it is accepted that there is a *continuum* of behaviour ranging from what *a particular culture specifies* as extremely feminine to extremely masculine, then there is no *absolute* criterion for assigning the word to any specific, invariant type of behaviour. As the italicised qualification emphasises, the term 'masculine' applies only within the framework of culturally defined criteria. What twentieth century Westerners call masculine is not what would be so judged in, say, a traditional New Guinea Highland, or Australian Aboriginal, tribe. It is well known that within certain cultures, biological males are typically passive, even 'maternal' (to Western eyes). To say that these men are not truly masculine is to impose the values of our own culture on another culture and to *judge* rather than *describe* that culture. This type of reasoning entirely ignores the cultural relativity of the criteria. Yet this, incidentally, is what Storr does, confusing biological inevitability with cultural determination by equating masculinity with what males generally do in his own society.

To be more subtle, Storr might better use the term 'masculine' when a person is judged to behave in a manner which, *relative* to other members of the male sex (and by some degree of contrast with females) in a *particular culture,* is towards the extreme of the continuum of behaviour typical of males. As is evident from the simplistically absolute dichotomies of Storr's quoted viewpoint, such qualifications are not mere pedantry; without them important questions can all too easily be begged.

6.4 'MISSING LINKS'

We have illustrated the tendency for psychology to rely on potentially over-simplifying dichotomies — especially when single causal factors are hypo-thesised. Another common weakness to which psychological argument is especially prone consists of outlining only in the most general terms the causal factors which are hypothetically responsible for a particular type of behaviour, without providing any details of how such factors might operate to produce the relevant effects. In other words there are 'gaps' or 'missing links' between the explanandum and the generalisation which purports to explain it. There are many examples of this, because, to some extent, it is inevitable that not all the mediating steps in causal accounts of complex phenomena will be known or spelt out at any particular time. Nevertheless some putative explanations lack so many details as to be of very limited value. The most instructive examples of such inadequacies are to be found where generalisations are proposed to explain a range of phenomena but in which neither the generalisation nor the phenomena being explained are described in precise terms. The vagueness of both the explanans and explanandum then serves to camouflage the insufficient (or non-existent) mediating factors.

Let us illustrate the way in which explanatory arguments may involve this weakness by discussing the 'common sense' generalisation that inadequate maternal care leads to psychological maladjustment, and by developing this generalisation into more sophisticated versions of the hypothesised relation-ship between these factors.

It will be argued that frequently there are two major inadequacies in examples such as this. We shall call these: (1) *Insufficient distinctions in terminology*; and (2) *Inadequate accounts of factors mediating between explanans and explanandum*. We will see that these are closely related in that the former makes the latter virtually unavoidable. In the present case, if one does not attempt to distinguish various types of 'inadequate maternal care', and some precise forms of 'psychological maladjustment' then it will be impossible to advance beyond very vague generalisations. Let us, therefore, turn to a detailed discussion of this example.

In recent years the controversy concerning the nature and duration of the effects of 'maternal deprivation' has centred on the theoretical writings of John Bowlby (e.g. Bowlby, 1969, 1973) and research findings from both non-human primates and human infants. It is a controversy which has direct relevance to a variety of social welfare policies, to arguments about the 'liberation' of women and the changing nature of the Western nuclear family. Unfortunately, popular discussion of the issue has frequently polarised into support for, or opposition to, generalisations which assert a simple causal relationship between 'maternal deprivation' (variously defined) and a variety of psychological 'abnormalities' (given names like 'delinquency' or 'psychopathy'). Such a polarisation glosses over the complexities of this area of psychological research in a way that illustrates only too clearly the lack of detailed analysis behind many psychological generalisations – especially those concerning the causes of 'deviant' or 'abnormal' behaviour.

Without discussing the details of research findings in this area, let us attempt to clarify the questions which fall under the topic of the generalisation, and itemise some of the possible links in the hypothesised causal chain between a child's maternal environment and his adolescent or adult personality. To facilitate this discussion, we shall refer to the monograph by Michael Rutter (1972) entitled *Maternal Deprivation Reassessed,* which approaches this issue by attempting to detail precise questions subsidiary to the generalisation we are considering. Very sensibly, Rutter makes relatively subtle terminological distinctions and, in the light of these, searches for possible mechanisms through which various types of deprivation might affect human development. Without outlining all these distinctions and possible mechanisms, we shall concentrate on the way Rutter attempts to fill in the missing links in the argument concerning only the long-term consequences of maternal deprivation (i.e. not the immediate short-term 'protest' and 'despair' that babies exhibit when separated from mothers and/or when placed in strange environments under certain conditions).

To overcome the gross simplifications inherent in generalisations such as the one with which we began this discussion, Rutter points to the need to specify (a) what types of 'maladjustment' are (hypothetically) produced; and (b) what precise aspects of the child's social, physical or maternal environment are associated with each. In relation to (a), at least five possible forms of maladjustment are distinguished: 'mental retardation, dwarfism, delinquency, "affectionless psychopathy" and possibly depression' (p.79). Hence any argument concerning the relationship between 'maternal deprivation' and 'maladjustment' must be judged on its ability to specify the (presumably different) factors involved in each of these outcomes. The issues then become quite complex. There are many possible psychological processes which need to be distinguished under the general heading of 'maternal deprivation' if the possible causal mechanisms are to be described in any detail. Indeed Rutter distinguishes over ten possible factors which might be (sometimes inappropriately) included under the general label of 'maternal deprivation'. Associated with each possible factor is a different conception of the manner by which the maladjustment or maladjustments is or are produced. In fact, some of the relevant factors may not involve deprivation of maternal care as such, at all! This is possible because the child's maternal environment may have been confused (i.e. confounded) with other aspects of the social and physical environment by various authors writing on the subject. Rutter therefore distinguishes the following questions (among others). The reader will notice how subtle some of the alternative interpretations of the nature of 'maternal deprivation' may be. Is the critical factor essentially the lack of maternal care as such, or is it one or more of the following?

1. The disruption of existing (social) bonds or the failure to form bonds with others generally;
2. The change of environment which might accompany that disruption (e.g. sudden hospitalisation);
3. Sensory privation or general social privation (reduced physical stimulation, lack of social interactions involving speech, smiling, etc.);
4. Nutritional privation;
5. Failure to form bonds specifically with the mother;
6. Distorted relationships generally, or with the mother in particular;
7. Imitation of 'faulty models' (i.e. parents). Or, perhaps, faulty imitation of models;
8. Some combination of these and/or other factors (e.g. specific, genetically determined predispositions).

To relate adequately the independent and dependent variables in the generalisation one would need to consider how each or some combination of these could produce each or some combination of the five 'maladjustments' referred to previously. We have therefore moved a long way from the original generalisation. The benefit of this type of analysis, however, cannnot be overestimated. Without making the types of distinctions Rutter makes, and without analysing all the possible causal connections between different types of 'deprivation' and different types of 'maladjustment', it would not be possible to propose any coherent argument on topics as complex as the one we are discussing. It is, therefore, essential to try to provide details as to how hypothetical causes actually function to produce their (assumed) effects. Even given the above analysis of the possible role of various types of environmental stress which were indiscriminately lumped together under the one term in the original generalisation, the precise biological and psychological processes by which these affect behaviour have still to be detailed. However, leaving this aside, the example illustrates the importance of going beyond vague generalisations, even those couched in what appear to be 'technical' terms (such as 'maternal deprivation'). It illustrates the value of asking precisely how the variables in the generalisation are causally related, thus allowing one to fill in the 'missing links' between the variables in the original generalisation.

6.5 'IS' AND 'OUGHT'

The last decade has seen renewed controversy about the social responsibility and the environmental impact of the physical sciences and resulting technological advances. It has become clear that questions of cultural value intrude into the study of even the most 'objective' science. Similar, and in some respects more important, questions of value and social responsibility and the issue of ethical controls arise in the behavioural and medical fields. The question which confronts the physicist – whether his discoveries are potentially dangerous to humanity or the environment – is one which is becoming increasingly difficult to separate from the more routine, physical questions which he studies. Similarly, psychological knowledge may be used or abused by social agencies. Furthermore, the questions regarded as warranting scientific study will be so judged depending on the cultural ethos and personal values of the individual scientist, be he physicist or psychologist. The result of this may be that psychological 'knowledge' frequently reflects, through what it assumes as much as through its explicit formulation, specific 'value-orientations'. When psychological expertise is cited as support for social practices, such orientations may be obvious only with the advantage of hindsight (e.g. the women's movement has pointed out the sexist biases inherent in much of the literature on personality development). At other times, however, the question of values is more explicit – especially when theories are to be 'applied' to alter an individual person's behaviour. Here the question of what *is* the case, and what *should* be the case, or what behaviour *should* be exhibited by an individual, is clearly controversial.

For instance, the recently developed techniques of behaviour therapy (or 'modification'), based on the principles of classical and operant conditioning, have been applied to the control of excessive drinking, to changing the sexual preferences and practices of homosexuals and to reducing the expression of aggression. As was indicated by the controversy surrounding the film 'Clockwork Orange', such psychological techniques raise (or at least highlight) some important issues. Among these are the following: What is the relevance of psychological knowledge and technology to social practice? What is 'deviant' or 'antisocial' behaviour? Should such behaviour be subject to psychological 'therapy'?

These issues are extremely complex, and can neither be summarily answered nor quickly dismissed. But this much can be said. They are not questions to which psychological theory or research can, *by itself*, provide answers. Indeed, it can be argued that such questions are essentially 'political', 'social' or 'moral' rather than psychological. Let us expand on this assertion in order to clarify the nature of the relationship between 'facts' and 'values', 'knowledge' and 'action', 'empirical statements' and 'moral statements'.

Briefly, moral statements either involve evaluative terms or else are imperative in form. They employ expressions like 'good' or 'should' (or their opposites). They may, of course, involve 'disguised' or implicit moral concepts. For example, it might be said that '*Democratic* child-rearing practices promote psychologically *healthier* children than *authoritarian* practices', or that 'Behaviour therapy *dehumanises* the persons on whom it is practiced'. In these cases, it could be argued that the concepts of 'health', 'dehumansiation' (and, indeed, of 'democratic' and 'authoritarian' practices) are essentially *evaluative,* rather than merely *descriptive.* By labelling them as evaluative we imply that their conventional use expresses either a positive or a negative value judgement concering the phenomena to which they apply. To take a clear example of this contrast, compare 'Jones killed Smith' with 'Jones murdered Smith'. Although these two statements may describe the same event, the second goes beyond the first in conventionally expressing the judgement that Jones was wrong to kill Smith. Frequently, of course, there is less unanimity about whether the terms express positive or negative value judgements. For the term 'murder' the situation is clear, but for many terms one needs to know details of the speaker's values or those of his audience in order to determine what type of judgement (if any) is being offered. A phrase like 'Fred is obedient' or 'Bill is ambitious' will involve a positive value judgement when used by some speakers, but will be used by others to express a negative judgement. Depending on who used the terms, 'development', 'artistic', even 'scientific' may imply differing value judgements of the phenomena to which they are taken to apply. We could say of such terms that they are 'theory-laden' in an even stronger sense than those to which the term was applied in Chapter 4. Their theoretical bias extends beyond any particular psychological assumptions and encompasses moral values.

Some philosophers concerned with the analysis of moral concepts have long held that arguments which attempt to derive evaluative or imperative conclusions from purely 'factual' premises are invalid. Many claim that there can be no logical implication between factual premises and imperative or prescriptive conclusions. This is usually expressed by saying that an 'is' can not imply an 'ought'. Any argument with a conclusion involving 'ought', 'good', or similar expression is, according to this view, invalid *unless* its premises include similar evaluative or imperative expressions. Supporters of this view might cite the following example:

> Social deprivation retards both the cognitive and emotional development of young children. *Therefore* children *should* be provided with intense social stimulation.

Although at first glance, this might look like a valid argument, it is not — at least not in the form in which it is presented here. Either the argument is incomplete (an enthymeme) or it is invalid. The conclusion does not follow from the premiss. If, instead of judging the argument as invalid, we take it to be an enthymeme, the missing premiss would seem to be linked with some judgement concerning the desirability of certain outcomes. A more complete form of the argument might therefore read:

> Social deprivation retards both the cognitive and emotional development of young children. It is desirable that children (should) develop these capacities as much as possible. Therefore children should be provided with intense social stimulation.

Now, the evaluative premiss, involving the concept of desirability, seems to make the argument valid. Unlike the first premiss, the additional premiss explicitly expresses a value judgement, although it may be a judgement that others find questionable.

But even when we thus augment the argument it remains invalid. It may be that social deprivation retards both the cognitive and emotional development of young children, and it may be considered desirable that children develop these capacities as much as possible, but it need not follow that children should be provided with intense social stimulation. For it may be possible that providing intense social stimulation adequate for the benefits outlined will also produce such deleterious side-effects that it can be objected that it should not be done. There may be such overwhelming reasons against providing social stimulation sufficiently intense to develop children cognitively and emotionally that the reasons cited in the premiss for this course of action are overridden. Hence, to improve the argument, it would need to be further augmented. For example, we could interpret the meaning of 'should' in the conclusion to mean, narrowly, 'should, for these reasons', or we could add a premiss to the effect that there are no undesirable side-effects of the recommended policy. (Yet even with these additions it would still be formally invalid. Why?)

This example suggests that one useful way of interpreting 'is-ought' arguments is to regard them as being incomplete. They may be seen as implicitly asserting conditional propositions: that is as being of the form *'If* situation *X* is desirable, good, etc., *then* facts *A, B, C* imply that conditions *L, M, N* should be implemented'. On this interpretation the only psychological content in an evaluative or prescriptive argument is in the second part of the conditional statement. But if there is no consensus about the evaluative clause of the conditional, then there need be no agreement about what the conclusion means with respect to desirable actions, no matter how voluminous is the psychological evidence which supports the factual premisses.

One of the main dangers of using evaluative terminology is that the evaluative terms seem to bridge the gap between factual statements and the policy statements that may be wrongly thought to follow from them. To return to our previous examples, no one is likely to be misled about the evaluative component of the term 'murder', but words such as 'retard', and 'development', taken from psychological literature, are usually stipulated to have only a descriptive meaning. However there may be a shift back to the evaluative assumptions that are implicit in the non-stipulated everyday use of the same terms when the terms are employed in examples such as that quoted earlier. It is therefore important to avoid covertly changing from 'descriptive' to 'evaluative' meanings and also to make explicit any evaluative assumptions which may be implicit in the use of psychological terms.

This point is at the foundation of some very important psychological controversies and needs to be recognised. It can be illustrated by returning to an example discussed previously. Let us again *assume,* for the sake of argument, that blacks, on the average, perform below whites on standard tests of intelligence. Let us further assume that the evidence favours the argument that this difference is largely genetically determined and not entirely due to environmental influences. It is natural to ask what relation this 'fact' would bear to moral questions. For example, racial discrimination is frequently justified (at least by its proponents) by such arguments as the 'biological inferiority' of black-skinned people.

Obviously, that one ought to practise racial discrimination is not *implied* by the presence of supposed racial differences in ability. To argue from these assumed differences to certain courses of action – either prejudice against, or increased facilities for, 'blacks', requires an additional premiss. This concerns desirable social outcomes, and it may differ from one person (including one psychologist) to another. Social values are not determined or changed by psychological research alone.

Hence it is possible to accept evidence concerning racial differences in ability but also to believe that either (a) black children require segregation from the general population from which they differ as a group; or (b) black children should be integrated and treated identically with other children, or to believe neither of these. It is not irrational to believe that there are innate racial differences in measured intelligence, yet to be quite 'liberal' politically. Similarly, prejudice is possible without the support of the 'evidence' of the inferiority of the rejected group. Although prejudiced people seek out (and frequently distort) evidence concerning the 'inferiority' of the groups they wish to reject, this 'justification' for their prejudice does not logically validate their position.

Perhaps a good example of the relationship between 'facts', prejudice and actions is the following: Identical twins, as a group, score slightly below the average of the general population on intelligence tests (Mittler, 1971). Yet no one would seriously suggest that this evidence implies that twins should be treated in special ways or denied privileges. Identical twins are not segregated into their own schools. The 'is' of evidence does not imply the 'ought' of action!

Therefore value judgements and imperatives to action might be seen as examples of rhetorical argument and criticised as such where appropriate. But students of psychology seldom accept this point, as the following quotations from essays indicate:

(i) Discussing the role of the mass media in encouraging violent behaviour, one student comments: 'The chief *offender* to the contribution of violent acts . . . is the television set'.

(ii) Discussing whether there is evidence for innate racial differences in intelligence, one student ended his essay with the essentially irrelevant comment: 'Many less intelligent people are warm and friendly and therefore make for a *much better world* than a person who feels insecure unless he knows he is better than someone else'.

(iii) Another example would be: 'The practice of aversive conditioning applied to homosexual behaviour is *reprehensible* because it makes the victim 'sexless' rather than heterosexual'. Here, although not fully specified, the evidence does not really imply that the practice of aversive therapy *ought* to be eliminated, unless one accepts (as one might) a further unstated premiss which places the value of active sexuality (including homosexuality) above that of inert sexuality. So the evidence could be used to support other points of view. It might be argued that aversive therapy is good, precisely because it has such a negative effect!

Students need to be aware of the distinction between 'facts and values', and sensitive to the subtle ways in which these are confused in psychological debate. This is because a counter-argument aimed at another person's political or moral assumptions, rather than at the substance of his argument, may be quite irrelevant in an academic context. On the other hand, it is sometimes possible to reject the alleged basis of various proposals for social action or prejudiced attitudes by pointing to this same distinction. As we have seen, if someone attempts to justify, say, racial segregation on the basis of the 'fact' that there are racial differences in intelligence, then a critic can point out that there is no logical relationship (of implication) between the practice advocated and the evidence cited. Indeed the critic need not even refute the evidence.

6.6 EXERCISES

1. The hypothesis that women, if only given the opportunity and encourage-ment, would equal or surpass the creative achievements of men is hardly defensible: and it is only those who exalt intellectual creativity above all else who are concerned to demonstrate that women can compete with men in this respect.

   It is a sad reflection upon our civilisation that we should ever be concerned with such a problem, for its existence demonstrates our alienation from our instinctive roots . . . Women have no need to compete with men; for what they alone can do is the more essential. Love, the bearing of children, and the making of a home are creative activities without which we would perish; and only a civilization in which basic values have become distorted would make these sterile comparisons (Storr, 1968, pp.88-89).

   (i)   What rhetorical strategies does Storr employ in this passage?

   (ii)   How does the passage rely on implicit and explicit value judgements to argue its case?

 (iii)   What assumptions (of a 'factual' nature) does the passage make?

 (iv)   What assumed dichotomies underlie the author's discussion of women's 'roles'?

2. The myth of early man's aggressiveness belongs in the same class as the myth of 'the beast', that is, the belief that most, if not all wild animals are ferocious killers . . . These myths represent the projection of our *acquired* deplorabilities upon the screen of 'Nature'. What we are unwilling to acknowledge as essentially of our own making, the consequence of our own disordering in the man-made environment, we saddle upon 'Nature', upon 'phylogenetically programmed' or 'innate' factors. It is very comforting, and if, somehow, one can correct it all with findings on greylag goslings, studied for their 'releaser mechanisms', and relate the findings on fish, birds and other animals to man, it makes everything all the easier to understand and to accept.

What, in fact, such writers do in addition to perpetrating their wholly erroneous view of human nature, is to divert attention from the real sources of man's aggression and destructiveness, namely, the many false and contradictory values by which, in an overcrowded, highly competitive, threatening world, he so desperately attempts to live. It is not man's nature, but his nurture, in such a world, that requires our attention (Montagu, 1968, p.16).

   (i)   What rhetorical devices does Montagu employ in this passage?

  (ii)   Is his nature/nurture dichotomy sufficiently subtle to allow rejection of the 'biological' arguments he attacks? Why or why not?

 (iii)   By adopting explicitly *evaluative* terminology, does Montagu strengthen or weaken his argument?

3. We have discussed the predicates 'intelligent', 'masculine' (and their opposites) as *relative* concepts. What other psychological predicates (of technical relevance) could also be called relative? In what sense are these concepts like the above?

4. Is there any genuine logical conflict between asserting that the 'neurotic-stable' distinction is one of degree (i.e. relative) and saying that a person has an illness called a 'neurosis'?

5. . . . just as there is not one physics for Aryans, and another for Jews, so there is not one intelligence for whites, another quite different type for blacks. The ability to reason, to abstract, to educe relations and correlates,

is fundamental to intelligent activity, to educational progress and to professional competence; the colour of a man's skin has nothing to do with the truth or otherwise of these statements. I.Q. tests, imperfect as they undoubtedly still are, are a first step towards a better understanding, and a proper measurement, of these important aspects of human nature (Eysenck, 1971, p.79).

(i)   Is this passage consistent with the arguments advanced in Chapter 6 for the *relative* nature of the concept of intelligence? Why or why not?

(ii) Is the analogy between 'Aryan physics' and 'black intelligence' an appropriate one to support Eysenck's views?

(iii) What might be meant by the 'proper' measurement of intelligence?

(iv) Compare this passage with that from earlier in Eysenck's book quoted in Chapter 4, exercise no. 1. Is the approach to definition in both consistent?

6. Obviously homosexuals are 'born' not 'made'. This must be the case because frequently only one member of a family exhibits homosexuality even though his/her siblings have been raised in the same (or very similar) home environment. If homosexuality were the result of one's interpersonal environment, it would not be expected that such diversity should exist in the same family. If, on the other hand, sexual role and preference are like the colours of one's hair and eyes, genetically determined, such diversity is easily accounted for.

(i)   What alternatives to being *either* 'born as', or 'made into', a homosexual, could be postulated?

(ii) Is it possible to consider environments as *similar*, in the absence of information about the person who is exposed to them: i.e. might not the one (objectively defined) environment be psychologically different for different people? How relevant is this point to the quoted argument?

7. Siegler *et al.* (Boyers and Orrill 1972, p.105) criticise R.D. Laing's opinions about the medical profession and 'medical model' of psychiatry in the following terms:

On the whole, people feel that the advantages of the medical model are such that it is worth preserving the social fiction which is required to sustain it. But not everyone is of this opinion; some people, for example Christian Scientists, feel that other values take precedence. As an individual, Laing is free to put forth any view on these matters that he chooses, but as a physician he is not free to put forth the view that the social fiction called medicine is more harmful than helpful.

(i)   Is this an argument?

(ii) What techniques does the passage employ?

8. You express astonishment at the fact that it is so easy to make men enthusiastic about a war and add your suspicions that there is something at work in them — an instinct for hatred and destruction — which goes halfway to meet the efforts of the warmongers . . .

> I can only express my entire agreement. We believe in the existence of an instinct for hatred and destruction . . . According to our hypothesis human instincts are of only two kinds: Those which seek to preserve and unite which we call 'erotic' . . . and those which seek to destroy and kill and which we group together as the aggressive or destructive instinct . . . Neither of these instincts is any less essential than the other . . . it seems as though an instinct of the one sort can scarcely ever operate in isolation; it is always accompanied — or, as we say alloyed — with a certain quota from the other side, which modifies its aims, or is, in some cases, what enables it it to achieve that aim . . . The difficulty of isolating the two classes of instinct in their actual manifestations is indeed what has so long prevented us from recognising them (Freud, writing to Einstein, 1932, quoted in Maple and Matheson, 1973, pp.21-22).

(i)   By dichotomising instincts into two apparently discrete, opposed classes, Freud seeks to explain human wars. In the light of previous discussion of misleading dichotomies and 'missing links', what criticisms can be made of the quotation?

(ii) How could one isolate, by 'their actual manifestations', the roles of such instincts?

9. It is a mistake to think that anything is achieved by destroying our enemies — we ought to struggle to preserve them. War provides an opportunity for stretching men and women to the limit (sic), thus not only proving their strength and heroism, but evolving potential undreamed of in peaceful conditions and ending their boring existence.

(i)   What psychological (as opposed to moralistic) content has this passage (from a student essay on the causes of aggression and the relevance of psychology to understanding war)?

(ii) List all the value-laden words in the passage. What percentage of the total do these words constitute?

10. Anatomy decrees the life of a woman . . . When women grow up without dread of their biological functions and without subversion by feminist

doctrine, and therefore enter upon motherhood with a sense of fulfilment and altruistic sentiment, we shall attain the goal of a good life and a secure world in which to live it (Rheingold, 1964), p.714; quoted in Weisstein, 1973).

(i)   List all the value-laden words in the passage.

(ii) What assumptions are embodied in the words 'Anatomy decrees'? How would the passage be altered by replacing these with 'Culture decrees'?

(iii) What ambiguity in the expression 'biological functions' is exploited by the author to further his case?

PURPOSIVE AND REDUCTIONIST EXPLANATIONS

Explaining metaphysics to the nation -
I wish he would explain his explanation.

Byron (of Coleridge)

IN THIS chapter we shall consider two types of explanations that persistently arise in psychological debate. Both are very common in colloquial discourse, and, for that reason alone, need to be carefully analysed. Moreover they are frequently asserted to be of peculiar or particular significance to psychology, compared to other disciplines. We will call these 'purposive' and 'reductionist' explanations, considering them as they occur in both informal and formal psychological discussion.

7.1   THE PROBLEM OF PURPOSE

In previous chapters we have indicated how different the language of informal, colloquial English is from more formal psychological discourse. For instance, in ordinary language we frequently 'explain' human behaviour ('actions', 'thoughts', etc.) in only the most superficial sense. Perhaps the most common of these explanations consists of attributing a 'motive' or a 'reason' to a person's actions[1] in an effort to explain those actions. Hence if one were asked 'Why did X steal food?', one would normally answer 'Because he was hungry', or 'To feed his wife and children', or provide a similar reason for the action. The 'reason' advanced here is like a 'motive' which is established in a court of law. The court establishes that a person stood to achieve some end (e.g. death of a hated rival, great wealth, etc.) by his alleged action. Similarly, in everyday conversation and thought most of us accept that such motives or reasons help reduce our puzzlement about a person's otherwise inexplicable behaviour.

However there are many psychologists who would not accept such reasons as adequate explanations of behaviour at all. They would argue that it must be assumed that all behaviour, including that of humans, is causally *determined,* and that any explanatory account of psychological phenomena must be consistent with the assumption that 'every event is caused'.

We will return to this problem later. Here, let it be noted that it does not normally matter if one appears to assume 'free-will', or fails to specify a causal explanation, but it may be very important if one is writing a psychological essay or report. To take an extreme case, one would not say that a rat 'chose' to press the bar in a Skinner Box, although it would not be regarded

---

1.   The word 'action' is sometimes interpreted as implying an 'agent' of the behaviour in question. We might arguably justify saying that persons *act* while, say, insects only *behave*. Whether there is any genuine difference between so-called 'actions' and other (less 'purposive') behaviour is the issue considered here. Without wishing to beg the question we will follow colloquial usage and use 'action' interchangeably with 'behaviour' for human subjects, although later we shall see that this colloquial usage may be misleading in certain contexts.

as naive to say that a person 'chose' to pull the lever of a poker machine. This is despite the fact that if one accepts a Skinnerian analysis of behaviour, the same type of explanation might be possible in both cases.

The suspicion that people proposing motives and/or reasons for others' behaviour are perhaps denying that such behaviour can be causally explained is one of the reasons why the issue of purposive explanations has been controversial in psychology. However, leaving aside this aspect of the problem, it is important to ask what status various types of informal explanations have when adopted in more technical contexts. There are a great many ostensibly different ways of answering questions about why a person behaved as he did. These may not all constitute equally adequate explanations according to the criteria discussed in Chapter 3. It will be recalled that in that chapter we emphasised the ease with which putative explanations of behaviour could be circular or incomplete. Therefore in order to describe more carefully what constitutes a 'purposive', as opposed to conventional, causal account of behaviour, let us follow Brown (1963) in distinguishing several interrelated varieties of explanations in the social sciences. It will be noticed that these are informally defined and occur in non-technical as well are in more formal arguments.

(1)   *Genetic:* Explanations of this type give a description or an outline of a temporal sequence of events (Brown, 1963, p.42). These are essentially historical sketches which, for example, might include case study information detailing a person's biography.

(2)   *Intentions:* We constantly refer to our intentions in our explanations of our own actions . . . When we give the intention of an agent's action we presuppose that the action was done by design. We exhibit his action as a means towards a goal – his aim or purpose (*Ibid.*, p.43).

Notice that intentional accounts of behaviour may make no reference to antecedent causal factors. The proposed intention removes puzzlement about a person's 'actions' by specifying its purpose or intended goal. Two rather similar types of explanation are what might be called 'dispositional' and 'reason-giving'. Rather than focusing on the nature of the end which the action is intended to achieve, these postulate some characteristic of the agent which predisposes him to certain actions or emphasises the reason he has for his actions – that is his belief about the world which he regards as sufficient reason for the action in question. Brown briefly characterises these as follows:

(3)   *Dispositions:* We can explain many of the things which people do and say by reference to the tendencies or dispositions that they have. The puzzlement behind the question 'Why does he insist upon going out into the pouring rain today?' may be removed by the answer 'Because being avaricious, he can't wait to collect his debts'. The explanation consists in

exhibiting, however sketchily, the particular example as an instance of a behaviour tendency – or disposition – in the person. Avariciousness can take many forms, one of which is an eagerness to obtain money. The fact that a person's haste to collect a debt is an instance of one of his personality traits accounts for his action, since it is the sort of behaviour which he exhibits when the appropriate conditions arise (*ibid.*).

(4) *Reasons:* 'The reason why I refused to speak to my wife yesterday was that she invited her sister to stay with us over the holidays and neglected to tell me. I was furious with her and I decided to teach her a lesson.' His wife's action is taken by the husband as his own reason for deliberately not speaking to her. Learning what his reason was would provide us with an explanation of his silence if we were puzzled by it. The husband has taken his belief about his wife's neglect as a sufficient reason for attempting to punish her. When we learn that he takes this particular belief to be such a reason we have accounted for his action (*ibid.*).

Clearly, intentional and reason-giving accounts are closely related. Each can be interpreted as emphasising a different aspect of what is essentially a purposive account of actions. That is both types of explanation (if that is not too strong a word to use in such cases) assume that human behaviour is purposeful – one specifies the intended *end* of the action, and the other, the *reasons* on which an action is based.

(5) *Functions:* There is a further type of explanation which is commonly found in psychology. This we shall call 'functional'. We frequently ask questions such as 'What is the function of the heart?' or 'What is the function of instinctive agonistic (fighting) behaviour?'. To these we might answer 'To pump blood', and 'To disperse a species over an ecologically viable territory', respectively. Such replies specify the function of the behaviours in question by showing how they fit into a set of functions which (ultimately) contribute to survival or to the biological health of the organism or species.

Different types of functional explanations may be given to questions such as 'What is the function of imitative play in infants?', 'Why did the Sioux Indians not wean their children until after they were three to four years old?', 'Why do some tribes of Australian Aborigines subincise the penis?'. In the first case, an answer might postulate the psychological value of imitation – its facilitatory effect on speech, social role-playing, etc. In the second and third, it might show how the social custom fits into a set of conventions, practices and values whereby the respective community maintains its own form of social cohesion. Hence the functions which imitation, late weaning or subincision serve are postulated to explain those activities. However there is no need to specify or assume an 'agent' who 'intentionally' achieves a 'goal' in such cases.

These five classes of explanation are, ostensibly at least, quite different from covering-law explanations or other causal accounts. This is certainly true of intentional, reason-giving and functional explanations. The first two of these could appropriately be called 'purposive' explanations and shall be distinguished from the last which does not assume an agent acting to achieve some goal or end. Hence in addition to causal accounts of behaviour (specifying the antecedent conditions sufficient for a phenomenon) there are purposive and functional explanations (or putative explanations). The *causal account* attempts to specify the conditions responsible for the explanandum – conditions which, if repeated, would produce identical (or similar) effects. *Purposive accounts* specify some reason for actions, or goals toward which behaviour is directed, assuming agency or intentionality of the animal or person exhibiting the behaviour. *Functional explanations* postulate the end or goal which behaviour achieves within some system of which it is part. The last need not assume intentionality or agency in the person or structure exhibiting the behaviour in question.

Although all these classes of explanation are ways of answering questions about many aspects of behaviour, this alone does not guarantee that they are adequate, informative explanations. In particular, two principal objections are frequently levelled at purposive answers to questions which ask why a person behaved in a particular way. The first asserts that postulated purposes ('reasons', 'motives', 'goals') are frequently (perhaps always) only partial accounts of behaviour; moreover they are particularly likely to be *circular* in the sense outlined in Chapter 3. The second equates the postulation of 'purposes' with the denial of determinism: i.e. proponents of this view argue that, frequently, if not always, purposive accounts of behaviour appear to reject the possibility of a complete, adequate, causal account of behaviour – especially of human behaviour. Let us consider these objections in turn.

To state that a person works 'in order to be highly regarded by his peers' does seem to tell us something about why that person works (as opposed to merely idling away his time). However whether this type of account is always adequate, even for human actions, is often debated. In particular, it can be argued that the postulation of goals (e.g. money or status) which an action achieves may often only be possible *post hoc* – i.e. after the occurrence of the event which it putatively explains. It is often possible to 'make sense of behaviour' after it has occurred by attributing some motive to it or stating what goal it achieves. But such a postulate may not be useful as a basis for *predicting* behaviour – it may fail to generate any additional, testable hypotheses about the person's behaviour. As such, the explanation may lack independent supporting evidence and even be so expressed that such evidence *could not* be observed (e.g. the proposed purpose might be so vaguely characterised that anything the person did would be compatible with it – for instance the goal of 'self-actualisation'; 'status' or 'power').

Of course purposive accounts are not unique in being potentially circular, but they are particularly prone to this weakness, Moreover when not unambiguously circular they may be only partially explanatory. For instance, working for wealth is different from working for status, although merely postulating one or the other purpose may not completely 'explain' the action in the sense of answering the most important psychological questions. In particular, it is likely also to be asked why the person worked for status rather than wealth. In other words, given the purpose postulated to explain a person's behaviour, it might still be asked what caused him to behave as he did (e.g. what sort of environment conditioned his motives, etc.).

Some psychologists see the last-mentioned question as an instance of the only genuinely interesting type of psychological question. That is they regard purposive accounts of behaviour as, at best, preliminary to *causal* accounts. Others adopt a more radical stance than that: they argue that purposive 'explanations' are frequently not merely circular, but also suggest the possibility that the behaviour in question *cannot* be causally explained. That is, saying that someone acted to achieve a goal may be taken to imply that he merely 'chose' or 'decided' to act in such a manner *regardless* of possible antecedent conditions. Just as proponents of moral responsibility often assume that people are capable of deciding to act morally, regardless of their personal history and circumstances, so psychological 'explanations' may appear to make a similar assumption when purposes or goals are postulated. The action of 'choosing' to achieve a purpose may carry the implied corollary that it is possible arbitrarily to 'choose' to seek any end or goal. Hence the claim that, regardless of one's past experience, one can always decide to act in a certain way. Of course, it is not necessarily assumed that all organisms can make such 'decisions' or 'choices', but it is frequently supposed that humans (mostly, if not always) can do so. Some persons holding this view of the uniqueness of human 'free will' hold that causal accounts are literally impossible in the case of some human actions. All that can be said of such actions is that they were aimed at achieving a certain outcome, 'chosen' by the agent, not predetermined by past events.

The opponent of purposive explanations asserts that there is nothing uniquely purposive (hence uncaused) in human behaviour. He argues that there is no more justification for assuming 'free will' in humans than there is in other animal species or in inanimate objects. To him the separation of humans from other physical systems by the criterion of purpose (and, it is held, therefore 'free will') is purely arbitrary. It results merely from our ignorance of the causes of human behaviour which we replace with informal descriptions of reasons or 'goals'. This process is also evident whenever there is ignorance about the causes of physical events. For instance, people once 'explained' large-scale physical regularities (like the movements of the sun, moon and stars) by reference to the will, purposes or goals of magical powers. But detailed hypotheses about the behaviour of physical bodies replaced these purposive accounts with more deterministic explanations. The determinist concludes that in *principle* this is also possible in the explanation of human behaviour: the postulation of free will in the guise of reason-giving or purposive accounts of human behaviour is merely a reflection of our ignorance of causes, not a justification for denying the existence of such causes.

The determinist's assertion that it is difficult to justify the need for purposive concepts in psychological explanation can be illustrated by what is perhaps the most famous attempt in modern psychology to define the essential characteristics of purposive behaviour. In 1923 William McDougall in his *Outline of Psychology,* proposed a set of seven such distinguishing characteristics. His 'seven marks of behaviour' demonstrate how difficult it is to define purpose without falling into the trap of naive indeterminism. McDougall's seven characteristics were:

1. 'A certain spontaneity of movement.' Thus an animal intitiates behaviour and 'is not simply pushed or pulled by forces *external* to itself'.

2. Once such behaviour is initiated, it persists 'independently of the impression which may have initiated it'.

3. This persistence is marked by variations in the direction of the movements (towards the goal).

4. When a particular kind of change is brought about by the animal's movements, such movements cease. This change in the animal's situation (goal?) is 'predictable in general terms from a knowledge of the species'.

5. The animal exhibits anticipatory or preparatory acts relative to the 'new situation'.

6. Such behaviour improves in effectiveness with repetition under similar conditions.

7. By contrast with reflex action, purposive behaviour commonly involves the 'whole organism'.

It is interesting to note that McDougall regards the first five marks of behaviour as jointly sufficient to allow one to infer the presence of 'mind', whereas neither the sixth, nor presumably the seventh, alone is sufficient for the inference of mental activity. For McDougall, 'mind' and 'purpose' are closely related. In this sense, at least, it would probably be fair to say that his view is quite similar to what we might call the naive psychological assumptions of ordinary language. Purpose is inferred from the persistence of goal-directed, spontaneous movements involving the whole organism and showing improvement with practice. Certainly, in a superficial way these characteristics seem to distinguish purposive from mechanistic movements by suggesting that the former involve mental activity. It is in this sense that the criteria might be said to confirm naive psychology or 'common sense'.

But McDougall's analysis has been widely criticised on a number of grounds. Generally critics point out that there are many examples which do not fit McDougall's classification. For example, there seem to be a large number of mechanically controlled systems whose behaviour satisfies his definition of purpose.

These would include any servo-mechanistic system in which the direction and continuation of movement are controlled by feedback from some environmental goal-state or target. For instance, a guided missile might be said to 'vary its movements' as the target moves. 'Information' concerning the relative positions of the missile and its target control the direction of the missile's flight. To a person who is unfamiliar with the mechanics of such a device, McDougall's first five marks of behaviour would apparently be satisfied. Yet one would be reluctant to attribute 'mind' or 'purpose' to a guided missile. This reluctance presumably reflects some additional criterion which McDougall has not formulated. But what might this be?

One possible way of distinguishing between (human) purposive behaviour and that of machines might be to assert that the former involves *conscious intention*. Hence the guided missile could not really be said to 'have a purpose' in the sense of being aware of some future state of affairs whose attainment would fulfil its intentions. But this way of speaking would presumably be quite appropriate when describing most human actions. We could say that the person who uses a guided missile to destroy enemy ships has an intention, but we could hardly say that the missile itself had such a purpose (in mind) in the same way.

Unfortunately this apparently obvious solution is somewhat illusory. For the issue then becomes one of deciding when it is appropriate to infer the presence of conscious intentions in the analysis of behaviour. Although most people would reject the possibility that inanimate objects or mechanisms (including electronic computers and guided missiles) possess consciousness, it is not always easy to decide where one is to draw the line in the case of living organisms. For instance, is a dog exhibiting purpose when it retrieves game? If the answer is 'yes', can we also say the same of a rat which runs a maze 'to get to the goal box' at the end? If we also accept that this indicates purposes because it implies conscious intention on behalf of the organism involved, then how does one decide when the interpretation is no longer justified? Is the behaviour of an earthworm purposive? Or the reflexive sucking of the new-born child?

To the non-purposivist, these problems demonstrate the inadequacy of analysing purpose in terms of conscious intention. They show that such an analysis is essentially *circular* and non-explanatory. It is circular in that conscious intention is really only specifiable on the basis of the apparently purposive nature of the behaviour which it is meant to explain. How does one decide whether the animal's behaviour is 'intentional' except by observing such characteristics as McDougall spelt out? In other words, purpose is defined in terms of conscious intention which is itself inferred from purposive behaviour! The purposivist's programme is non-explanatory owing to this circularity. We cannot explain the target-seeking behaviour of a guided missile by stating that the missile's purpose is to seek targets any more than we can explain a rat's journey to the goal-box of a maze by saying that it intends to eat the food to be found there. These descriptions do not indicate the (possible) causes of the behaviour in question.

Such arguments do not exhaust the debate between the proponents and opponents of purposive accounts of animal (especially human) behaviour. In order not to suggest that the purposivist has no parry to the last thrust of his opponents' attack, let us make one final point on his behalf. Although he may concede that it is difficult to avoid circularity in the definition of purpose, he claims it nevertheless appears to be necessary in specific cases for the following reason: saying that someone behaves in a certain way in order to achieve a certain goal or purpose (i.e. providing a reason for his behaviour) does at least provide some information relevant to explaining that behaviour. If it did not, then it would be irrelevant, whether the reason advanced were true or false. In other words, it is a genuine empirical question whether a particular person is acting to achieve the end, goal, or purpose attributed to him.

It follows, says the purposivist, that reasons can answer (at least partially) questions about why someone behaved in a certain way. The amount of information provided will depend on the actual explanation sought, but, at the very least, reasons can indicate the irrelevance of specific possible causal explanations. For example, if one says that someone jumped off a high building *in order to* kill himself, one will certainly not investigate wind velocities, etc., to explain his fall. Hence reasons provide informative, if incomplete accounts of behaviour.

This reply by the purposivist constitutes a much weaker claim than the one we originally considered. In its diluted form, it may be reconcilable with deterministic assumptions. Whether this is a strength or weakness of the analysis must be left for the reader to decide. At this point we merely wish to reiterate that the issue of purposive and reason-giving accounts of behaviour raises fundamental questions about the appropriate language in which to attempt to explain behaviour. In particular, it serves to warn students of psychology against assuming that colloquial English is a viable, let alone ideal, medium by which to analyse or describe psychological phenomena.

The practical implication of this discussion is to caution against adopting purposive descriptions of behaviour — especially non-human behaviour — in one's formal psychology writings, unless one is prepared to justify the use of such language. But this is not to say that purposive and causal accounts of behaviour are necessarily incompatible.

7.2 REDUCTIONISM

As the issue of purpose clearly demonstrates, there are perplexing problems of meaning in the most elementary psychological discussion. Even the preliminary analysis presented here raises such perennial philosophical problems as the reality of 'mental' phenomena and the question of 'free will'. A common reaction to these problems is to argue that all 'psychological' accounts of behaviour (including both mentalistic and more behaviouristic formulations) can be replaced ultimately by means of the language of the physical sciences. It is asserted that the premise of this programme is twofold: not only can the inconsistencies and questionable assumptions of colloquial language be avoided, but the whole range of mentalistic concepts in psychology can also be precisely and unambiguously redefined.

This radical proposal is known as *reductionism*. In its most popular form it asserts that all scientific information will ultimately form a unified body of knowledge encoded in a self-contained language of the physical sciences. Therefore psychology is but a transitory discipline which will be 'reduced to' physiology (especially neurophysiology) and biochemistry. These two disciplines will eventually be subsumed under the laws of microphysics, as is already apparent in many fields of chemistry. Thus there is a hierarchy of sciences, all resting ultimately on physics, and all capable of being replaced by its concepts and laws — at least at some time in the future. At the present time psychology appears to be far removed from physics, but according to this view it will be redefined within the conceptual domain of this fundamental science. Indeed it could be claimed that intermediate stages in this reductionist programme are already evident. For example, both behaviourism and some of the findings of contemporary neurophysiology provide adequate explanations of some phenomena without recourse to traditional psychological (or at least mentalistic) concepts.

Using the physical sciences as a model, many argue that the process of 'reduction' is continuously occurring. To support this point of view the example of successful reduction of a concept of one science to the domain of a 'more general' or 'more basic' discipline, which is frequently cited, is that of 'temperature'. Long before detailed knowledge of molecular theory and thermodynamics, regularities ('laws') involving temperature changes in gases had been formulated by Boyle and Charles. With the development of microphysical theory it became evident that the expression 'temperature of gas X' could be taken to refer to the 'mean kinetic energy' of the particles of that gas. That is, the expressions 'temperature' and 'mean kinetic energy' were accepted as *contingently identical* — they referred to the same phenomenon despite their different meanings.

Or to put this point in the language of Chapter 4, the two expressions, although of different 'intension', were shown to have identical 'extensions'. New theories and more sophisticated measurement procedures allowed what was previously a useful, well-defined concept to be subsumed under physical laws having a range of application which is far broader than the phenomena to which the concept was originally relevant. Although Boyle and Charles were not aware of the actual details of what nowadays temperature is taken to be, their laws were both empirically supported and theoretically viable within the context for which they were devised. The laws were nonetheless reducible to instances of more general micro-physical regularities.

It is not surprising that this example is frequently cited to suggest that psychological concepts will ultimately be reinterpreted in a similar manner as referring to physico-chemical processes. This is despite the fact that these psychological concepts may appear quite adequate within their current range of application.

For example, Moss (1965) provides a vague suggestion concerning the possible reduction of 'hypnosis' to physiological variables when he asserts (p.50):

It would be comforting if evidence were available concerning the physiological concomitants of hypnosis. *Because all behaviour must be ultimately reduciable to biological processes (and eventually to Physics and Chemistry)*, identification of neurophysiological mechanisms involved could constitute a long stride towards alleviating the array of competing interpretations now in existence on the molar level of behavioural description. However, it must be acknowledged that reduction of hypnotic behaviour to physiological events at the present state in our knowledge would constitute little more than a substitution of one set of terms for another [emphasis added].

Although there is much that could be objected to in this statement, it illustrates the tendency to assume that reductionism is both possible and desirable, without offering any detailed justification for this view. Similar, unsupported assertions can also be found which deny the possibility (and/or desirability) of reductionism.

The issue of reductionism is important in elementary psychology for precisely this reason. Students all too often *assume* either that mentalistic concepts are appropriate and/or essential to psychology (i.e. irreducible) or, on the contrary, that no explanation which is not behaviouristic or physiological can be regarded as adequate. In either case, the student may easily overlook important aspects of the explanatory adequacy of alternative theories, or the value of certain concepts. Therefore in the following brief discussion we shall attempt to spell out some of the difficulties involved in maintaining a consistent conceptual framework in one's approach to psychological argument in the face of assumptions concerning the possibility or impossibility of reductionism.

Behaviourism is one form of reductionism which confronts students of psychology very early in their careers.[2] As a form of reductionism it seeks to redefine phenomena treated by a variety of theoretical perspectives into 'physical' more directly observable, concepts pertaining to stimuli and responses. It might be regarded as an intermediate or transitional stage in the ultimate rejection of traditional mentalistic concepts in psychology. Although, in some sense, all psychologists study 'behaviour' (broadly defined), there are great differences between them on the issue of reductionism.

Consider, for the sake of argument, the rather vague concept 'anxiety'. In both informal and psycho-analytic language the word refers to mental states involving fear, tension or apprehension. Psycho-analysis even allows 'unconscious' anxiety. Indeed unconscious anxiety concerning sexual and aggressive wishes is hypothesised by Freud to be of great significance in personality development. Therefore in psycho-analytic literature anxiety is indicated by a variety of indirect manifestations — in the 'symptoms' of neurosis, the thematic content of dreams and fantasies, defensive personal reactions, and so on. The reductionist asserts that, in fact, anxiety consists only of particular behavioural reactions. The term actually refers to physico-chemical processes such as cardiovascular, respiratory or muscular conditions associated with the activity of the sympathetic nervous system. He further argues that knowledge of such processes is both necessary and sufficient to explain the more 'mentalistic' aspects of anxiety. By this he means that anxiety is *nothing more than* a set of physiological reactions. Hence when our knowledge of physiology is more fully developed, the reduction of anxiety to some set of defining characteristics of a physiological type will be successfully effected.

This example is analogous to the case of 'temperature' which we mentioned previously. Temperature was once indicated only by changes in the mercury volume of a thermometer and/or by its subjective psychological effects (whether the substance being measured felt hot or cold, etc.). But without knowing more precisely 'what temperature was', it was nevertheless possible for scientists to discuss it informally (as it is now for people who know nothing about microphysics) and also to incorporate the concept into a precise and heuristically valuable set of 'laws'. Similarly, not knowing what

2.   Two schools of behaviourism are sometimes distinguished:

    (i) *methodological behaviourism,* which does not deny the existence of 'mental' phenomena, but asserts that these are inherently 'private' and, therefore, cannot be scientifically studied; and

    (ii) *philosophical or metaphysical behaviourism,* which denies the existence of mental phenomena as distinct from physical processes, and therefore focuses on observable 'behaviour' (because 'that is all there is!').

anxiety 'really is', we can still employ the concept quite fruitfully in psychology or in day-to-day affairs. One need not be a neurophysiologist to understand what it means to be anxious about one's examinations, for instance. Ultimately, however, psychologists may need to reinterpret the expression in the light of information from the biological or physical sciences. Just as we now take 'water' to refer to H_2O molecules (within a certain temperature range), and 'temperature' to refer to the mean kinetic energy of the particles of a substance, so we may ultimately take 'anxiety' to refer to specific physiological reactions and to nothing over and above such reactions.

It comes as no surprise to find many arguments being advanced against both behaviourist and other reductionist programmes. However because these are usually directed at the materialist or physicalist foundations of reductionism, they raise questions of philosophical analysis beyond our present scope. Consequently we will leave this issue open and proceed to make a number of general, yet important, observations which have direct practical implications for psychological argument. These should help students avoid some common conceptual confusions associated with this issue.

7.2.1 Facile or Trivial Reductions

Reductionism offers deceptively simple solutions to some very complex problems. It is tempting to try to avoid virtually all explanations phrased in conventional psychological terms by replacing these with other 'ultimate' or 'basic' explanatory terms from physiology, for example.

In previous discussion of circularly-defined concepts used to explain behaviour (e.g. 'instinct', various 'mental faculties', etc.) we saw how easy it was to propose essentially trivial (non-informative) 'explanations' of complex human behaviour. Reductionist accounts of behaviour are also open to this abuse: what appears to be a reductionist claim may, in fact, be merely a convenient, arbitrary or *post hoc* postulate having little or no *independent evidence* in its support. That is, apart from the behaviour being explained, there may be no reason for postulating the particular explanatory concepts. This is sometimes referred to as 'transforming a problem into a postulate'. By this it is meant that the problem (e.g. what is 'hypnosis') is gratuitously converted into an 'explanation' (e.g. 'Hypnosis is a physiological state which causes people to behave in certain specified ways'). The explanandum is used to explain itself with the help of an unsupported reductionist assumption. In colloquial discourse examples of this are easy to find. One relevant case is the frequent assertion that being a criminal or a homosexual, etc., is 'in one's blood' in such a way that all further discussion of possible causes is superfluous. Such accounts are not informative unless some specific hypothesis about the genetic bases for the relevant behaviours can be advanced *on grounds other than the occurrence of those behaviours.*

Genuine reductionist arguments seek to subsume a 'secondary' science (e.g. psychology) within the more generally applicable concepts and laws of a 'primary' science. They are not merely facile claims that there must be a physiological cause for all behaviour. It is the details of the reductionist explanation which are crucial in any particular case.

The important point to emphasise from this discussion is that precise, informative explanations are preferable to vague or circular postulates, whether or not the latter appear to be reductionist and therefore 'fundamental' or 'basic'. Because all explanations are proposed within particular contexts, as answers to specific questions, it may be impossible to decide which of two explanations is the more 'fundamental'. Certainly the primary consideration should not be whether or not a putative explanation is reductionist.

7.2.2 Inconsistent Terminology

'Psychoneurobiochemeducation' is the title of a paper by Krech (Gordon, 1971). This facetious title suggests that psychology is not an isolated discipline but is constantly interacting with numerous other branches of science. This view of psychology generates the enthusiasm that many psychologists show for reductionist arguments. But the title also suggests the danger of indiscriminately adopting parts of the vocabulary of diverse disciplines for describing the one set of phenomena. This practice may create considerable confusion, whether or not a reductionist argument is, in fact, appropriate to the phenomena being discussed.

For example, although Krech is speaking only in very general terms, he sometimes gives the impression that psychological words such as 'memory' are likely to be replaced by physico-chemical expressions. He says, that '. . . for every separate memory in the mind we will eventually find a differentiated chemical in the brain — 'chemical memory pellets' as it were' (Gordon, 1971, p.94). Such futuristic speculations are often quite justifiable and need not raise any serious conceptual issues. However they do not really demonstrate, in detail, how the reductionist programme is to be effected. For instance, it might be asked how one could define 'separate memories' in a manner that would equate them with Krech's 'memory pellets'. Given that there is dispute about the best description of 'what is learned' or what aspects of information are stored in memory, and the manner of their storage, the assumption that 'separate memories' will correspond to distinct physical structures in a manner analogous to pellets is naive, to say the least. Like all pseudo-reductionist speculations, its simplicity is superficially appealing. But the cost of thinking in such simple terms may be confusion between psychological descriptions of memory (concerning information encoding, storage and retrieval) and physiological hypotheses which, although concerned with the same phenomena, do not necessarily relate to what is known of memory in the psychological literature.

Other examples suggest the ease with which serious conceptual confusions may result from the premature assumption of reductionism. This is particularly apparent in students' written work, where the vocabulary of one discipline is employed indiscriminately to explain phenomena more usually described in language of a different kind. Lacking any detailed procedures for relating the two sets of concepts, it is all too easy to create complex theoretical anomalies in one's written arguments. These anomalies are generally indicated when an author-vacillates between theoretical terms from different scientific 'disciplines'. The author shifts his argument from one 'level of explanation' to another in quite an arbitrary manner.

In the example of premature or pseudo-reductionist explanation to be considered subsequently it is emphasised that criticism is primarily on the grounds of explanatory inadequacy rather than reductionism *per se*. It is not sufficient to categorically reject explanations simply because they are reductionist, but it is legitimate to evaluate their explanatory force in the light of the general criteria for adequate explanation which were outlined in Chapter 3 — especially those concerning circularity.

Most students of elementary psychology are familiar with the observations and 'laws' of perceptual organisation proposed by *Gestalt* theorists such as Wertheimer and Kohler. The major tenets of Gestalt theory might be stated very briefly as:

(a) An emphasis on the structured 'wholeness' of perception. Visual experience consists of organised 'wholes' rather than discrete, disjoint components. The whole is greater than (or more accurately, qualitatively different from) the sum of its parts.

(b) A number of 'laws' of perceptual organisation are proposed. These state that properties such as the similarity, proximity and closure of elements lead to their perceptual organisation.

(c) But such organisation is not intrinsic to the perceived stimuli; it is 'imposed on' them by the perceiver.

(d) Therefore, a principle of *Psychoneural Isomorphism* is proposed to account for these organisational properties. This asserts a one-to-one correspondence between 'brain fields' and the perceived organisation of stimulus configuration. That is the structural properties of the brain bear a precise relationship to the aspects of perceptual experience emphasised in the laws of organisation.[3]

The Gestaltists are somewhat ambiguous concerning whether this is a 'causal' relationship between two distinct phenomena or whether the physiological and psychological regularities are two aspects of the same reality. In

3. Prentice provides a detailed, basically sympathetic account of Gestalt theory (as a theory) in S. Koch (ed.), *Psychology: A Study of a Science*, vol. 1, N.Y.: McGraw-Hill, 1959, pp.427-55.

either case, the principle is essentially reductionist, for the physiological process would be regarded as 'basic' on both interpretations. Prentice, calling the concept of isomorphism a hypothesis, states: 'it comes nearest, perhaps, to what has sometimes been called the 'double aspect' theory, the view that cortical events and phenomenal facts are merely two ways of looking at the same natural phenomenon, two faces of the same coin, as it were' (Koch, 1959, p.435).

Granted that isomorphism is a hypothesis, it is, nevertheless, possible to employ the language of the hypothetical physiology of perception to 'explain' psychological phenomena in a deceptively facile manner. The result is a mixture of inconsistent concepts and expressions. For example, Gestalt effects like 'closure' can be spoken of as 'field effects' in the sensory projection areas of the cortex. These field effects (which are hypothetical, at best) may be described as 'forces', 'valences', etc., in pseudo-physical terminology. Hence it becomes difficult to distinguish between 'field' or 'force' as applied to some (possible) cortical event and the metaphorical description of psychological (mental) phenomena in similar terms. Rather than being 'reductionist', such accounts may not be essentially explanatory at all and may merely generate considerable confusion due to the vacillation between 'physical' and 'psychological' levels of explanation.

Recall that reductions are effected by establishing the *contingent identity* (i.e. the identical extension or denotation) of two or more expressions. However in the arbitrary equation of perceptual effects and 'brain field' properties, one is *asserting,* rather than demonstrating, such an identity. In fairness to Gestalt theorists, the lack of independent evidence for such hypothetical cortical properties has long been acknowledged and the claim of reductionism is seldom explicitly argued. Nevertheless the frequent confusion between the description of perceptual experience and (hypothetical) neurological states renders the theory difficult to evaluate. It provides the shadow rather than the substance of a reductionist explanation – not because it is not reductionist, but because it is not adequately explanatory.

7.3 CONCLUSION

The problems of purpose and reductionism are important to elementary psychology because each has implications for a wide range of psychological arguments in diverse areas. In this chapter we have tried to suggest some of the verbal distinctions which need to be made between various types of explanations if one is to discuss particular psychological questions consistently, without making naive, unanalysed philosophical assumptions, be they of 'free will', 'purpose', the need for reductionist explanations, or the denial that these are possible.

To conclude, let us re-emphasise two very widespread conceptual confusions which result from ignorance of the issues discussed in this chapter.

First, there is frequent confusion between reason-giving, intentional ('purposive') accounts of behaviour on the one hand, and causal accounts on the other. The English language embodies this confusion so generally that one may simply not notice it. It is for this reason that one must ask questions *about the use of language itself*, if one is to avoid the conceptual confusion of purposive and non-purposive explanatory paradigms.

Second, the ease with which apparently reductionist explanations can be provided for psychological phenomena may cause one to combine two sets of concepts (e.g. mentalistic and neurological) as though both had identical meanings, without justifying this assumption with respect to the phenomena being considered. As we saw in the case of Gestalt theory, this may involve quite facile, essentially circular argument. The result is a confusion of physical and psychological terms, the relationships between which have not been established by any detailed analyses.

7.5 EXERCISES

1. (a) Unless, as scientists, we are to allow non-material 'substances' to intrude into the domain of psychology, we must use the word 'dreaming' to refer to certain patterns of electro-physiological activity in people's brains. Only then can scientists study the phenomenon without recourse to the mentalistic speculations of the Freudians and similar groups. Science, being concerned with what dreams *are* (not with what they *mean*) must accept this step if it is to explain dreaming in relation to other activities of the brain.

   (b) It would not matter whether dreaming occurred in one's 'brain' or one's toenail — if it is experienced as a series of images and sounds which 'make sense (to varying degrees), then it cannot be 'reduced' to non-mental phenomena. It is an essentially psychological event, although of course, it does 'take place in the brain'. Psychological explanation is concerned with what dreams mean and why a particular person's dreams have a particular meaning. This cannot be established by looking at the electrophysiological activity of his brain.

   (i) What implicit definition of science is proposed in (a)?
   What definition of psychology is assumed in (b)?

   (ii) Do these definitions, in effect, beg the question concerning the best (or only) 'scientific' way of studying dreaming?

   (iii) Although (a) is a reductionist and (b) an anti-reductionist argument, are they really contradictory, or could they be more accurately described as addressing different issues?

   (iv) If the latter, can the two viewpoints be reconciled?

2. We are rapidly approaching the time when purely physical tests of intelligence will be possible. It is already known that the evoked (electrical) potentials ('brain waves' on the electroencepalograph) recorded after a sudden stimulus, differ for 'bright' and 'dull' subjects: The brighter the subject, the 'quicker' the waves. Hence, conventional (so-called 'psychological') tests of intelligence will disappear as brain function is measured directly; after all, what is intelligence if it is not brain function?

(i) What reductionist claims are made in the passage?
Is the supporting argument convincing?

(ii) Discuss the problems involved in *defining* intelligence in terms of brain function(s) alone.

3. Consider the following accounts of simple animal behaviour:

(a) After three previously reinforced trials, the food-deprived rat ran up the main alley of the *T*-maze and turned right, entering the goal box 3.5 seconds after being placed in the start box.

(b) After three previously reinforced trials, the hungry rat ran up the alley of the *T*-maze to the choice point and turned right in order to acquire the food in the goal box. This took 3.5 seconds.

(i) Does (b) make assumptions not made in (a)? What are these?

(ii) How important might these be if one wished to explain why the animal behaved as reported?

(iii) If it were a human, not a rat, involved, would the second description be any more defensible? Why or why not?

4. (i) How are the following two passages different from each other?

(ii) Are they incompatible in terms of the explanations they propose?

(iii) Is either of greater *explanatory value* than the other? Why or why not?

(a) The burglar's purpose in stealing the jewellery was to seek revenge on its owner. This was his real motive, not wealth, for he stole the jewels with the most sentimental value, not necessarily those of greatest monetary worth.

(b) The burglar's behaviour in stealing the sentimentally valuable jewels was the result of his neurotic fixation on jewels as symbolic of their owner, who had previously frustrated his sexual advances.

5. That human beings possess an instinct for survival cannot be doubted. Their behaviour inevitably leads to their survival — eating, breathing — copulating, etc. All are directed towards the survival of the individual, and through him, the species.

(i) Does the postulating of abstract 'instincts for survival' or 'life forces' help to explain any particular aspect of human behaviour? Why or why not? (i.e. Even allowing that eating, breathing and copulating are all necessary for survival, and that humans are biologically predisposed to these behaviours, what further information is provided by saying that these behaviours have a certain purpose?)

6. Consider the statements in each of the following sets (a), (b), and (c), asking of each:

(i) Are the sentences equivalent in meaning? Why or why not?

(ii) What (if any) assumptions seem to be made by each?

(a) (i) The male stickleback fish's purpose in doing the zig-zag dance is to attract a mate.

(ii) The purpose of the male stickleback fish's zig-zag dance is to signal that it is ready to mate.

(iii) The significance of the male stickleback fish's zig-zag dance is that it provides a signal to the female of the species which causes it to approach the male (as a forerunner to mating).

(iv) The function of the male stickleback's zig-zag dance is to elicit the early phases of mating behaviour in the female.

(b) (i) The purpose of traffic lights is to control the flow of traffic.

(ii) The function served by traffic lights is to regulate the flow of traffic.

(iii) Street lights change colour in order to regulate traffic flow.

(c) (i) During the hot sunlight hours, the leaves of the eucalypt orient their smallest surface towards the sun with the purpose of minimising the effects of dehydration.

(ii) During the hot sunlight hours, people use protective clothing or shelter for the purpose of minimising the effects of dehydration.

PART II PRACTICE

8

RESEARCHING PSYCHOLOGICAL PROJECTS

Knowledge is of two kinds. We know a subject ourselves or we know where we can find information upon it.

Samuel Johnson

8.1 USING THE LIBRARY

UNDERGRADUATES use library resources for two main purposes: (1) for researching essay or thesis topics; (2) for study preparatory to examinations, usually concerned with text-book information which supplements lecture material. In either case, psychological literature often appears either too specific (e.g. journals are too advanced or esoteric), or too general (e.g. introductory texts tend to summarise only rather superficial aspects of various well-defined content areas such as 'learning', 'motivation', 'individual differences'). Additionally there is a wide range of 'survey' books, or collections of important papers which focus on specific topics at the level of generality and technical detail more appropriate for an undergraduate essay. For example, there are books on the works of Piaget, Freud, aspects of motivation, theories of personality, learning and so on. These do not suffer from the inevitable problems of all-purpose introductory texts. There are also journals which present research findings in a relatively non-technical way (e.g. *Psychology Today*), and which are appropriate as *preliminary* reading in undergraduate literature searches.

Literature searches generally begin with a list of references relevant to an essay topic or project specified by a staff member. These references are essential reading for the project. In some cases, however, no such list is provided, the object being to encourage the student to approach the topic in his own way, using the resources of the library on his own initiative. In the case of more advanced thesis preparation, it is essential that the student initiate and execute a thorough library search.

In this chapter, a general guide to the use of library resources and their function in essay and examination preparation will be provided. This is particularly necessary in psychology, as much of the relevant literature is classified under general headings more naturally associated with other disciplines such as medicine (e.g. psychiatry), sociology, physiology, education or philosophy.

8.1.1 Library Systems of Classification

University libraries most commonly employ the Dewey Decimal System of classification, although this is not the only system possible. The United States Library of Congress (L.C.) system is being employed with increasing frequency. However, in this discussion we will concentrate on the more common Dewey System to exemplify the principles of searching psychological sources.

Library classification is from the general to the specific, beginning with headings as global as 'Intelligence, 'Social Psychology', etc., and moving to more detailed subcategories such as 'The Use of Psychological Tests' or 'Public Opinion'. However these latter categories are still quite broad and are by themselves no guarantee that all and only the information relevant to a specific topic is contained therein. For this reason, there is little to be said for the practice of searching through such general classifications in the hope of discovering precisely relevant information. Even the more specific Dewey classifications are unlikely to guide one to literature that would not otherwise have been found through different methods (e.g. the use of abstracts — see section 8.1.3).

The Dewey System. There are two general Dewey sections for psychology: 130-39, 150-59.

(i)   *130-139 Branches of Psychology and Pseudo-Psychology*
       This includes:
       130.1 Theories of Mind and Body (i.e. philosophical aspects of psychology — 'mental' events, etc.)
       130.3 Mental Hygiene (including Psycho-analysis, 131.34)
       132.1 Mental Illness
       133.4 Witchcraft
       134.5 Hypnotic Phenomena
       137.7 Graphology (the art of 'interpreting' handwriting)

Notice that these headings are often somewhat misleading and certainly do not reflect the relative importance of a subject area in contemporary psychology. For instance, given its historical importance, *Psycho-analysis* would seem worthy of classification either separately, or, at least, under 132, *Abnormal Psychology,* rather than as a subsection of the anachronistic *Mental Hygiene* area. *Mental Hygiene* is a category of 131, *Physiological Psychology,* which effectively classifies Freud's theories as outcomes of physiological investigation — the antithesis of their actual origin. Hence the Dewey system can be quite misleading as to the type of material its classifications demarcate. Moreover in (i) above, *Graphology* appears to be a more important topic of psychological research than *Psychoanalysis.* Examples such as these greatly reduce the value of searching through the library from the general to the particular if the categories one explores are specified solely by the Dewey classifications.

(ii)   *150-159 General Psychology*
       This section includes:
       151   Intelligence
       152   Sensation and Perception
               152.1 Visual Sensation and Perception
               152.8 Psychophysics
       153   Cognition
       159   Volition and Motivation

The main limitations of this section are the omission of *Educational Psychology* (370.15), and of physiological aspects of psychology, some of which are included under 612, *Human Physiology. Social Psychology* (301.15) and aspects of *Criminology* and *Delinquency* (364.3, 364.2) are also excluded.

To some extent, the Dewey system reflects the historical development of modern psychology. It begins with philosophical issues and psycho-analysis — the latter defined by rather archaic terminology (as in 'Mental Hygiene'). Then follow categories reflected in the chapter headings of general introductory textbooks, with irregular entries for related disciplines like criminology and neurophysiology.

Because it is less widely employed, the L.C. system is not discussed in detail here. However, Sarbin and Coe (1969, pp.102-4) provide a listing of subjects and numerical classifications under that system.

8.1.2 Library Card Catalogues

Most university libraries have two categories: (i) a 'subject', and (ii) an 'author-title' listing.

(i) *The Subject Catalogue* lists titles of books under headings which indicate the general topic to which the book is most closely related. Subjects may include persons. (For example, books about Freud, Piaget or their respective theories would be listed under headings such as 'Freud, S., books about'.) It is best to use this catalogue before consulting the author-title catalogue because the information in the subject catalogue is general and somewhat arbitrarily classified. This means that the student's classification of the subject he is pursuing need not correspond closely to the library's classification, thus reducing the value of searching the subject catalogue if one pursues only books listed under a small number of topics, however relevant these topics may appear. Of course, the cards do refer the user to related topics, but this process may be somewhat time-consuming, with no guarantee of exhausting the relevant material.

(ii) *The Author-Title Catalogue* is a list of all the monographs (books) and serials (journals, periodicals) held by the library. Monographs are entered under author or editor, and the card contains details of the Dewey (or other) classifications; these include:

Title; place of publication; publisher; date of publication; information about the number of copies held in the library (or in other university departmental libraries) and the number of pages in the book (if a monograph).

The 'classification number' denotes the subject of the book, while the 'shelf number' distinguishes different books on the same subject.

e.g. Dinkmeyer, D. *Child Development*
155.4
6

'155.4' is the Dewey classification for books on child psychology, whereas '6' is the shelf number given to this particular book. If there is more than one copy of the book, the numbers '6A', '6B' . . . would distinguish the various copies.

The author-title catalogue is used for locating books whenever one knows the author's name. Clearly, to use this catalogue more specific information is needed about a book than for the subject catalogue.

Serials (journals, periodicals) are generally listed under the author-title catalogue[1] by their respective titles or under the name of the organisation by which they are issued. Those which some libraries call 'distinctive' titles are listed by title: e.g. *Journal of Clinical Psychology; Journal of the History of the Behavioural Sciences.* Those issued by a society or institution which include the name of that body as an important part of the title are listed under such names. These are often called serials with non-distinctive titles (e.g. reports of the proceedings of various professional organisations). Catalogue entries for serials usually provide the following information:

Title; place of publication; the dates (issues) held by the library – e.g. vol. 1 (1945) +; the frequency of publication (e.g. annual, quarterly); whether additional copies of the journal are available in the library or associated libraries, and if so at what call numbers.

It is not advisable merely to 'browse' through serials in the hope of encountering relevant information for an essay or project. Journals publish very specific papers which will look quite foreign to students simply leafing through their pages. Journals are more fruitfully consulted by means of abstracts (see below).

However, students should remember that there are serials concerned with every conceivable aspect of psychology, and that their titles are usually an accurate indication of their general content. Sarbin and Coe (1969) list many of these, describing their particular orientations. These authors concentrate exclusively on American journals. There are, of course, British journals of (general) psychology, educational psychology, etc., as well as Canadian, Australian and other national series, usually published under the auspices of the professional Psychological Society of their respective country. Of the better known internationally read journals originating in America, the following might be representative:

Psychological Bulletin – a monthly publication which focuses on critical reviews of research in specific areas, rather than publishing original empirical research papers.

1.   Libraries generally issue a special, regularly revised, computer listing of serials also.

Psychological Review — a bi-monthly collection of theoretical articles of considerable sophistication.

Other general journals include:

Psychological Record
Journal of General Psychology
Journal of Psychology

These, and similar, journals should be consulted for specific papers, rather than as potential sources of information on particular research areas or project topics. The latter function is better served by journals which concentrate on research from particular fields of psychology. These would include:

Journal of Verbal Learning and Verbal Behaviour
Journal of Psycholinguistic Research
Journal of Social Psychology
Perceptual and Motor Skills
Genetic Psychology Monographs
Journal of Personality
Journal of Clinical Psychology
Psychoanalytic Review
Journal of Abnormal Psychology
Journal of Experimental Psychology
Journal of Counselling Psychology
Child Development
Journal of Experimental Child Psychology

and very many more.

8.1.3 Guides to Psychological Literature

(i) **General.** A large number of general guides to psychological literature are to be found in all major libraries. These provide both information and advice on the use and documentation of psychological literature. They include:

Elliott, C.K.	*A Guide to the Documentation of Psychology.* London: Bingley, 1971.
	A relatively recent guide to periodicals and reference books, plus advice on various kinds of information problems. Not focused exclusively on American literature.
Sarbin, T.R., & Coe, W.C.	*The Student Psychologist's Handbook.* Cambridge, Mass.: Schenkman/Harper & Row, 1969.
	An excellent introductory guide to American sources of information — especially journals — with advice on

organising and writing papers. Includes appendices listing Dewey and Library of Congress (L.C.) classifications of psychological literature. However it does not cover British or European (or Russian) literature, except as this has found its way into the American serials. It does include a section entitled 'glossary of statistical terms', which may be most useful to students of elementary psychology.

Borchardt, D.H.   *How to Find Out in Philosophy and Psychology.* Oxford: Pergamon, 1968.

A general, comprehensive guide to reference material in the two disciplines.

There are also a number of general bibliographies. For instance:

American Behavioural Scientist: The A.B.S. Guide to Recent Publications in the Social and Behavioural Sciences. N.Y.: 1965.

This may be supplemented by

Recent Publications in the Social and Behavioural Sciences (1966), 1967 . . .).

More specialised bibliographies include:

Brackbill, Y.   *Research in Infant Behaviour: A cross-Indexed Bibliography.* Baltimore: Williams & Wilkins, 1964.

Mental Retardation Abstracts. These are arranged under broad subject headings; this series includes subject and author indices.

Perceptual Cognitive Development. Published bi-monthly, this is a bibliography of articles, books and research projects in a rapidly expanding field of psychological research.

Bulletin Signaletique. Section 390: Psychologie, Psychopathologie, Psychiatrie. This extensive bibliography covers mainly European material. Given the more ubiquitous sources of information on American literature, this is a most useful complement.

Some journals publish reviews of large numbers of books in psychology. The best known of these is:

Contemporary Psychology, vol. 1 (1956), published annually; reviews over 200 books and lists others published during the year.

Useful survey and annual review journals bring the reader up-to-date in various areas of psychological research. The most widely read of these is probably

Annual Review of Psychology, vol. 1 (1958). This reviews literature in particular areas (e.g. personality, maturation, statistics, abnormal psychology) in a most comprehensive manner. Experts in the particular field describe, interpret and evaluate the year's progress in that area. A cumulative author and subject index is included.

Dictionaries include:

Drever, I.   *A Dictionary of Psychology*. Harmondsworth: Penguin, 1952.

Chaplin, J.P.   *Dictionary of Psychology*. N.Y.: Dell Publishing Co., 1968.

A more advanced, technical source, providing detailed explanation of many terms is:

English, H.B., and   *A Comprehensive Dictionary of Psychological and*
English, A.C.   *Psychoanalytical Terms*. N.Y.: Longmans, 1958.

The terminology of psycho-analysis is sufficiently complex to warrant its own dictionary:

Laplanche, J., and   *The Language of Psycho-analysis*. London: Hogarth,
Pontalis, J-B.   1973.

(ii) **Psychological Abstracts**. Perhaps the most important and useful sources of information for psychology students are the editions of psychological abstracts. These abstracts consist of short (100-150 word) summaries of original material published in all major (and very many minor) journals throughout the world. Each month, a publication of up-to-date research abstracts appears, and author and subject indexes are added every six months. There are eleven major sections and coverage includes books, articles, films psychological tests and unpublished doctoral theses.

It is usual for students undertaking theses, extensive literature searches, or searching for, say, all the works of a particular author, to consult the psychological abstracts as the first stage of their enquiry. Undoubtedly, all students wishing to pursue advanced study of psychology would be well advised to familiarise themselves with the use of these sources of information in their own university library.

8.2 READING THE LITERATURE

Given that one is confidently familiar with the use of the library, how should one read the literature that is set for a particular project? To provide some reasonably specific guidelines for this important task, let us restrict discussion to cases where the student is required to research an essay topic for which a reading list has been provided. The hypothetical essay is to be about 2,000 words long.

Just as there are strategies and techniques for writing psychological essays (see next chapter), so there are some general strategies for reading and preparing for writing such essays. First, it is virtually useless to read psychological literature as one might browse through, say, a news magazine. Unlike reading for personal pleasure or searching for interesting information on a number of topics, reading in preparation for writing an essay or academic paper must involve deliberate, strategic attempts to gain specific information. The difference might be stated thus: one does not read an essay reference with the aim of merely 'understanding what it says', but more with the goal of answering specific questions, or of *testing certain statements against the author's point of view or research findings.*

As we put it in the first chapter, one should read for conceptual understanding, not merely for linguistic understanding. Let us try to explain this by means of a hypothetical case. Consider an essay of 2,000 words to be written on the topic 'In what sense might the process of stereotyping be regarded as irrational?'

If the reading list is adequate it should include references which cover the following two aspects of the topic:

(1)   They provide definition(s) or at least some analysis of the terms 'stereotype' and 'irrationality'.

(2)   They provide evidence, or analyse examples, of the process of stereotyping, by which that process can be compared with criteria for judging behaviour as 'irrational'.

Hence *before* reading any of the literature one must understand the question. That is, one must interpret the question and decide (even write down) what an adequate answer would need to cover. When this is done, one should focus one's proposed reading on these specific aspects and select the references to this end. To do this, the title alone may suffice; if not, the abstract (if one is available) is usually adequate. In some cases, a preliminary reading may be required. So the second step in researching the essay is *to order the references according to the interpretation of the question.* Although in practice it is sometimes difficult to decide in advance in what order the references should be studied, it is desirable to impose order whenever possible. This should at least reduce the amount of re-reading that would otherwise be necessary.

Given a tentative, logical ordering of the references, the next step is to *study*, not merely *read,* each paper and book. Study involves reading, taking descriptive or summary notes, making written critical comments arguing for or against the paper, and, most importantly, relating the paper to the topic being researched (i.e. to the topic as interpreted). In the present example, one should try to analyse the argument and summarise the evidence presented concerning the two aspects of the question which have been previously distinguished. One's commentary should concern analyses and evidence of irrationality (e.g. the paper may argue that stereotypes are often logically inconsistent, are 'overgeneralisations' or 'oversimplifications', or that they do not change even when contradicted, and so on).

The notes which summarise and criticise a paper should include a paraphrase of its major thesis (or theses), plus a brief description of the evidence provided in its support. Should particular quotations be reported verbatim, they should be completely documented and marked so that they are not confused with one's own notes. A third section of the notes might be headed 'Comments' of 'Criticisms' or 'Discussion'. This section should note inadequacies, inconsistencies or peculiar interpretations made by the paper which differ from those of comparable papers, as well as relevance of the paper to the topic as interpreted, and so on.

To facilitate writing the essay, it is recommended that one use either large (8" x 5") filing cards or loose-leafed paper. In both cases, these can subsequently be re-ordered as the structure of one's proposed essay requires. A typical card or page of preparatory notes should include (perhaps at the top, or in a margin) the author's name, title of paper, and library location. A margin, in which page references of important quotations or paraphrases are recorded, is essential. All too frequently one wishes to quote an author's words in an essay, only to find that one has to retrace their exact page of origin by re-reading the paper. This can be avoided by the consistent application of a clerical procedure such as the one recommended here.

Therefore a student's essay preparation should produce a series of documented notes on interchangeable cards which summarise the thesis and supporting evidence from each relevant paper, and include quotations and critical commentary. This greatly simplifies the organisational and clerical work involved. For instance, one of its advantages is that the essay's bibliography can be listed simply by sorting the cards into alphabetical order (by author) and copying down the respective titles, after the essay has been written.

A Note on Photocopying: The Seduction of Reproduction. Easy access to inexpensive photocopying machines has greatly altered methods of research for undergraduate essays. It is now possible, though possibly illegal, to copy all references and use the copies as one's sources of information. One can underline and annotate the copies of papers and (it might be hoped) avoid the study processes that have been briefly outlined in this chapter.

However, it is generally *not* a good idea to rely on photocopying to reduce study time if this means that one avoids writing summaries or critical commentaries. First, this reliance will lead to a very uneconomical source of information from which to write an essay or report. As we have emphasised in preceding chapters, being able to translate others' ideas into one's own words and to draw implications from these ideas are essential aspects of understanding. If no notes are taken, one may read, but not necessarily understand, an article or monograph. Second, photocopying carries the temptation to avoid reading altogether while collecting ever-increasing stocks of unpleasant-smelling paper. There is a curious tendency to believe that merely photocopying an article is tantamount to committing it to memory. This is obviously a dangerous (but quite common) misconception. So it is probably a good rule not to photocopy material until *after* one has read it. Certainly it is advisable not to photocopy more than can be properly studied before one has further access to the tempting machine. It is pointless to amass piles of unstudied material which is merely left to gather dust — the unfortunate fate of much psychological literature.

9

WRITING ESSAYS

My words fly up, my thoughts remain below:
Words without thoughts never to heaven go.

Shakespeare

9.1   INTRODUCTION

WRITING psychology essays is not a simple matter. In addition to the formal aspects of definition and argument which we discussed in the first sections of this book, and the detailed research of the relevant literature which is necessary preparation, there is the problem of actually formulating one's ideas in coherent, lucid English. The last problem is the focus of this chapter.

Ideally, an essay should contribute something to the area it discusses. At the minimum it should show that its author knows what he is talking about — that he understands the subject. Assessors may hope to learn something about their speciality from a student's essay, but failing this, they will be looking for evidence of a student's grasp of the topic. They will be looking for evidence of breadth of information, depth of understanding and level of critical skills. It is important not only that the student have such information, understanding and critical skills, but that, especially in writing essays, he demonstrate them. His essay must show unequivocal evidence of them.

In the preceding chapters, we were concerned with evaluating the written work of others. But in essay writing the tables are turned: Instead of being the audience trying to evaluate critically the material received, the student has to produce material which will stand up to critical scrutiny. Nevertheless the advice given earlier is still highly germane, for all essayists, in the selection of their material, must be their own critics. They must produce ideas and arguments that can not only be clearly understood, but that will also stand up to critical evaluation.

Essays should, at least, show that their authors *understand* the topic, i.e. that they have critically evaluated relevant information. Critical evaluation is shown by the use of arguments, which, as we have seen, demonstrate not only what authors assert to be true, but, more importantly, *why* they make such assertions.

Since understanding is so important, it is worth recalling (and re-reading) a number of distinctions made in section 1.1. There we distinguished two levels of understanding — the linguistic level and the conceptual level. The former concerns understanding material to the point of being able to express it in one's own words; the latter involved seeing both the implications of statements and the questions they answer. Both these levels were seen to be essential for the evaluation of statements and arguments, and their importance will be apparent throughout this chapter, for an essay is an attempt to show these levels of understanding.

We have chosen, by means of two examples, to introduce the very considerable difficulties which confront many students when writing essays. We have selected segments of two essays written by students as part of a course in elementary psychology. The topics chosen are sufficiently non-technical to illustrate some important features of essay writing without requiring the reader to possess any specialist knowledge of their respective contents. Although the person assessing the essays would be familiar with the relevant literature, it is nevertheless instructive to read the excerpts without the benefit of similar background information. The following general features should be noted, for these are clearly important to the assessor of essays, regardless of the topic under discussion.

(a) The coherence and soundness of the arguments presented are largely due to the way in which the author 'organises his ideas'. There are at least three levels at which such organisation can be analysed:

   (i) Within sentences: Are the ideas (propositions or statements) expressed by the one sentence closely related, or would they be more appropriately separated into individual sentences? Does the structure of the sentence reflect the relative importance of its component statements?

   (ii) Within paragraphs: How do the statements included within each paragraph contribute to the one central idea? What is this major idea which the topic sentence of the paragraph embodies? (This assumes that it is possible to isolate such a 'topic sentence'. In an extended argument this should usually be identifiable as an intermediate conclusion to the major point at issue.) Are the paragraph boundaries appropriate? Are the lengths of the sentences within the paragraph varied in a manner appropriate to their content?

   (iii) Overall structure: How do the various subarguments embodied in particular paragraphs develop or reinforce the major argument(s) being advanced in the essay? Is the direction and structure of the essay clearly indicated by means of the sequence and prominence of the paragraphs, or is the order somewhat random?

(b) Vocabulary and style: Psychological essays are not assessed by purely 'literary' criteria, but the communication of ideas demands lucid, economical prose. Choice of the appropriate word, varied and interesting sentence structure, unpretentious expression with minimal jargon — all contribute to the impact an essay makes on the reader.

(c) Conventions: Failure to follow certain organisational and linguistic conventions can lead to uneconomical essays. Precise rules concerning the documentation of sources also need to be followed if the suspicison of plagiarism is to be avoided.

9.2 SOME INSTRUCTIVE EXAMPLES

The following examples violate, in various ways, the fundamental requirements of a lucid, carefully argued essay. The first example is particularly unsatisfactory. Few essays are as poor as it. However such essays do find their way into markers' hands, even in universities. By beginning our discussion with a very poor essay we hope to emphasise the importance of preparation and organisation of written work.

Example 1

The question: 'What psychological factors are important in the 'mirror-image phenomenon' in international relations? How might this phenomenon be reduced or eliminated?'

The mirror image phenomenon refers to the tendency of national groups who see themselves as enemies to attribute similar (negative) characteristics to each other. Hence, for example, it is held that during the Cold War the Russians and the Americans regarded each other in quite similar ways.

Excerpts from one student's attempt to answer this question show how inadequate some written essays are. In this example virtually no information about the topic is communicated clearly.

Par. 1   There are many factors important in the so-called 'mirror-image' phenomenon in international relations. The most major is the fact that it blinds one side from the truth — it presents false realities — in such aspects as aggression, politics, governmental forms and economic policy. It is necessary for one thing — war — be it cold or real. This phenomenon must be reduced or the consequences could easily be war. This is best illustrated by Soviet-American relations and the actions of individuals.

Par. 2   The mirror-image phenomenon in international relationships is the same as cognitive dissonance displayed by individuals and on the individual scale this phenomenon is best explained.

Par. 3   Cognitive dissonance is actually the upgrading of an object or system on its being chosen from two reasonably attractive alternatives which is virtually an attitude that is opposite that of the established 'grass is greener on the other side'. Thus if the Soviets choose Communism over Democracy then dissonance will occur that will bias them in favour of the governmental system they chose. It is this that causes the mirror-image effect and whose important factors and hopeful elimination will be discussed. For each factor in international relations there are two sides both of which are firmly believed in by their supporters.

Par. 4   An example of this is the belief held by democratic countries that communist countries are aggressive . . . as evidenced in the communist takeovers of China, Indochina, Czechoslovakia, Hungary and Cuba. The communists also veto all proposals for disarmament by refusing to let anyone check on their state of armament.

Par. 5   The Communists on the other hand believe that America is a war monger that vetoes communist disarmament proposals by expecting the right to check their state of arms at any time. They also have bases all around the borders of the Soviet Union and Communist China. America also has spy planes and ships to try and inspect Communist military bases. It has also intervened in every war since World War I, including Korea and Vietnam.

The essay continues in this vein for about 500 words, detailing in a rather naive manner the way Russians and Americans see each other. The final point made in this section of the essay is:

Par. 6   If a war were to break out then the cognitive dissonance would serve a useful purpose which would cause both sides to really believe they are on the right side [sic!].

The writer then discusses the second part of the question. He makes fairly obvious suggestions concerning increased international travel and cultural exchanges, although he fails to indicate if there is any evidence of their psychological effectiveness. He then writes the following concluding paragraph:

Par. 7   The mirror-image phenomenon is not impossible to break. The means open to us to aid in the breakdown are many and varied as are its causes. An analysis of its causes is necessary to allow an insight into the other side's mind and thus allow a change in the mental processes which cause the mirror-image phenomenon to occur. Some of these causes are: the aggression displayed by both countries. Each sees itself as pacifist and the other as unrealistic ... Each side's peace manoeuvres are seen by its opposition as nothing but propaganda. This shows a basic mistrust between the parties involved and on an analysis of the situation it seems that mistrust is the cause of the mirror-image phenomenon. If this mistrust could be removed, the mirror-image phenomenon could be abolished. If this phenomenon is not broken down then a situation could occur from which civilization might not recover — World War III.

This essay is unsatisfactory for many reasons. It would not be judged adequate in even the most elementary psychology course. However for this reason it is very instructive. Let us examine it in detail, noting the major criticisms applicable to each paragraph.

The most that could be said of the first paragraph is that it provides only a confused introduction to the essay. The following comments might be made:

(a)   The paragraph fails to suggest any definition or general interpretation of the phenomenon to be discussed. Indeed the vague discussion of the concept under consideration is quite misleading. For example, it is stated that the mirror-image phenomenon blinds *one* side from 'the truth'.

(b)   It does not indicate how the essay as a whole is to be approached. For instance, it fails to say which 'factors' are to be considered. The only psychological factor mentioned is really just an instance of a possible *consequence* of the phenomenon, not a factor which defines or contributes to it. Consequently, the rest of the essay never really discusses what *causes* the mirror-image phenomenon at all (e.g. defence mechanisms like 'projection' and 'rationalisation' are ignored).

(c)   As a result there is no indication of how, in general, the phenomenon might be reduced or eliminated (yet this is one part of the essay question).

In short, the opening paragraph does not *interpret the topic, analyse the principal concept or concepts,* or indicate *the general orientation of the essay as a whole.* Rather, it mentions one debatable aspect of the mirror-image phenomenon and then asserts that it 'must be reduced'. But the question is not whether it should be reduced, but how this might be achieved, given an understanding of its psychological basis.

Examining the paragraph in more detail, one is struck by the very poor verbal expression. Consider, for example, the second sentence: It includes 'most major' (redundant) and 'false realities' (self-contradictory).

But worse is to come. Paragraph 2, which consists of only one sentence, effectively *equates* 'cognitive dissonance' (which it does not define) with the mirror-image phenomenon. Then, in the next paragraph, the writer attempts to explain the latter as one instance of the former. The writer's confusion about the psychological concepts is increased by his failure to construct simple precise sentences.

The first three paragraphs are ostensibly introductory to the discussion of evidence and examples relevant to the mirror-image phenomenon. But the result is simply incoherent. The first sentence in paragraph 3 is too long. It contains both a general definition and a concrete example which neither complement nor clarify each other at all. Second, the sentence confuses two grammatical subjects. The second-last sentence in the paragraph is badly structured, containing two major, but distinct, ideas, which are arbitrarily connected by 'and'. Generally, it is the failure to distinguish abstract statements and definitions from concrete examples which renders this paragraph so incoherent. The problem would be partly overcome by providing a precise, yet general, definition of the phenomenon (in one or two sentences), then illustrating it by relevant examples. There is a difference between *defining* a concept and *exemplifying* or *illustrating* it (see Chapter 4).

Without going into further details, the importance of this example should be clear. The first three paragraphs could easily have been made into a reasonably coherent introductory discussion with a little care for elementary aspects of English expression. So, before dealing with other quoted sections of the essay, let us try to rewrite these paragraphs in the light of our discussion. In doing this we shall not utilise information additional to that in the original. We shall merely restructure and re-express the ideas which the original author apparently intended to communicate.

Par. 1   Many factors are important in the so-called mirror-image phenomenon in international realtions. Most importantly, this phenomenon blinds one side from the truth by producing misperceptions of many characteristics of the other side — its politics; form of government; economic policy and its attitude to aggression. The mirror-image phenomenon is a vital aspect of international affairs — especially war — both 'cold' and 'real'. Consequently, it must be reduced or such situations will never be eliminated. This is best illustrated in two ways: firstly, by the political relations between the U.S.A. and U.S.S.R.; and, secondly, by the attitudes and actions of individuals within these nations.

Par. 2   The individual person's attitudes which generate the mirror-image phenomenon are due to what is sometimes called 'cognitive dissonance'. It is in terms of individual psychological processes that the phenomenon is best explained.

Par. 3   It is very difficult to amend this paragraph because it is so confused and disjointed. But what it seems to express is something like:

When a person chooses between two reasonably attractive alternatives, 'cognitive dissonance' may result. The alternative which has been chosen is upgraded in order to reduce the dissonance of the original decision. This process is virtually the opposite of that which leads to the attitude that 'the grass is greener on the other side'. Therefore if the Soviets choose communism over democracy, then dissonance will occur which will bias them in favour of their choice. This process is (partly) responsible for the mirror-image effect. The effect consists of each of two opposed national groups believing similar (unpleasant or negative) things about its opponent. The important aspects of this phenomenon and ways by which it may be eliminated will now be discussed.

The remainder of Example 1 is less incoherent than the first three paragraphs, but still capable of great improvement. The most important general comments that should be made would include the following:

First, taken as a whole, paragraphs 4 to 7 do not directly answer the original question. Recall that the essay question consists of two parts. The first concerns the factors involved in the mirror-image phenomenon: the second, methods for reducing it. In answer to the first, the essay merely discusses various examples of the mirror-image mentality. But it fails to consider the psychological factors contributing to this mentality at either the international or individual levels. Consequently the question is never really answered! The final paragraph demonstrates this very clearly. Were one to break the 'argument' advanced here into its component propositions, it would be difficult to detect any logical development culminating in a specific conclusion directly relevant to the essay topic. The paragraph consists of *assertions*, not arguments.

Given that there is no detailed argument about the causes of the phenomenon, there is no way of clearly demonstrating how it might be reduced or eliminated. Obviously, an essay which fails to answer the question asked is inadequate, no matter what its virtues might be.

Second, the essay does not cite any detailed evidence relevant to the topic. It offers, instead, a list of examples of the phenomenon being explained. But examples alone are insufficient to the task: they merely illustrate the phenomenon; they do not explain the factors which contribute to it.

Third, the essay offers no formal recognition of the sources of what meagre information it includes. No references are cited for the brief mention of the concept of 'cognitive dissonance', nor for the expression 'mirror-image phenomenon'. At the very least the essay should cite such sources, as their information is incorporated into the argument.

Example 2

Our discussion of the previous example was organised around three major sections of the essay:

    (i)   The introductory paragraphs;
    (ii) The general discussion of evidence (pars 4-7);
    (iii) The conclusion (par. 7).

We found that essay seriously deficient in each segment.

The next example is considerably better in all sections for a number of reasons, although it is by no means an ideal treatment of its topic. On the credit side, it attempts to describe properly documented, relevant evidence and to develop general themes, if not detailed arguments. We will discuss its demerits after presenting four of the most important paragraphs verbatim.

The question: 'It has often been suggested that watching violent films and reading about violent acts encourages aggressive and violent behaviour. Critically discuss this claim.'

Par. 1   Violence has increased at a rapid rate in western societies such as the U.S.A. since the turn of the twentieth century. During this time there has also been an enormous increase in strength and power of the media (i.e. newspapers, T.V., motion pictures). These are dominated by tales of violence depicted in various ways. It is doubtful if the above is just coincidence.

Par. 2   Aggression may be defined as 'behaviour intentionally causing physical harm to another person'. Violence and aggression may expend a great amount of energy but in this modern age they may also be carried out in a cool, calm and impersonal manner. Many theories have been expounded on the causes of aggression in the human race. Ardrey (1967) and Storr (1968) view aggression as innate in man. However, contrary evidence is available. Studies of two primitive tribes indicate that aggression is learnt during childhood. In child-rearing, the Arapesh tribe sows seeds of passiveness. They treat the child as a soft vulnerable thing which they protect continuously and feed often. The Mundugumore, on the other hand, are vicious and quarrelsome head-hunters, who rapidly instil such characteristics in their offspring.

The essay then summarises evidence for the statement that aggression is 'learnt' — mentioning child-rearing studies, imitation of aggressive models in films and surveys of the amount of violence in T.V. programmes. Next it treats the issue of whether viewed violence can have a cathartic (emotionally releasing) effect. Typical of these paragraphs is the following:

Par. 3   Experiments by Bandura support Berkowitz's beliefs (concerning imitation of violence). His experiments involved children viewing an adult engaged in violence on T.V., film, cartoon, and in real life. The child was then mildly annoyed and his free-play observed. As well as finding 'twice as much aggressiveness', Bandura observed that the children were 'not too inclined to give precise imitations (of cartoon characters) but many behaved like carbon copies of real-life and filmed models.

The concluding paragraph follows immediately:

Par. 4   This reinforces the view that aggression and violence under certain conditions are learned and later adopted by people. If the violence and aggression viewed are appealing, and in carrying out that violence one feels in some sense morally justified, one's inhibitions to violence are decreased. The portrayal of violence on T.V. and film does tend to lead people astray.

This example is sufficiently well organised to allow us to discuss it in three general sections.

(i) Introductory paragraphs : 1,2

The first paragraph is quite typical of those found in mediocre undergraduate essays: It is rhetorical and vague, containing assertions for which no documentation or evidence are deemed necessary. With its occasional redundancy ('strength and power') and patent generalisations, the paragraph is quite innocuous. However, given the question being answered, it could be claimed that the entire paragraph is really unnecessary, for it avoids, rather than confronts, the question.

The second paragraph is considerably better than any of those from the first example discussed, although that is not to say that it is ideal. The writer does attempt to define aggression, however cursorily. Second, he cites two proponents of an important point of view concerning the origins of human aggression and indicates the relevance of empirical methods to settling the issue raised. On the other hand, in doing this, the author does set up quite rigid dichotomies ('instinct' or 'learning') and offers no detailed justification for selecting either the authors or ideas he introduces. Moreover the definition of aggression which he offers is very specific, and could easily be confused with a definition of 'violence' (the two are not usually taken to be synonymous). He mentions impersonal violence but does not relate this point to his general discussion. More importantly, there is no analysis of the concept of instinct, not even an outline of Storr's or Ardrey's definitions. Had this concept been examined in detail, the rigid dichotomisation of the 'nature-nurture' issue in the essay might have been qualified or replaced by more workable categories. Were this done, the very relevant anthropological evidence mentioned in the final section of the paragraph could form a separate, quite extensive section in its own right.

(ii) Discussion of evidence

Paragraph 3 of our example attempts to summarise one study (by Bandura), with only limited success. Although the general findings of the study are reported, a more lucid summary could have been given. Generally, however, this paragraph is typical of those found in students' essays. It does confirm and extend the writer's argument quite well. In conjunction with other evidence (which we have not quoted) the 'body' of this essay is relevant to the question under discussion and is adequately documented.

(iii) Conclusion

The concluding paragraph (4) is not very satisfactory. Instead of drawing together the major themes of the evidence reviewed and showing how these relate to the question, the writer is content merely to repeat the results of one series of studies and attach a generalisation with which to end the essay. However an ending is not necessarily a conclusion. Although not entirely irrelevant, the last paragraph could be more precise and its conclusions qualified so as to explicitly answer the question. The final statement is essentially moralistic ('. . . lead people astray') and much too vague to answer the question adequately.

So far our discussion has been essentially negative. Therefore keeping in mind the examples we have quoted, let us approach the task of writing essays in a more positive way, beginning where the student begins — confronted by a question (which he may or may not understand).

9.3 THE QUESTION

It is surprising how many students write essays on topics which bear only indirect or tangential relevance to the question assigned. Leaving aside those students who fail completely to understand the question, many others tend to write vaguely about issues related, but not central to, the question. But there is a distinction between 'topic' and 'question': the 'topic' is the more general concept or subject area about which particular questions can be asked.

Example 1 (above) illustrates the failure to observe this distinction. Look carefully at the wording of the question 'What psychological factors are important in the so-called mirror-image phenomenon in international relations? How might this phenomenon be reduced or eliminated?' Notice that it does *not* merely read: 'Write an essay on the mirror-image phenomenon'; it is more specific than that. Second, notice that there are two parts to the question. Hence the student must decide

(a) what the question means. In this case, one would have to ask what the words 'psychological factors' might refer to, as well as how the major concepts might be defined; and

(b) how the component questions are to be answered in relation to each other. This involves deciding which (if either) is the major question and how much importance should be given to it and the subsidiary issues. It is not sufficient to write an essay about one aspect of the total question and simply append a cursory sentence or two which pay lip service to the minor issues. In Example 1, considerable discussion would be required of how (in the light of the answer to the first part of the question) the phenomenon being discussed could be reduced or eliminated. It would probably require about one third of the total essay to discuss this question adequately.

A second issue arises in direct relation to the way the question is phrased. An essay question almost invariably requires elementary logical analysis before it can be properly answered. By this we mean that the logical structure of the question needs to be elucidated. For example, consider the essay question ' "Stereotypes are necessary for prejudice". Discuss.' First, it is important to notice what the question does *not* say. It does not merely say 'Discuss the relationship between stereotypes and prejudice', or 'stereotypes may lead to prejudice' (or vice versa).

Therefore, without knowing too much about either 'stereotypes' or 'prejudice', one can analyse the logical structure of the question in this negative way. What is more, this analysis can be very revealing. In the present case, it demonstrates that one would have to answer the original question negatively (i.e. disagree with the quoted statement) unless one could show that prejudice always involved stereotypes. It would not be sufficient to demonstrate that stereotypes sometimes or frequently lead to prejudiced attitudes: it would have to be shown that prejudice could not occur without stereotypes. One of the authors has actually marked essays on this topic and found that very few students are aware of the *logic* of the question which they discuss. Students are strongly advised to analyse the logical status of each question they consider and ask what (possible) evidence would provide arguments for or against answers to the question *before* reading the relevant literature. Otherwise they will have no way of knowing which literature actually is relevant to the question. At the risk of repeating our earlier recommendation, it is not just what the question asks, but what it does *not* ask, that must be understood before one searches for answers.

Once the logic of the question is clear, the next step is to analyse the major concepts involved. In Chapter 4 we noted the importance of clarifying and defining one's terms whenever there is some possibility of misunderstanding between a writer and some of his readers. In essay work, the writer is the student and the reader (assessor) is likely to have been his teacher, which may seem to reduce the need for clarification and definition of terms. However the processes are still important, owing to the double purpose of essay writing. The student has not only to write competently on a particular topic, but to show as unequivocally as he can that he understands what he has written. This often requires that he define and clarify some of the more important terms being used — particularly new terms and those which are used in a technical sense which differs from their everyday usage.

We have seen that many psychological concepts are open to a variety of interpretations and can be defined by a variety of procedures. In Essay 2 (above) the writer defined 'aggression' as 'behaviour intentionally causing physical harm to another person'. But aggression could be defined more broadly than this. For instance, it could include 'psychological' assaults such as insults and other interpersonal 'attacks'. Second, the writer of that essay offered no definition of violence as distinct from (or as one aspect of) aggression. Yet the essay question implied that aggression and violence were not synonymous.

Other essay topics may involve even less precise terms than these. For example, the following: ' "The behavioural control techniques in current use dehumanise man." Evaluate this claim discussing specific examples.' The word 'dehumanise' is very difficult to define. Consequently, many students who wrote on this topic during a course on the principles of behaviour control were content to assume that no definition was necessary. As a result, they usually failed to relate the techniques of control to any relevant evaluative concept. They may have shown, for example, that such practices raised a number of ethical problems, involved practical difficulties, caused pain or eliminated 'human responsibility', but failed to argue how any of these should necessarily be regarded as 'dehumanising'.

This example raises another problem involved in the interpretation of essay topics. Although the above question does not explicitly require it, it seems to ask implicitly for some kind of comparison. It is certainly possible to interpret the question as requiring a comparison of current behaviour control techniques with other forms of psychological intervention in people's lives. It would be of limited interest to show that the behavioural techniques were 'dehumanising' if it could also be claimed that all forms of psycho-therapeutic intervention were equally likely to restrict individual freedom and dignity.

Consequently, one must look beyond the explicit question to see if comparisons and contrasts are called for, and ask how relevant these are to the answer one proposes. This is a very important point and arises in relation to many psychological questions. Recall the discussion of the comparative nature of evidence (Chapter 5) where the *relative* effect of variables was stressed. The present points are an extension of the argument advanced there.

9.4 EVIDENCE

The importance of thinking carefully about the meaning and internal logic of the question can be seen when one attempts to research the topic. Without such an analysis one cannot read the literature with specific questions in mind. One will scarcely comprehend, let alone remember, technical arguments from the literature unless they can be related to issues about which one has formulated precise questions. The general strategy one might adopt, given a coherent interpretation of the major questions at issue, should focus on the following: *What evidence would refute possible answers to the question?* (This is not a question of what the evidence *is,* but of what it *could* be.) As a corollary, the student should ask *What evidence would confirm (support) possible answers to the topic question?*

In keeping with the (admittedly oversimplified) version of the logic of scientific argument outlined in Chapter 3, it is suggested that these questions are of crucial importance. Although the first appears rather negative, its prac-tical value is considerable. In particular, it is important to formulate, *in advance* of reading specific studies, the evidence that could be relevant to both positive and negative conclusions regarding the question being discussed. To do this, the points considered in Chapter 5 should be studied carefully — especially the distinction between correlation and cause, and the need for appropriate comparison conditions which it would be redundant to discuss again in this chapter.

9.5   THE CONCLUSION

Most students' essays *end* rather than *conclude* (i.e. reach a conclusion). However there is a great potential difference between merely ending a discussion and concluding an argument. Trivially, this difference is shown by the fact that the conclusion of an essay-form argument need not be presented in the final sections of the essay. A conclusion may be presented prior to the supporting argument and evidence, although this is not generally the case. But, regardless of where it occurs, some conclusion is essential to any argument.

In its most mundane form, a conclusion may simply consist of a paraphrase of the question, preceded by an appropriate word or phrase like 'thus', 'therefore', or 'it can be seen that . . .'. However this is seldom ideal. Usually the conclusion of an essay involves a number of careful qualifications. For example, the concluding paragraph in Essay 2 (above) attempts to specify the precise conditions under which aggressive behaviour may be encouraged by the media. Although that example is rather vague and brief, the attempt is preferable to asserting dogmatically that 'the media cause aggression', for instance. Such glib generalisations are unlikely to reflect the complexity of the psychological literature relevant to an undergraduate essay. It is much more likely that conclusions will be of the form 'certain people, under certain conditions, for certain duration (perhaps at certain ages) will be influenced in particular ways . . .'. It must be admitted that the formulation of essay questions may predispose students to look for crude general solutions to issues, for the questions themselves usually involve brief, unqualified phrases. It is part of the skill of essay writing to be able to avoid merely reproducing the oversimplified categories assumed in many questions.

Finally it is emphasised that the conclusion of an essay does not need to pretend to be the ultimate statement that is possible on the topic. Highly qualified and conditional conclusions are preferable to dramatic overstated assertions which one often finds in students' work. Essays are not dramatic literary exercises: they need no emotional climax or rousing final scene. Assessors do not need to be told that 'the issue of racial prejudice is the most important problem facing the world and must be solved for fear of World War III', nor that 'Behavioural Control Techniques are the realisation of society's gravest fear of a 1984 situation, where its every detail is controlled'. The soundness of a conclusion is not necessarily proportional to its rhetorical vigour.

9.6   STYLE

In discussing the verbal style of psychological essays we do not wish to propose unduly restrictive guidelines, for there is no particular style which is obligatory in such cases.[1] However there appear to be three common stylistic weaknesses in undergraduate essays which are relatively easily rectified. These will be called (1) personal informality; (2) pseudo-scientific jargon; and (3) inappropriate choice of words.

9.6:1 Personal Informality

Whenever writers adopt the first person singular ('I'), or worse, the first person plural ('we'), there is a tendency to intrude unnecessarily into the text. Typical phrases which signify this type of intrusion are:

> 'I think that . . .'
> 'It is my opinion that . . .'

or worse,

> 'It is my considered opinion that . . .'
> 'It is my firm belief that . . .'

Sometimes the first person locution may be used to argue more 'authoritatively':

> 'When I was in Alabama, I saw . . .'

or

> 'Having been to New Guinea, I know what village conditions are like . . .'

or

> 'Having studied genetics, I can vouch for the validity of X's arguments.'

Such appeals to personal authority and experience should be avoided whenever possible for reasons outlined in Chapter 6.

The first person plural ('we') is often used by an individual author as a device for taking the reader into his confidence. For instance, the writer of a text-book might proceed:

> 'If we now study the evidence from Freud, then we can see clearly that . . .';

or

> 'We have seen that . . .'.

1. Prose style is discussed in Alsip and Cjezik's *Research Guide in Psychology* (1974), while G.H. Vallin provides a comprehensive treatment of the use of English in *Good English* (1951) and *Better English* (1953).

This is sometimes unpretentious and appropriate, although it is difficult to justify the rather intimate (and condescending) tone in some essays. Further, 'we' is sometimes used in what amounts to a 'royal plural' and is quite unnecessary.

9.6.2   Jargon

All disciplines have their own specialised vocabulary and psychology is no exception. Students are expected quickly to acquire knowledge of a technical vocabulary as they study this subject. They will talk about 'ego strength', 'reafference', 'operant conditioning' and so on. Some technical terminology is necessary and, in most cases, quite efficient for communication.

But excessive jargon (cant) may be used to obscure and inflate rather than to clarify and explain one's ideas. Students are given plenty of examples by their mentors of the use of pseudo-scientific vocabulary. Psychologists seem to be capable of manufacturing a new word for any phenomenon they study. The danger is that the technical vocabulary may be redundant, obscure, or both. A recent symposium on computer technology included references to a 'voice-oriented, point-to-point channel switched network' (a telephone system); 'the informationarisation' of society, and to computer-controlled cities as 'computopolises'. One speaker (one hopes facetiously) referred to a 'computer peace corps' which included an 'uneducated people eradication team'.

Psychological jargon, we hope, has not reached that stage, but many examples of cant may be found. The reader might attempt to paraphrase the following:

(a)   The input to the child's neural structures;

(b)   Developing competence for coping with negative emotions;

(c)   The study of environmental processes from the point of view of a particular participant in that process creates a situation dichotomised into participant on the one hand, and all other environmental components on the other (Proshansky *et al.*, 1970, p.35).

(d)   In other words, when we speak of design, the real object of discussion is . . . the ensemble comprising the form and its context . . .

There is a wide variety of ensembles . . . The biological ensemble made up of a natural organism and its physical environment is the most familiar; in this case we are used to defining the fit between the two as well-adaptedness (*ibid.*, p.43).

These examples are replete with rather inflated, 'scientific' words and phrases. Some may well have more precise meanings than less formal expressions which would be more readily comprehended by non-specialists. But other expressions seem to be unnecessarily 'technical' (e.g. 'neural structures';

'negative emotions'; 'biological ensemble', 'well-adaptedness'). It is not merely the choice of such words but the very passive grammatical structure which each author adopts that makes the passages very 'dense' (e.g. 'process creates a situation dichotomised . . .'). Jargon is even more noticeable when it is interspersed with non-technical language in students' essays, especially if there is the suggestion that the student is not totally familiar with the meaning of the jargon he employs. Unfortunately the specialist also sometimes falls between the excesses of glib jargon and more prosaic expression, as the following examples indicate:

> Of particular interest were territoriality patterns with respect to beds, chairs and parts of the room and social distances maintained by team-mates in free-time activities. It was anticipated that isolated and non-isolated groups, and groups formed according to different personality compositions would differ in spatial behaviour. Prior research had shown that incompatibility and compatibility of dyad members on need affiliation, need achievement and dogmatism affected performance stress and interpersonal exchange in isolation (Altman and Haythorn, in Proshansky *et al.*, 1970, p.227).

The density with which technical expressions are packed into this passage concerning the way sailors use the space and furniture in their living quarters renders it almost incomprehensible on first reading, even to someone familiar with the area of research. It is amusing to compare the passage with part of a satirical paper entitled 'An Ethological Analysis of Reproductive Behaviour' (Germana, 1971). Under the heading 'The male-female sexuality as a mechanism of social organisation', Germana writes:

> Whenever a group of animals is first brought together, they demonstrate little or no social organisation. Such social structure is produced through the establishment of dominance-submission relationships; only in terms of this social hierarchy can an individual demonstrate an appropriate differentiation of behaviour. This behaviour differentiation permits the survival of the individual within the group — that is, it is the 'primary behaviour adaptation' to which all other behaviours interrelate (p.55).

This passage sounds informative; it seems to be quite impressively so! Notice, however, that this results from the passivised formality and the cliches borrowed from, or invented to imitate, conventional jargon (especially 'primary behaviour adaptation'). Unfortunately, students' essays are sometimes unintentionally satirical in a rather similar way. as the following quotation attests:

> When faced with a problem, an organism will respond in a certain way. His decision or reaction will be a variable, dependent on many differing intervening variables . . .

It is hard to imagine a less informative statement, despite the words 'organism', 'decision', 'reaction' and 'intervening variable'.

Even worse is the passage from a final-year sociology student's formal thesis which a colleague brought to our attention:

> The individual is a set of potentialities which are actualised (in temporal sequence) by operating in the social dialectic. He is born into a particular social situation inhabited by significant others who mediate those aspects of the objective world according to their socio-economic location, and as ongoingly experiential selves with idiosyncratic and peculiar biographies.

Another example of jargon is the use of 'systems' and 'computer' language in psychology. In some cases this has been of great benefit in formulating old problems in new ways (e.g. in the psychology of language acquisition and use). Too often, however, students have adopted the jargon in a glib, pretentious manner. Humans are now 'encoders of input', which may result in various 'output' or 'throughput'. (Presumably, potential input which is ignored or rejected is 'backput'!)

An allied trend is the proliferation of hyphenated combinations of older words or prefixes and words. Hence we hear of 'socio-political factors', 'intra-dyadic communication', 'sociograms', 'sociofugal spatial arrangements', 'neuropharmacological studies', and so on. Again, without wishing to proscribe the use of all such terms, it is probably fair to argue that these should be used sparingly, and not at all if not properly understood by the writer of an essay or report.

9.6.3   Choosing the Right Word

Much of the difficulty that students find in writing psychological essays is that they do not really understand the meanings of many of the words they have read in the literature. It is only when they are required to express ideas precisely and unambiguously that this becomes apparent. The result may be that a student chooses slightly inappropriate words, which, in a technical essay or report can seriously mislead the reader (or irritate the marker). The following is a very simple example of slightly inappropriate words in a technical context:

(a)   The participants in the study were all white teenage boys.

(b)   Subjects in the experiment were all Caucasian males aged between 13 and 19.

These two sentences are very similar, and either might be acceptable in most contexts. Yet the words chosen in (b) are more appropriate to formal psychological literature than the alternatives in (a). This is because each word in (b) is more precise, and its meaning is more limited and unambiguous than its counterpart in (a). Without being too pedantic, the following comments might be made: 'participants' is vague enough to include the experimenter as well as the subjects; 'study' might refer to things other than experiments (e.g. field research); 'white' suggests racial classification solely on the basis of skin colour (which in some contexts may be difficult, if not impossible, to use).

Recall that when we discussed the assumptions inherent in various definitions, it was emphasised that the choice of particular words could have a crucial bearing on the theoretical orientation of an argument. The point being emphasised in this section relates to the precision and scope of the meaning of words, regardless of their more theoretical functions. But it is still an important practical aspect of the language of psychology that each word needs to be carefully chosen and its precise meaning fully comprehended. Words which appear to have identical meanings may be different in subtle ways which greatly affect the force of particular arguments. Consider the italicised words in the following brief discussion of group differences in intelligence:

The Irish *race* has been shown to score below the English in tests of *intellectual ability*. Such differences in *intelligence* are probably *inborn* because the educational systems of both countries are *comparable*. This *proves* that the difference is *instinctive* rather than learned.

This might be compared with:

The Irish *population* has been shown to score below the English population in tests of *I.Q.* Such a difference in I.Q. is probably *innately determined* because the educational systems of both countries are *similar*. This suggests that the difference is *not due to environmental influences*.

The most appropriate way to emphasise the importance of precision in one's written work is to participate actively in constructing sentences which reflect the differences between the meanings of pairs of words which are frequently confused in psychology. The list which follows offers some typical examples: Try to construct pairs of sentences using one of each illustrative pair of words in as precise and appropriate a manner as possible. If in doubt about the exact meanings (and hence exact differences between the pairs) consult dictionaries (e.g. J. Chaplin's *Dictionary of Psychology*) or glossaries of standard, including introductory, textbooks.

instinctive	genetic
intelligence	I.Q.
test	task
abnormal	sick
deviant	pervert
motive	cause

```
diagnosis . . . . . . . . . . . . . . . . . . . . . . . . . . . . . . . . . classification
gender . . . . . . . . . . . . . . . . . . . . . . . . . . . . . . . . . . . . . . . . sex
behaviour . . . . . . . . . . . . . . . . . . . . . . . . . . . . . . . . . . . actions
language . . . . . . . . . . . . . . . . . . . . . . . . . . . . . . . . . . . . speech
prejudiced . . . . . . . . . . . . . . . . . . . . . . . . . . . . . . . ethnocentric
innate . . . . . . . . . . . . . . . . . . . . . . . . . . . . . . . . . . . . . . inborn
supports . . . . . . . . . . . . . . . . . . . . . . . . . . . . . . . . . . . . proves
disconfirms . . . . . . . . . . . . . . . . . . . . . . . . . . . . . . . disproves
race . . . . . . . . . . . . . . . . . . . . . . . . . . . . . . . . . . . ethnic group
imitation . . . . . . . . . . . . . . . . . . . . . . . . . . . . . . . identification
```

Notice that it cannot be assumed that these words have exactly the meaning assigned to them in common speech, but even there, the differences between members of the pairs are generally quite important.

If further evidence of this is required, the reader might re-examine the examples with which this chapter began, especially the sections comparing original student essays with more carefully worded alternatives: Apparently very simple differences (e.g. between 'aggression' and 'violence') were seen to have critical consequences for the meaning of an argument. It cannot be emphasised too strongly that one's ideas are capable of being judged only through the medium of words, the choice of which requires the most careful consideration.

9.7 CONVENTIONS

Like most technical disciplines, psychology has evolved a set of widely accepted conventions with which students need to be familiar. These conventions relate to bibliographies, the acknowledgement of sources of information, certain stylistic practices, and, although less well-defined, the general format of empirical reports. Being aware of these conventions greatly facilitates the research for an essay, as well as its actual organisation and presentation.

In itemising and illustrating the major conventions to be found in the literature, we do not wish to imply that these are completely unchangeable. Minor variations will often be found if one covers a wide range of material. However such variations need not cause any real confusion in students' written work. By definition, conventions are somewhat arbitrary. Their justification is that they are both economical and unambiguous, if adopted generally.

9.7.1 Identification of Books and Journal Articles

Books are usually identified by the following means (acceptable punctuation is indicated): Author's name, Initials. *Title of book.* Place of publication: Publisher, Date of publication (year only). Examples follow:

Bandura, A. *Aggression: A Social Learning Analysis.* Englewood Cliffs, New Jersey: Prentice-Hall, 1973.

Where there is more than one author:

Redl, F., and Wineman, D. *Children Who Hate: The Disorganisation and Breakdown of Behaviour Controls.* Glencoe, Ill.: Free Press, 1951.

Should there be *editors* rather than authors, the format is:

Wrightsman, L.S. (ed.). *Contemporary Issues in Social Psychology.* Belmont, Calif.: Brooks/Cole, 1968.

Maple, T., and Matheson, D.W. (eds.). *Aggression, Hostility and Violence: Nature or Nurture?* N.Y.: Holt, Rinehart & Winston, 1973.

Journal articles are identified thus (punctuation again being indicated): Author's name, Initials, Title of paper, *Title of journal,* Volume, Year of publication, Page numbers.

Festinger, L., Pepitone, A., and Newcombe, T. Some consequences of de-individuation in a group. *Journal of Abnormal and Social Psychology,* 47, 1952, 382-89.

In cases where the conventions do not literally apply, it is advisable to give too much, rather than too little, information while remaining within the broad framework of the above. For instance:

Mann, J., Sidman, J., and Starr, S. Effects of erotic films on the sexual behaviour of married couples. In *Technical Report of the Commission on Obscenity and Pornography. vol. 8: Erotica and Social Behaviour.* Washington, D.C.: U.S. Government Printing Office, 1971.

The rule to observe in all cases is to provide sufficient information for the reader to locate the source to which the author refers. The conventions are not merely pedantic rituals but are very functional. This is often overlooked by students who hastily list references by title and author only.

It should be noted that the manner of identification of books and journal articles varies according to the 'house style' of the publishing house concerned.

Whenever written work is submitted as part of an academic course, all the books and journal articles to which reference is made should be listed in alphabetical order in accordance with these conventions.

9.7.2 Plagiarism and the Use of Sources

Plagiarism is the cardinal academic sin. Yet it is committed by a very large number of students whenever they are required to submit essays and reports.

This may be due to ignorance rather than deliberate intent, so let us examine the practice in some detail.

A typical dictionary definition of 'plagiarism' might read 'to steal another's thoughts and pass off as one's own; to publish ideas or writings of another under one's own name'.

In a world where university teaching staff must frequently take the role of academic Robin Hoods, stealing from the intellectually rich to give to the educationally poor, the dividing line between plagiarism and teaching may be difficult to draw. Similarly, a student cannot always recall the origin of every idea proposed in the course of a lengthy essay. Nevertheless both teacher and student are responsible for acknowledging sources whenever possible. This is so for quotations and paraphrases, as well as for summaries of other authors' ideas.

Failure to acknowledge direct quotations must be considered deliberate plagiarism. If a student copies large segments of text or reference books and passes these off as his own work, then the assessor will have no option but to call for a resubmission of the essay, or award zero credit for the work. (Sometimes even more serious consequences follow!) Strictly speaking, any phrase or sentence which is quoted without being acknowledged as deriving from another source is an example of plagiarism, although this would seldom be penalised if only an isolated instance. However it is not uncommon to find extensive sections of essays stolen from books which the student apparently hopes will not be familiar to the marker. There are also instances of students jointly writing essays and submitting the same work as their respective individual efforts. This practice will also be regarded as plagiarist.

In addition to the obvious moral reasons against all forms of plagiarism, there are also excellent practical, educational reasons. Recall that one of the qualities an assessor is looking for in an essay is some evidence of a student's understanding of the topic. If the essayist simply 'borrows' an author's exact words he will not show that he understands those words even in the limited sense of being able to paraphrase them. To repeat another's words (parrot fashion) is not to *show* that one understands his ideas (even if it is true that one does!). Consequently, if the aim of writing an essay is to display one's understanding of authors' works, it is best not to rely solely on direct quotations, even if these are acknowledged.

Similarly a simple grammatical paraphrase does not demonstrate understanding. Anyone who speaks English can turn 'Differential reinforcement inhibits generalisation' into 'Generalisation is inhibited by differential reinforcement' without understanding any learning theory. It shows at most that the grammar of the sentence has been understood. Such turns of phrase are also best avoided, if one wishes to give unequivocal evidence of understanding. Specifically, in this case, it is wisest to give evidence that one understands the technical terms the sentence uses.

Paraphrases of books and papers are much more common than direct quotations. Students frequently argue that unless they paraphrase other sources they could not compose an essay at all! They point out that virtually every idea they originate will inevitably be found somewhere in the extensive literature on a given topic. Though this is true to some extent, it does not really justify plagiarism. On the contrary, it is a simple matter to indicate when one's original ideas coincide with some published argument without simply 'borrowing' that argument and paraphrasing it without acknowledgement. Moreover if one has to express these ideas in an original manner rather than by merely altering a similar presentation in superficial respects, one becomes aware of important subtleties that may pass unnoticed if one merely paraphrases. Hence it is best to formulate one's thoughts *in one's own words* and acknowledge their relation to other authors' arguments where necessary, rather than merely to present a series of paraphrases of other sources.

There are simple conventions regarding the acknowledgement of sources in psychological literature. These both avoid plagiarism and provide consistent, thorough documentation of all sources relevant to a particular piece of work.

Two classes of sources may be distinguished — primary and secondary. *A primary source* is any book, report, or journal article *actually consulted* during the preparation of an essay. *A secondary source* is any book or article which furnishes information about another article, report or book, the latter not being consulted itself. For example, summaries and critical discussions in textbooks of original research published elsewhere are secondary sources of information about that research.

The most generally accepted conventions are:
Direct quotations (all sources): place the entire quoted passage in quotation marks; cite the author's name and the date of the publication to which reference is made, together with the page(s) from which the quotation is taken. These particulars are placed in parentheses. If only one phrase or sentence is quoted, these details can precede or follow the quotation, depending on context. For example

1. Brown (1964, p.167) argues: 'There is considerable consensus concerning the origins of juvenile delinquency.'

or

2. 'There is considerable consensus concerning the origins of juvenile delinquency', argues Brown (1964, p.167).

Such short quotations would normally be integrated into a paragraph without any other emphasis. Longer passages, such as complete paragraphs, are frequently accentuated by means of indentation and/or different spacing (if typewritten). Usually they are indented and single-spaced if the rest of the essay is double-spaced. Otherwise their acknowledgement is as above.

Should more than one publication by a particular author during one year be referred to in an essay, then each title may be distinguished thus: Brown (1964, a); Brown (1964, b), and so on.

Where a figure (e.g. graph) or table of data is to be reproduced from a primary or secondary source it also needs to be acknowledged by reference to author, publication date and page number.

Notice that these conventions obviate the use of any footnotes. The reference list at the end of the essay adequately identifies the source of the quotation.

Direct quotations from a secondary source are also possible. For instance, if Smith (1970) in a textbook on, say, aggression, quotes a passage from a journal article or book by Jones (1964), then the passage may be used in one's essay, provided that it is acknowledged appropriately. Because one has not read the primary source, one must indicate this when quoting. For example,

3. Jones argues that 'aggression is a bio-social phenomenon in all primates' (Smith, 1970, p.200).

The convention is important for distinguishing primary from secondary sources. It would be necessary to record only the secondary source in one's references in the above example.

Paraphrases and summaries: When material from either primary or secondary sources is summarised or paraphrased, conventions apply which are similar to those employed when making direct quotations. For instance,

4. Brown (1964, p.167) considers that there is general agreement about the causes of delinquency (cf. example 1).

Or, for secondary sources,

5. Jones (Smith, 1970, p.200) sees aggression as a bio-social phenomenon (cf. 3).

When longer arguments or reserach projects are summarised, similar acknowledgements are quite adequate. Of course, many stylistic variations are possible which provide subtle differences of emphasis, but these will develop as one's reading of psychological literature progresses.

9.8   EXERCISES

1. Consider the following hypothetical essay topics, assuming that you are to

write 2,000 words on each question. In each case,

(i) Specify which terms require interpretation and/or definition.

(ii) Explicate the logical nature of the question (i.e. spell out what is the *precise* relationship between the variables in the question as was done for the example discussed in 9.2).

(a) 'The theory of the Authoritarian Personality is relevant to, though not sufficient to explain all, racial prejudice.' Discuss.

(b) 'Language acquisition is a function of complex maturational variables with which environmental factors interact. It is not simply a matter of "learning" in the sense of classical or instrumental conditioning.' Discuss.

(c) 'Perceptual illusions are the necessary consequence of perceptual constancies, There cannot be the latter without the former.' Discuss.

2. Throughout this book we have cited numerous examples of good and bad arguments, careful and careless definitions, etc., concerned with the issue of human aggression. The following passages are taken from students' essays on a question about the origins of human aggression. Each involves errors, omissions, verbal imprecisions, conceptual and stylistic confusions, or poor organisation. Putting yourself in the position of a marker, consider how well each of the quoted passages *introduces* an essay on the topic:

'Although man is often claimed to be the most aggressive creature on earth, this alone does not mean that humans possess instincts which cause them to engage in acts of war.' Discuss.

Of each passage, ask the following specific questions.

(i) What, if any, interpretation is given of the logic or meaning of the question as a whole and of its major terms?

(ii) Does the passage *assume* rather than argue an answer to the question, at least implicitly? Where?

(iii) Although introductory paragraphs do not usually cite evidence, they may anticipate the type of evidence to be considered in the body of the essay. Does the passage do this? Where? With what success?

(iv) Are there any generalisations which lack empirical support in the passage?

(v) Does the passage require reorganisation, either within or between sentences, or between paragraphs? Suggest changes.

(vi) More theoretically, does the passage assume purposivism or reductionism (or their opposites)?

(vii) Is the style anthropomorphic?

(viii) Is there unnecessary jargon?

(ix) Is the passage properly *documented*?

(a)   The fact that man has an instinct of aggression seems to be supported by arguments of many people such as Freud and Storr, but the way in which this aggression is directed or the reason why it exists has been expressed in many different ways. Freud argues that aggression is a death instinct in that the aggressor is trying to bring living matter back into an inactive condition. On the other hand, Storr sees aggression as an attempt by a person to find his own identity by asserting himself as an individual. The fact that man has an instinct of aggression seems to be quite well founded because when a man is cornered or attacked he will fight to free himself and he seems to meet aggression with aggression. That is, a person will seek revenge for a wrong done to him . . . But is man the 'most aggressive creature on earth'?

(b)   The history of man's civilization is the history of man's aggression; a history of conflict between nations, of conquest, of subjugation or rebellion. What makes man unique in the animal kingdom in that he is the only species which commits acts of mass murder against other members of the species. The reason often given is because man is naturally aggressive. *Although man is often claimed to be the most aggressive creature on earth, this alone does not mean that humans possess instincts which cause them to engage in acts of war.* The answer lies in man's *innate aggressive nature,* his territorial behavioural pattern, and as a result of his cultural evolution.

Before any discussion of this broad statement (italicised above) can take place one must clearly define the meaning of the principal terms. What is aggression? Does its field of definition cover all forms of aggressive behaviour – the 'pushy' salesman trying to make a sale, the strong competitor striving to reach the summit of his field, the keen executive trying to reach the top position in his company. All these people exhibit aggressive behaviour, but not behaviour that could be termed hostile or physically injurious to other persons. Because the latter part of the statement refers to 'war', this essay shall regard the terms 'aggressive' and 'hostile' as synonymous, and denote any behaviour described by these terms as that which is aimed at the injury of other persons. Following on from this, 'war' is defined as an armed contest between two independent groups by means of organised military force, in the pursuit of a tribal or national policy. The term 'instinct' must also be clearly defined. An instinct is an inherited tendency to action of a specific kind, usually set off by a limited range of stimuli, and having definite survivial or biological value in the struggle for existence.

Having provided a basis for discussion of this statement, one is now confronted with a series of questions which must be answered. Does man possess an aggressive nature? If so, is this aggressive nature instinctive or is it 'learned'? Given that he does possess this aggression, what set of circumstances lead him into acts of war? In his book 'African Genesis', Robert Ardrey says: 'Man is a predator whose natural instinct is to kill with a weapon'. This appears to be an over-simplified analysis of an exceedingly complex problem.

Klineberg, O. *The Human Dimension in International Relations.* N.Y.: Holt, Rinehart & Winston, 1964, p.10.

3. The following are two concluding paragraphs from student essays on the topic considered in (2). Compare these, asking the following questions:

(i)   How successful is each in formulating a concluding statement about the question asked?

(ii) What rhetorical and moralistic comment does each contain? Is this relevant to the question asked?

(iii) What stylistic faults and organisational or conceptual confusions need to be rectified in each?

(a)   In the main, man's aggression is more than an instinctive response to frustration − it is an attempt to assert himself as an individual, to separate himself from the herd, to find his identity. This aggression only becomes dangerous when it is suppressed or disowned. The man who is able to assert himself is seldom vicious, it is the weak who revert to aggression. It is impossible to believe that all aggressive potential springs from frustration.

... It seems probable that the denial or repression of our aggression is liable to cause disharmony within ourselves. We are constantly seeking opportunities for the vicarious expression of aggressive drives, such as sports, alcoholism and suicide. In war these impulses used to find an acceptable channel for discharge. Abolition of war would only cause an increase in civilian aggression which is already occurring.

(b)   In conclusion we can say that there is no clear cut answer to the question of whether humans possess instincts which cause them to engage in acts such as war. We have seen that definitions of the three terms 'aggressive', 'instinct' and 'war' are so vague or broad that this adds extra complexities to an already complex area. All that can be concluded is that among psychologists, there appears to be a weakening of the idea that aggression is an instinct which makes war inevitable, and a strengthening of the idea that aggression is both biologically and socially determined and therefore that war is not inevitable.

4. (a)   Poor and under achievers exhibit *inappropriate affect*; restricted ego development, a certain tendency to self-consciousness in *dyadic interpersonal communication* situations and poor *super-ego functioning.* They are also *disproportionately representative of family systems* with a *less-than-adequate monetary income* and certain disadvantages on other *socio-economic indices.*

   (b)   Language acquisition is thus a linear process starting from a primitive form of *behavioural control,* which involves some kind of *tangible reinforcement* through a succession of approximations, involving shifts in *response typography,* the *antecedent controlling stimuli* to the *point in time* where the *verbal behaviour* typifies the form and *omission pattern* of adult verbal behaviour.

(i)   Attempt to paraphrase these passages.

(ii)   What stylistic improvements are required to render them more intelligible?

(iii)   Are the words in italics essential to the meaning of the passage, or could they be replaced by less 'technical' expressions?

10

REPORTING EXPERIMENTS

When, as becomes a man who would prepare
For such an arduous work, I through myself
Make rigorous inquisition, the report is often cheering.

Wordsworth

PSYCHOLOGY students may write several empirical reports in each year of study. These describe simple projects such as demonstrations of perceptual illusions, naturalistic observations of animal behaviour, elementary learning experiments, or small-sample attitude surveys. In the final year of study, a student may decribe an original, technically sophisticated experiment, similar in form to those reported in technical journals. In both the elementary and more sophisticated projects, there is a set of widely accepted conventions that govern the form which such reports follow. Therefore, in this chapter, techniques and conventions of writing empirical reports are outlined, and particular attention is paid to the economical verbal style which reports demand.

Let us first clarify a possible ambiguity: the word 'experiment' is some-times restricted to observational studies in which there is deliberate manipu-lation of the conditions in which subjects are treated. But it might be used more generally to cover any empirical study, including field studies, attitude surveys, evaluations of methods of therapy, and so on. In this chapter the word will be employed in the latter, more general (if somewhat ambiguous) sense. This is because in all cases methodology and findings need to be presented economically, yet with sufficient detail to allow the study to be either replicated or amended by other researchers. When replication is not possible (e.g. psychiatric case studies could not be replicated in further research), the methodology must be explicit enough for comparisons to be made with similar studies or cases. This means that many technical details (such as specification of sample size, equipment and materials used and statis-tical methodology) have to be included. However these should not be allowed to obscure the major theoretical arguments which give rise to the hypothesis being tested. To achieve this balance, the empirical report needs to be organised around a set of unambiguous headings such as one finds in technical journals. Typically, these include:

1. Introduction (sometimes untitled)
2. Method — Subjects
          — Materials
          — Procedure
3. Results
4. Discussion
5. References (discussed in Chapter 9)

10.1 INTRODUCTION

The major aim of this section is to present the theoretical argument and summarise the empirical literature relevant to the hypothesis evaluated by the subsequent experiment. This should be done briefly, yet with sufficient documentation of sources to allow readers to research the literature relevant to the report.

For example, Daehler and Bukatko (1974) described an experiment investigating discrimination learning in two-year-olds. In two paragraphs they are able to outline the reasons for the study (i.e. the motivation for conducting this particular experiment), some of the methodological problems in the area, and also to describe the general hypotheses to be studied. In the quotation which follows, notice the economical descriptions of research findings in paragraph 2 (e.g. 'Rossi and Rossi (1965)...'), and the reasonably lucid presentation of the problems to be investigated:

The perceptual and conceptual abilities of very young children, that is, children between 1 and 3 years of age, have received little attention in comparison to the abilities of preschoolers and, more recently, newborns and infants under a year of age (cf. Siegel 1967). Among the deterrents to research on learning with 2-year-olds is a general suspicion that such children are highly distractible and will display a variety of error factors (e.g. Harlow 1950, 1959) or task-irrelevant behaviours. Successful discrimination learning in children under 2 years of age has been relatively difficult to demonstrate (e.g. Hill 1965; Weisberg & Simmons 1966; Welch 1939), and many investigators report children over 3 display various response and stimulus biases (e.g. Berman, Rane & Bahow 1970; Greene 1964; Levinson & Reese 1967). But research on a limited number of 2-year-olds suggests that under appropriate conditions, discrimination learning may proceed with very few errors, particularly after the initial discrimination has been acquired (cf. Gellermann 1933; Hayes, Thompson, & Hayes 1953; Welch 1939). Stimulus and response biases have been reported for this age group as well as older children (e.g. Gellermann 1933; Graham, Ernhart, Craft & Berman 1964), but it remains unclear whether these biases dominate and generally interfere with cue-guided behaviour or whether they are simply initiated because of inadequate understanding of instructions or other aspects of the learning task. Thus, one purpose of the present study was to determine how rapidly two-choice discrimination learning tasks can be solved by 2-year-olds and how pervasive stimulus and response biases are in performances on such problems.

Even fewer studies have attempted to assess the very young child's knowledge of conceptual categories and their use in problem solving. Rossi and Rossi (1965) found that 2-year-olds frequently recall together items belonging to a common category and Goldberg, Perlmutter and Myers (1974) have found that recall in this age group is facilitated if pairs of items belong to a common category. However, there have been no investigations on the influence of class membership of simple problem solving at this age. As an exploratory attempt to investigate this question, some children in the present study were given discrimination-learning problems in which the positive instance was always a member of a common category. Other children received problems in which the stimuli were unrelated. Of interest, of course, was whether learning would proceed more rapidly when the positive instances belonged to a common category (p.378).[1.]

The terse prose of this example is neither unduly compressed, nor cryptic. It is informative and unpretentious without being unduly bland. Although some typical academic phrases occur ('research ... suggests ...'; 'it remains unclear whether ...'), these are not noticably repetitive and do not reduce the precision or economy of the passage.

Notice that there are no passive sentences. When writing introductions it is tempting to put the description into the passive voice in the (mistaken) belief that this is a more 'objective', scientific style. Undergraduate reports abound in phrases such as 'In an experiment by Brown (1968) it was found that ...'; 'It has been demonstrated by Brown that ...'. However these stylistic variations are less economical and add no information to the active voice style: 'Brown (1968) showed that ...'. It is advisable to avoid the passive altogether rather than risk its over-use, especially in empirical reports.

The quoted study is typical of most papers in its use of the past tense, both for describing past research, and for proposing the hypotheses ('Thus, one purpose of the present study was to determine ...'). Unless there are some special reasons for not doing so, all empirical reports employ the past tense.

Given these general points, the introduction to an empirical report should (1) outline the aims (including hypotheses) of the study; (2) describe research relevant to these hypotheses (experiments should be summarised very briefly, with one or two sentences usually being sufficient for each); (3) present methodological or theoretical criticisms of these studies insofar as such criticisms relate to the hypotheses being investigated; (4) if necessary, define the terms of major importance, perhaps mentioning the relationship between the proposed definitions and operational criteria adopted in the experiment.

10.2   METHOD

It is conventional to report experimental method under at least three subheadings: Subjects, Materials (and/or Apparatus), and Procedure. This classification will be followed in our discussion, although the convention is not rigid. The choice of subheadings in the Method section of a report is determined by the information one wishes to report, not by prescribed rules. For example, Daehler and Bukatko report their study using the subheadings Subjects; Apparatus and Stimuli; Conditions (i.e. experimental 'treatment' conditions) and Procedure.

The Method should describe all details of the study which would be

---

1.   Daehler, M.W., and Bukatko, D. 'Discrimination Learning in Two-Year-Olds'. *Child Development*, 45(2), 1974, 378-82.

relevant should another researcher wish to replicate it. Hence even apparently inconsequential details such as the brand name of toys used, or the size of tables at which subjects sat might be reported in a study of child development. Beginning with the subheading 'Subjects', let us illustrate the detail and style typical of the Method section of a report:

> *Subjects:* 20 male and 20 female undergraduate psychology students, 19-22 years of age, served as subjects. All were of European descent and attended the University of X. All spoke English as their first language and none had a history of auditory or visual defects of any kind.
>
> W.A.I.S. I.Q.'s ranged between 110-23 (median 117).

As in this example, 'background' factors such as age, social class, ethnic group, potentially relevant medical information, I.Q. and/or school grade are reported in this section. These factors may be quite important to readers wishing to compare the reported study with others investigating similar phenomena. For instance, the socio-economic background of children in two otherwise comparable studies may be slightly different. This may affect the results of the studies quite significantly. So although background information may often appear to be pedantic or unnecessary, it can be most important. Even in cases in which background variables are not controlled or in which their range is not restricted, they might still need to be mentioned: Hence, Daehler and Bukatko (above) report that

> All Ss (the conventional abbreviation for 'subjects') were brought to the university as part of a series of studies on cognitive development in very young children. Participants lived in the Amherst area and most came from highly educated, middle-class families . . . and were probably intellectually above average (p.379).

Should animals be the subjects in an experiment, information about age, breeding strain, body weight and even cage history may be relevant. When one is in doubt as to the necessary detail, it is best to consult literature on comparable research as a guide, for there can be no general rules to cover all possibilities.

Materials/Apparatus: As for the previous section, the general principle to follow when reporting the materials and/or apparatus used in one's research is to err on the side of too much, rather than too little, detail. Particulars concerning all materials (T.A.T. cards; ability tests; verbal stories, etc.) should be presented in replicable detail. 'Apparatus' covers technical details of equipment such as display panels, timing mechanisms, Skinner box dimensions, response-recording devices, E.E.G. machines, etc.

Such details may be very important: For instance, Milgram (1965) reports a series of experiments in which a facsimile of a 'shock generator' was employed on which subjects ostensibly administered electric shocks to other subjects. This study could not be replicated unless details of the shock generator were copied very closely, for it is crucial that subjects accept the authenticity of the apparatus. Hence Milgram describes it very precisely, even mentioning the engraving of the fictitious manufacturer's plaque.

Similar, if more mundane detail, is provided in our ongoing example of Daehler and Bukatko's report. Under the heading 'Apparatus and Stimuli' they report:

> The apparatus, located on a child-size table, consisted of an upright mason-ite panel 33 x 33 cm in size. The panel contained (1) a hook in each upper corner on which stimulus cards could be hung; (2) a delivery chute pro-truding from the centre and through which bead reinforcers could be delivered, and (3) a 10 x 15 cm opening at the bottom into which the positive stimulus could be placed.
>
> Stimuli consisted of cards 9½ x 10 cm in size which depicted common objects in stylized colored drawings. The cards were part of a pegboard series produced by the Ideal School Supply Company. When placed on the panel, the two stimuli for each problem were 10 cm apart.
>
> An assistant out of sight behind the panel operated a hand puppet at the top of the panel. The puppet was used to encourage responding and to provide social reinforcement for correct responses (p.379).

Notice that much of this detail might have been judged as incidental rather than essential (e.g. the size of the stimulus cards). In the interests of potential replication, however, it is described quite completely.

Procedure: A similar criterion determines procedural description, for slight differences in procedure may have important psychological consequences. Instructions by the experimenter (abbreviated E) are reported verbatim. The nature and number of trials, stimulus changes, reinforcements, etc., must all be outlined in terse, unambiguous prose. Daehler and Bukatko begin their Procedure section thus:

> Procedure — After becoming acquainted with the female E in a nearby playroom, both child and parent were invited to play a game with a puppet in the experimental room. The child was introduced to the puppet and given the following instructions. 'Do you see these pictures (E pointed back and forth to each)? "Herman" (the puppet) likes one of these. You put the one he likes here in the window (E pointed to the opening).' The puppet essentially repeated the instructions, but if S failed to respond after repeated encouragement, the E modeled the appropriate behaviour. No more than two modeling trials were required for any S and these occurred only on the first problem. The pictures were never labeled by the E or the puppet (p.379).

Reports of more conventional experimental procedures (such as typical Skinner Box conditioning studies, or Piagetian tasks) may not require as much detail, provided that one's potential readers can be assumed to be familiar with such procedures.

10.3 RESULTS (Including Statistical Analysis)

Conventionally, this section reports the data yielded by the experiment, but does not discuss their theoretical significance. It presents both the methods of statistical analysis and the decisions which these tests allow concerning the hypothesised outcomes of the experiment. In a typical analysis involving parametric inferential statistics (t-, F-tests) these decisions and the data on which they are based are presented in tabular form. The summary of the means, and standard deviations (or variances) for the respective experimental (comparison) conditions provides a comprehensive, yet not a confusing, picture of the major trends in the data. These trends may be highlighted and clarified by means of graphs, which should be presented in the simplest possible way and which should be closely related to the relevant verbal description of results.

It is sometimes argued that all empirical reports should present the 'raw data' on which the statistical decisions are based, not merely the summary details (means, variances) suggested above. The justification for this viewpoint is that only then can the data be reanalysed by another researcher should he consider that the original analysis was either inappropriate or insufficient for the conclusions drawn. In most cases, however, reporting this much detail would be impractical, given the volume of data resulting from many studies. Nevertheless, when theses are submitted, it is usual to meet this condition by including raw data in an appendix – a practice worth following in shorter reports should the method of data analysis employed require any unusual justification or atypical assumptions. When this is so, the likelihood of reanalysis by another researcher is greater and the justification for complete data presentation correspondingly stronger.

To return to more typical cases. In a conventional learning experiment involving, say, four conditions, the data might be summarised in a series of tables, each accompanied by relevant verbal description. Typical tables might include:

TABLE 1

Mean Errors on All 20 Trials for All Four Training Conditions

Training Conditions	Mean Errors	Standard Deviation
1	6.8	1.9
2	3.5	0.9
3	2.9	1.7
4	4.1	1.4

TABLE 2

Mean Response Latencies on Correct Trials for All Four Training Conditions

Training Conditions	Mean Response Latency	Standard Deviation
1	0.356 sec.	0.090 sec.
2	0.290 sec.	0.131 sec.
3	0.389 sec.	0.122 sec.
4	0.412 sec.	0.087 sec.

Notice that tables are generally headed in this manner and numbered with arabic rather than Roman numerals. Graphs would be similarly labelled Figure 1 . . . n, and integrated appropriately into the text.

Statistical analyses are best presented in a manner which reflects the hypotheses being investigated: details of statistical methods (e.g. F-, t-tests, planned contrasts, x^2-tests) may be presented in tabular form (e.g. Anovar tables as presented in conventional statistics texts), and/or verbally described in relation to relevant hypotheses. Significance levels and degrees of freedom are always reported. It is best to report *all* statistical decisions relevant to one's hypotheses, not only those which are consistent with predictions made at the outset. This is because unconfirmed hypotheses may provide as much information as those which are confirmed (recall our discussion of 'falsifiability' in Chapter 3).

10.4 DISCUSSION

The *Discussion* should be limited to the theoretical argument and the resulting hypotheses adumbrated in the Introduction. This ensures strict relevance. To this end it is advisable to refer frequently to the Introduction when planning and writing the Discussion. One will also concentrate on extending the Results section, placing the reported statistical decisions in theoretical context. The principal difference between the Results and Discussion is that the latter draws together the information yielded by the experiment in the light of the explicit aims of the study. That is to say it considers results (data and statistically based decisions) in relation to theory by way of the hypotheses tested.

Insofar as one can specify a general format for the organisation of the Discussion it is of the following type: first, one reports the general support for, or refutation of, one's hypotheses. The initial paragraph of the Discussion in Daehler and Bukatko, for instance, reads:

The results of this study leave little doubt concerning the ability of many

2-year-olds to perform successfully in two-choice discrimination-learning problems. Very young children do not inevitably display stimulus or response biases even though they are frequently reported to interfere with discrimination learning and even though children at many ages will display such behaviours when noncontingent reinforcement is used (p.381).

The second stage of the Discussion typically expands and qualifies these general conclusions. For example, the degree to which one is justified in extrapolating from the results (e.g. to other age-groups, species, situations) might be considered, the student focusing on details in which the present study differs from comparable research. This might lead to an examination of possible reasons for the failure or success of the reported experiment to yield predicted results, by considering peculiarities of method or by suggesting inadequacies in comparable experiments. In this way, Daehler and Bukatko explain the difference between the general results they obtained and those of similar studies:

> Certain procedures employed in the present study differed from those of most other discrimination-learning experiments, and these methodological changes may have assisted the child in understanding the nature of the task. For example, instructions emphasized selecting the stimulus the puppet liked. Such instructions specify that it is something about the stimuli which is important, and that someone other than the child has defined which of the stimuli is relevant. In contrast, many discrimination-learning studies emphasize 'winning' or 'finding' the reinforcer; the instructions fail to indicate that the cues should be noticed or that one cue has been preselected as more appropriate than the other for 'winning'. Both social and material reinforcers were used in the present study, but their purpose was to complement and reinforce the goal of completing the activity for the puppet (p.381).

This expansion and qualification serves to place the reported findings in the necessary context and leads naturally to the discussion of possible avenues of future research. Usually suggestions for further research follow additional theoretical discussion which arises from the results. These may be quite technical. In the example to which we are referring, the authors propose some relatively informal theoretical ideas concerning the infant's possible understanding of 'category membership':

> There was little evidence that children made use of the categories to facilitate learning. Since problems were presented successively, the task may not have been very effective in encouraging awareness of the categories. More important, since learning could and did occur very rapidly, the benefits of category membership were considerably diminished and a much less useful aspect of the learning situation. Thus, the question of whether very young children can use category membership to facilitate learning remains unanswered (p.382).

The authors then reiterate the major findings of the study as a concluding paragraph, emphasising what they regard as the general importance of the results:

> Two-year-old children can perform exceptionally well in a two-choice discrimination-learning situation. Failure to rapidly learn such a task may not be an indication of lack of capability, but rather evidence of ambiguously defined task goals, reinforcement or motivational variables, response factors, etc. The results of this study suggest that certain techniques optimize our ability to better appreciate the learning capacity of very young children (p.382).

This quite typical, yet relatively non-technical example illustrates that the Discussion section of an empirical report must be carefully organised and expressed in order to draw out the (justified) implications of the reported findings and to place these briefly in a theoretical context. As with other aspects of report writing, there are not simple rules which can be slavishly followed, but there are guidelines. Careful organisation under appropriate subheadings, concise unpretentious language and attention to detail will allow one to present lucid (even interesting) reports. It is advisable to consult publications in the area of psychology studied and to compare them with one's own draft report prior to its submission. Second, because the most interpretive sections of a report are the Introduction and Discussion, and because these need to be clearly integrated, it is also advisable to compare these with each other before writing the final draft. At all times it must be remembered that a very strict criterion of relevance applies to empirical reports, and this alone necessitates such a comparison.

REFERENCES

Adorno, T.W., Frenkel-Brunswik, E., Levinson, D.J., and Sanford, R.N. *The Authoritarian Personality*. N.Y.: Harper & Row, 1950.

Altman, I., and Haythorn, W.W. 'The Ecology of Isolated Groups'. In H. Proshansky *et al., Environmental Psychology*. N.Y.: Holt, Rinehart & Winston, 1970, 226-39.

Ardrey, R. *The Territorial Imperative*. London: Fontana, 1969.

Ardrey, R. *The Social Contract*. N.Y.: Atheneum, 1970.

Barker, S.F. *Induction and Hypothesis: A Study in the Logic of Confirmation*. N.Y.: Cornell University Press, 1957.

Bowlby, J. *Attachment*. London: Hogarth, 1969.

Bowlby, J. *Separation: Anxiety and Anger*. London: Hogarth, 1973.

Bridgeman, P.W. *The Logic of Modern Physics*. N.Y.: Macmillan, 1927.

Brown, R. *Explanation in Social Science*. London: Routledge & Kegan Paul, 1963.

Buss, A.H. *The Psychology of Aggression*. N.Y.: Wiley, 1961.

Cattell, R.B. 'Factor Theory Psychology: A Statistical Approach to Personality'. In W.S. Sahakian (ed.), *Psychology of Personality: Readings in Theory*. Chicago: Rand McNally, 1965, 388-414.

Chaplin, J.P. *Dictionary of Psychology*. N.Y.: Dell Publishing Co., 1968.

Craig, W. 'Why Do Animals Fight?'. In T. Maple and D.W. Matheson (eds.), *Aggression, Hostility and Violence*. N.Y.: Holt, Rinehart & Winston, 1973.

Dubos, R. 'The Social Environment'. In H. Proshansky *et al., op.cit.*, 202-8.

Elms, A.C. *Social Psychology and Social Relevance*. Boston: Little, Brown & Co., 1972.

Eysenck, H.J. *Race, Intelligence and Education*. Melbourne: Sun Books, 1971.

Freud, S. *Three Essays on the Theory of Sexuality*. N.Y.: Avon, 1962.

Germana, J. *Contemporary Experimental Psychology: In Flagrante Delicto*. Monterey, California: Brooks-Cole, 1971.

Goldschmid, M. (ed.). *Black Americans and White Racism*. N.Y.: Holt, Rinehart & Winston, 1970.

Greenspoon, J. 'The Reinforcing Effect of Two Spoken Sounds on the Frequencies of Two Responses'. *American Journal of Psychology*, **68**, 1955, 409-16.

Gregory, I. *Psychiatry: Biological and Social*. London: Saunders, 1961.

Gregory, R.L. *Eye and Brain: The Psychology of Seeing*. London: Weidenfeld & Nicholson, 1966, a.

Gregory, R.L. 'Visual Illusions'. In B.M. Foss (ed.), *New Horizons in Psychology*. Harmondsworth: Penguin, 1966, b.

Harlow, H.F. 'Love in Infant Monkeys'. *Sci. Amer.*, June 1962.

Harlow, H.F. *Learning to Love*. San Francisco: Albion, 1971.

Harlow, H.F., and Harlow, M.K. 'Social Deprivation in Monkeys'. *Sci. Amer.*, Nov. 1962.

Harman, G. *Thought*. N.J.: Princeton University Press, 1973.

Hempel, C.G. *Aspects of Scientific Explanation and Other Essays in the Philosophy of Science.* N.Y.: Free Press, 1965.

Hempel, C.G. *Philosophy of Natural Science.* N.J.: Prentice-Hall, 1966.

Hunt, J.M.V. 'Has Compensatory Education Failed? Has It Been Attempted?'. In *Environment, Heredity and Intelligence.* H.E.R., 1969, 130-52.

Klineberg, O. *The Human Dimension in International Relations.* N.Y.: Holt, Rinehart & Winston, 1964.

Krech, D. 'Psychoneurobiochemeducation'. In I.J. Gordon (ed.), *Readings in Development Psychology.* Glenview, Illinois: Scott, Foresman & Co., 1971, 93-100.

Laing, R.D., and Esterson, A. *Sanity, Madness and the Family.* Harmondsworth: Penguin, 1970.

Lovell, K. *An Introduction to Human Development.* London: Macmillan & Co., 1968.

Maas, J.B. (ed.). *Readings in Psychology Today, 3rd ed.* Del Mar, California: C.R.M., 1974.

McClelland, D. 'Some Social Consequences of Achievement Motivation'. In R.A. King (ed.), *Readings for an Introduction to Psychology.* N.Y.: McGraw-Hill, 1961, 80-85.

McDougall, W. *Outline of Psychology.* London: Methuen, 1923.

Mandler, G., and Kessen, W. *The Language of Psychology.* N.Y.: Wiley, 1959.

Maple, T., and Matheson, D.W. (eds), *Aggression, Hostility and Violence.* N.Y.: Holt, Rinehart & Winston, 1973.

Milgram, S. 'Liberating Effects of Group Pressure'. *Journal of Personality and Social Psychology,* 1, 1965, 127-34.

Mitchell, J. *Psychoanalysis and Feminism.* Harmondsworth: Penguin, 1974.

Mittler, P. *The Study of Twins.* Harmondsworth: Penguin, 1971.

Money, J., and Ehrhardt, A.E. *Man and Woman; Boy and Girl.* Baltimore: John Hopkins University Press, 1972.

Montagu, A. (ed.). *Man and Aggression.* London: Oxford University Press, 1968.

Moss, C.S. *Hypnosis in Perspective.* N.Y.: Macmillan & Co., 1965.

Newell, A., Shaw, J.C., and Simon, H.A. 'Report on a General Problem Solving Program'. In *Proc. Int. Conf. on Information Processing.* Paris: UNESCO, 1960, 256-64.

Prentice, W.C.H. 'The Systematic Psychology of Wolfgang Kohler'. In S. Koch (ed.), *Psychology: A Study of a Science, vol. 1.* N.Y.: McGraw-Hill, 1959, 427-55.

Quine, W.V., and Ullian, J.S. *The Web of Belief.* N.Y.,: Random House, 1970.

Rachman, S. 'Schizophrenia: A Look at Laing's Views'. *New Society,* 26 April 1973, 184-86.

Rosenthal, R. 'Experimenter Outcome-Orientation and the Results of the Psychological Experiment'. *Psychological Bulletin,* **61**, 1964, 405-12.

Rosenthal, R. *Experimenter Effects in Behavioural Research.* N.Y.: Appleton-Century-Crofts, 1966.

Rosenthal, R., and Jacobson, L. *Pygmalion in the Classroom: Teacher Expectation and Pupils' Intellectual Development.* N.Y.: Holt, Rinehart & Winston, 1968.

Rutter, M. *Maternal Deprivation Reassessed.* Harmondsworth: Penguin, 1972.

Salmon, W.C. (ed.) *Statistical Explanation and Statistical Relevance.* Pittsburgh: University of Pittsburgh Press, 1970.

Salmon, W.C. 'Theoretical Explanation'. In S. Korner (ed.) *Explanation.* Oxford: Basil Blackwell, 1975.

Sampson, E.E. *Social Psychology and Contemporary Society.* N.Y.: Wiley, 1971.

Sarbin, T.R., and Coe, W.C. *The Student Psychologist's Handbook.* Cambridge, Mass.: Schenkman/Harper & Row, 1969.

Seigler, M., Osmond, H., and Mann, H. 'Laing's Model of Madness'. In R. Boyers and R. Orrill (eds), *Laing and Anti-Psychiatry.* Harmondsworth: Penguin, 1972.

Skinner, B.F. *Beyond Freedom and Dignity.* Harmondsworth: Penguin, 1973.

Storr, A. *Human Aggression.* Harmondsworth: Penguin, 1968.

Vallins, G.H. *Good English: How to Write It.* London: Pan, 1951.

Vallins, G.H. *Better English.* London: Pan, 1953.

Weisstein, N. 'Psychology Constructs the Female'. In P. Brown (ed.), *Radical Psychology.* London: Tavistock, 1973, 390-420.

Weisz, P. (ed.). *The Contemporary Scene.* N.Y.: McGraw-Hill, 1970.

NAME INDEX

SUBJECT INDEX